An Unfinished Odyssey
Lebanon and Beyond
Books I & II

Cecil Hourani

Antoine

Copyright © Cecil Hourani, 1984 and 2012

All rights reserved. No part of this publication may be reproduced, stored in a retrieval system, or transmitted, in any form or by any means, electronical, mechanical, photocopying, recording or otherwise, without the prior permission of the copyright owner.

Book I first published in Great Britain by
George Weidenfeld & Nicholson Limited in 1984
Reprinted in Lebanon by Antoine S.A.L. in 2012

Book II first published in Lebanon by Antoine S.A.L. in 2012
Forest Building, Horsh Tabet, Sin al-fil, Beirut, Lebanon

ISBN: 978-9953-73-458-3

Printed and bound in Lebanon by Rouhana Antoine Chemali

Front cover picture *Baghdad Garden Party* by Kenneth Wood

An Unfinished Odyssey

Book I

For Furugh and Zelfa

Contents

List of Illustrations	ix
Preface	xi
Map of Lebanon	xiii
I A Manchester Childhood	1
II Return to the Sources	26
III Discovery of America	50
IV Wars of the Middle East	75
V An Arab Leader: the Tunisian Experience	97
VI Hammamet: a Cultural Adventure	123
VII Rival Nationalisms	146
VIII Marjayoun Besieged	160
Epilogue	189
Notes	194
Index	201

Illustrations

(BETWEEN PP. 130 AND 131)

Fadlo and Soumaya Hourani with their children, c. 1918.
The author's grandmother with her son and daughters.
Zelfa and Furugh in Tunisia.
The author with President Bourguiba *(Tunisian Press Agency)*.
Musa Alami with his boys at Jericho.
The theatre at Hammamet *(photograph by L. Laouini)*.

Preface

This book is not an autobiography nor a history of the Arab countries and peoples among whom most of my life has been spent, but rather a memoir in which I trace the various stages in my voyage of self-discovery. How did it come about that Lebanon, the country from where my parents came almost a century ago, exerted an attraction for me more powerful than the society into which I was born in England, and where I received all my formal education? What were the influences which shaped my character and which determined the path I have followed?

Had I been for all of my life a private citizen leading a life of comfortable obscurity, I would have needed an ego of exceptional size to induce me to publish this memoir: but the positions I have occupied, and the activities in which I have participated, have sometimes placed me in the limelight, and sometimes too made of me a figure of controversy, so that I have found it not only useful to myself, but perhaps also interesting to others, to try to understand my motives and to explain my ideas. It is my hope that my readers will find in these pages things which will shed light on problems and events in which I have been involved, and stimulate thought and discussion: and perhaps also help those who, like myself, have found themselves born into two worlds, to discover where they wish to belong.

Cecil Hourani
Beirut and London, November 1983

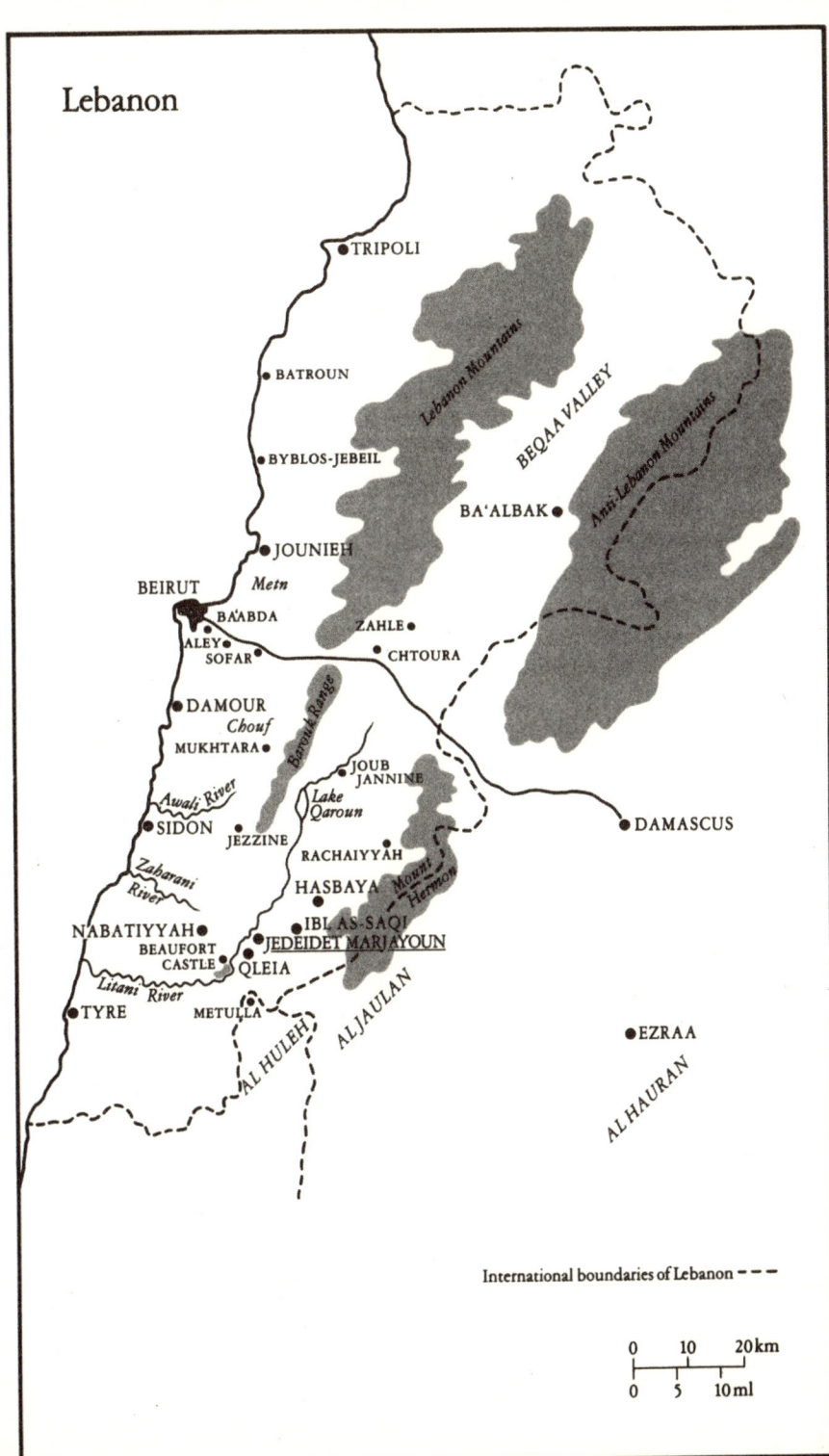

I
A Manchester Childhood

A happy combination of action and reflection is what I have sought to achieve in my life, sometimes successfully, sometimes less so. A period of enforced retirement from the activities in which I had been for ten years engaged in Tunisia gave me the opportunity and the motive to put down on paper, partly for myself and partly for others who might tread the same paths, some reflections distilled from recollections of my earlier days and more recent past. Events in Lebanon in which I was both emotionally and physically involved distracted me from my self-appointed task, and it is only now, when Lebanon is slowly emerging from its dark night, that I feel the urge to take up my story again.

To memory there are two dimensions: the one is private, peculiar to oneself, the result of particular events and happenings which for one reason or another leave their marks on memory's cells; the other collective, in which events, some historical, some mythical, combine to create a social and cultural identity in which the individual participates. For those born into families who are completely integrated into the society in which they live, the private and collective memories fit into each other and create no problem of identity: but in my case the collective memories which my parents brought with them to Manchester where they came from Lebanon at the end of the nineteenth century were not those of the society in which they made their new home and into which I was born. From where did I come, and who was I? These were questions which, dimly at first, more consciously later on, dominated my childhood and youth, and so I must attempt to describe not only the time and place into which I was born, but also the mythological past from which my parents came and which they transplanted to the Victorian dream-city, Manchester.

Among the great myths which still dominate the historical imagination of the Arabs is that of an ancient fertility and prosperity in the vast Arabian peninsula: the language and poetry of pre-Islamic Arabia have preserved intimations of an earlier, richer, more stable life before nomadism and the tent established 'the shrunken republic of the desert'.[1] Another myth, based upon fact as are all valid myths, tells how a great dam at Marib in Yemen, the remains of which can still be seen today, was slowly eaten away by mice and finally collapsed, flooding large areas of that fertile land, and driving northwards, in search of new lands to cultivate, the townspeople and villagers of Yemen who in successive waves and over many decades moved into present-day Iraq and Syria.

In Syria many of these new immigrants from Yemen settled in the Roman province of Auranitis, today the Hauran, then as now a great wheat-growing area. There they were converted to Christianity, transformed the black-volcanic temples into churches, but retained their Semitic language and their south Arabian ways of life. When, in the seventh century, the new religion of Islam brought Arab invaders into Byzantine Syria, the Yemenite people of the frontier province of Auranitis, under their princes of the family of Ghassan, sided with their fellow Arabs, and remained as Christian, Orthodox communities from whom most of the Orthodox inhabitants of Lebanon and Syria are descended.

Centuries later, when the great Arab empires had disintegrated and Ottoman rule taken their place, small groups of townspeople from the Hauran moved into Lebanon and northern Syria under the impulse of insecurity and poverty, still retaining dim memories of their earlier history and of their south Arabian origin. One such group settled in the seventeenth century on a barren hillside overlooking Mount Hermon near what today are the frontiers between Lebanon, Syria and Israel. This new town – el-Jedeidet – developed in the nineteenth century into a prosperous and dynamic community, whose members traded throughout southern Syria and as far away as Egypt and Najd in the Arabian peninsula.[2]

From this town of Jedeidet-Marjayoun, or the 'new town of

the valley of the springs', my father came to Manchester in 1891, carrying with him the memories of his family's past, mythical and historical, which stretched backwards in time from Marjayoun to Hauran and finally to the Yemen.

But on these collective memories of the village where he was born had been imposed another cultural tradition. Although the majority of the town were Orthodox, my grandfather was the first to become a Protestant. American missionaries of the Presbyterian Church were active in the area, and my father, orphaned at a very early age, was educated by the Americans and sent to their recently founded Syrian Protestant College. There he graduated in Arabic literature and language, but was also strongly influenced by the religious and ethical outlook of the American teachers and by their President, Dr Daniel Bliss. In his mind, and on the bookshelves of our house in Manchester, there lay side by side the sophisticated verses of Mutannabi and Ma'ari,[3] the Psalms in their metrical version, and the poems of Robert Burns. In Manchester he joined the Presbyterian Church of England, of which he was for many years an elder.

Thus to my earliest memories in Manchester, where my three sisters and two brothers were born before me, there were two faces: the one Near Eastern, Lebanese, full of poetry, politics and business, the other partly Scottish Presbyterian, full of Sunday churchgoing and Sunday school, partly English through an English nanny and a succession of English and Irish cooks and maids. Nothing epitomized this dichotomy more than the diet on which we were raised: on Saturdays, when my father lunched at home with his Lebanese and Syrian fellow businessmen and clients from abroad, we ate the food of the Lebanese villages – *kibbé*, and the traditional dish of Saturday, *mujaddara*, or Esau's pottage:[4] on Sundays there was an English roast, followed by an apple pie or a milk pudding.

Although our parents had at quite an early stage in their life in England decided that they would make it their permanent home, they retained all their lives a nostalgia for their villages, partly appeased by frequent visits home and by a permanent stream of uncles, aunts, cousins, friends and clients from 'the old country', as well as from Brazil, North America and West

Africa. This nostalgia they succeeded in passing on to me long before I knew the country from where it came. By importing every year the basic ingredients of a typical Lebanese family's diet, we were never cut off from the tastes and smells of the East. It was one of the most exciting events of my childhood when the wooden cases arrived from Beirut, and I would wait to scrounge whatever titbits came my way from the tins and jars and cloths which held olives and olive oil, cheeses, jellied quinces, grape molasses, dried figs, apricot paste, sesame oil, cracked and roasted wheat, and even large bundles of mountain bread, all of which took their place in our ample cellars alongside the pots of damson jam and marmalade which were England's contribution to our daily diet.

These intimations of another world beyond the flat horizons of Didsbury where we lived took a more tangible form when a young brother of my mother came to live with us. I was six years old and Munah Racy was in his early twenties: he came straight from my mother's village, and brought with him into our house that mixture of simplicity and sophistication which I was to discover later characterized the people of Ibl as-Saqi, to whom music, poetry, story-telling and fantasy were just as important as money. My father tried to interest him in his business, with little success, for poetry and painting were his loves: the writings and drawings of Khalil Gibran were his inspiration, and he drew on the rich resources of his village's folklore to sit by my bed and tell me stories which, like Scheherazade's, would never end, but which had always as their closing phrase – 'and the wheel would turn'. In his world of symbols wheels had a special place: they represented time, destiny, change, repetition and return, and everything mysterious was deemed 'wheels within wheels'. Where he got this obsession with wheels I do not know, but his imagination combined stories from the *Arabian Nights* with those from his village in which the real and the mythical merged in the personalities of his heroes and villains.[5]

Another intimation of a world and a life more glamorous than that of Manchester was brought by a classmate of my father at the Syrian Protestant College, Amin Kisbany, who, after a career of adventure which took him as salesman for

Singer sewing-machines to Morocco, missionary to the Moroccan Jews (of whom he told us he only converted one), and partner in my father's business, finally joined the group of Lebanese and Syrian patriots who rallied round King Faisal I in Baghdad after the collapse of his Arab kingdom in Damascus. In Baghdad his qualities of learning and scholarship – he knew Hebrew, Aramaic, Turkish and Persian in addition to Arabic and English – his integrity, sense of humour and political vision made him many friends, among whom one of the closest was Hussein Afnan, Secretary of the Council of Ministers, who had read the proclamation of Faisal as King of Iraq, and whose daughter I was to marry. Amin Kisbany, who on more than one occasion became our guardian during the visits of my parents to Brazil and Egypt, told us stories of his wanderings in Arabia and Morocco, of his involvement in the events which led to the creation of modern Iraq, of his encounters with T. E. Lawrence, and of his unsuccessful business ventures in Brazil and North America. Wherever he travelled he would leave behind him trunks and cases of books and papers 'to be collected later': from one such trunk left in London fifteen years earlier he gave me a history of the Arabs which first awakened my serious interest.

A visitor to our house in Didsbury who contributed further to the growth of my imagination, my curiosity to visit countries and people far away, and my first insight into revolutionary politics, was a Palestinian sailor from Bethlehem called Boutros Khouri, or Peter as we knew him. He had killed a man on his ship and landed in prison in Liverpool, from where he contacted my father. His origins and history are obscure, but he was a Communist – the first I had met – Lenin and Trotsky were his heroes, and took their place in the fertile ground of my imagination alongside Sherif Hussein and Faisal.[6] Later on Peter went to West Africa and spent several years wandering in the area between northern Nigeria and Lake Chad, and his long and detailed letters to my father, part descriptive and part political, widened still further the horizons of my childhood.

Other frequent visitors to our house were the business clients and friends of my father, who came from Brazil and

New York and brought into our life the habits and customs not only of 'the old country', Lebanon, but also of the countries and societies of their adoption. Their presence in Manchester, where often they stayed as guests in our house, was the occasion for lavish banquets: my mother, assisted by other ladies from the Lebanese community, would spend days in the kitchen preparing the *kibbé*, the sweet *ma'mouls* and other delicacies of the Lebanese table. These parties were the occasion for much shouting, arguing and jollity, and were often followed by games of backgammon, which I was later to learn from my father.

But there was another more austere, more sober side of life which coloured my Manchester childhood. My father and mother were both active members of the Presbyterian church in Didsbury, and counted among their friends the pastor and many of the Scottish and English congregation. My mother's father, Yuakim Racy, had been himself a Protestant pastor in the village and headmaster of the American missionary school in Sidon. My father retained all his life an admiration for the earnest men and women who had left their homes in America to teach in Lebanon, and he had taken from them not a theoretical interest in their Calvinist beliefs so much as a conscious effort to follow their example – sobriety in dress and conduct, avoidance of extravagance and ostentation, help to one's fellow men and good works – these rather than a serious belief in predestination or the idea of an elected few were the canons of behaviour set before us at home and in the church in Didsbury to which on Sundays we were dutifully led.

Dimly at an early age, more clearly when I grew a little older, I became aware of an ambivalent quality in our family life. On Saturdays it was permitted for our elders to give lavish parties at which whisky, port and madeira flowed, backgammon, bridge and solo were played for money; but on Sundays no games, not even tennis, were allowed, and the only distractions in the gloom which had descended on the house were sessions of hymn-singing, on which my father sometimes insisted to break the monotony of those Sunday afternoons. An English, or rather Scottish, sabbath was hard to reconcile with a Levantine Saturday.

Already on Saturday evening I used to sense the oncoming of the Sunday gloom; next morning I would dally in dressing as much as I dared in the hope, rarely to be fulfilled, that my parents would go off to church without me, satisfied to be accompanied by my sisters and brothers. Sometimes I would feel suddenly sick or queasy at around half past nine in the morning, but when I risked that ultimate stratagem it had one unfortunate drawback, that the recovery could not always be rapid enough to permit attendance at lunch, so that I had to choose between missing church and missing the Sunday roast. Perhaps it was at this early age that I learnt that life does not always offer a choice between objects desired, but too often between evils to be avoided, and from this childhood dilemma perhaps sprang a later difficulty in making any choice at all, and a strong propensity to procrastinate.

So strong was my aversion to the churchgoing on Sunday morning, Sunday-school in the afternoon, and the hymn-singing which sometimes followed tea in the drawing-room, that even now, sixty years later, I derive a positive pleasure from the thought on a Sunday morning that nothing obliges me to go to church – though I sometimes do – and that I am free, free, free. It took me many years, however, before I was able to lie abed on a Sunday morning and savour the extraordinary pleasure of doing nothing, enhanced in me by the fact that deep down in the recesses of my Calvinistic childhood subconscious lurks the conviction of the sinfulness of sloth, so that I have a double joy – both the sensation of idleness and the pleasure of sin.

Between the always exuberant and sometimes mysterious intrusions made into our life at home by figures from the Levant and from its outposts in the New World, and the sober and often gloomy presence of the Presbyterians, a child would naturally be attracted to the first rather than to the second. The problem of where I belonged, and from where I came, did not present itself in my early childhood: our home was essentially a Lebanese one, our friends the children of other families from the same oriental world, and it was only when the outside world began to impinge on my consciousness that I began to feel that perhaps I was different from the English children whom I began to meet at nursery school.

My first memory of such a feeling is connected with a family happening when I was seven years old. My eldest sister, who in her youth was as dark and oriental-looking as any of her Yemeni or Haurani ancestors, was marrying a young man from Haifa, himself unmistakably a member of *Qahtan*, a collective name by which the Arabs sometimes call themselves. The marriage was to take place in a suburb nearby in the most conventional and respectable way. My mother had evidently consulted her English friends, or perhaps it was the shopfitters at Kendal Milnes where she bought our clothes who advised her on the appropriate outfit for the three young brothers of the bride. The decision was reached – naturally without consulting us – that we should wear black-striped trousers and jackets, and on our heads, on our way to and from the church and the hall where the wedding reception was to be held, little black bowler hats. When the hats arrived, and we tried them on, I became acutely aware that the effect, especially on me, was ludicrous: my narrow Semitic head, sallow complexion, and a profile marked by a long nose and a receding chin fitted uneasily and unconvincingly into that little hard black horror. I refused to put it on, although ordered by my parents to do so as we set out for the church, and kept it hidden as far as possible from the view of the other children at the wedding. For me the wedding was ruined, and I have never since been able to wear a hat of any sort.

Later on, at public school, I became more conscious of the fact that among English children, and also to some extent among grown-ups, physical appearance is an important element in belonging, and that there is a racial and physical aspect to the English national consciousness. I was more hairy than most English boys, although I remember the satisfaction it caused me when a new boy arrived who, though his name was undoubtedly English, was covered all over his body with a much thicker and more extensive growth of hair than was I. In the England of today these differences have ceased to have much importance, but fifty years ago they mattered, at least to me.

That my father was aware that his children – I at least – might feel handicapped by the more obvious signs of our foreign origin was revealed to me by a curious conversation he had with me just before I went up to Oxford: if I should find that our family name marked me as non-English, and this caused me embarrassment, he would have no objection to my changing it. I do not know if he ever made such a suggestion to my brothers, but I rejected it with indignation. I *liked* our name, and was happy that it made us different. Perhaps the suggestion had some basis in his own experience. Had he felt, perhaps, some disadvantage, some handicap in his doubly foreign name, Fadlo Hourani? He had taken the precaution of giving his children two names, the first English, the second Arabic – in my case, Amin – and perhaps he felt in himself a conflict or contradiction between his Lebanese Arabic personality and his acquired English one which he did not wish his children to inherit. These are questions I never felt I could ask him. To the end of his long life, though attached by sentiment, memory, loyalty to the land of his birth, he remained convinced of the superiority of English life and government, business methods and personal values to those of the East, and even claimed that he owed the healthy ruddiness of his cheeks to the English climate which, he believed, had saved him from the sallow complexion of many of his fellow countrymen.

When my father looked for a school for my two elder brothers, he had to choose between sending them to the local primary school, which he found too rough and rowdy, or to the best private school in the area. He went to meet the headmaster of this snobbish institution, but was told that it only accepted English boys. To my father, who had by now, more than thirty years after he had first come to Manchester, integrated himself, in his own mind at least, into the business society of the city and the predominantly Scottish society of his Presbyterian church, this came as a shock and a challenge. He decided to set up his own school; he found a headmaster, took a house, and thus was created the 'Didsbury Preparatory School'.

The students of this unique school were never more than about thirty-five in number, and of these one third were the children of Lebanese and Syrian families like my own, one third English, and one third the children of Jewish families, mostly of oriental origin from Beirut, Damascus, Aleppo, Baghdad, Cairo, Istanbul and Tripoli. Majdalani, Matar, Racy, Bardawil, Hourani, Chiha, Ydlbi, Saidi, Moukhaish, Ramadan, Haffar, Silvera, Levy, Nahum, Anzarout, Shou'a, Shashoua, Jeddai, Bigio were the names of some of the families of our oriental community from whom came most of our fellow students and friends. That some were Christian, some Muslim, some Jewish I was hardly conscious: our Jewish friends, for example, ate the same food as we did, and frequented the same greengrocer from Lebanon whose shop, after service was over in the Portuguese-Spanish synagogue in West Didsbury, was filled with Jewish families talking Arabic while picking and choosing the vegetables and fruit exactly as my mother and her friends did, and as the English greengrocers would not permit. If anything, the Jewish families were more attached to their oriental origins than were some of us Christians: our families did not make any attempt to teach us Arabic, convinced as they were that we were going to grow up totally English, whereas the Jewish boys were taught by Rabbi Mendoza not only Hebrew in preparation for their bar-mitzvah, but also Arabic. Of Palestine, and Zionism, we were completely ignorant, and I do not believe that at that time the oriental Jewish community knew or wished to know anything about the Zionist movement, although Manchester was one of its strongholds, and one of our schoolfriends, Daniel Sieff, came from a family which was one of its pillars.

Outside of home and school there was another world in Manchester which formed my childhood imagination. To visit my father's office and warehouse in Major Street in downtown Manchester was one of the principal treats in which he would indulge me. In what seemed to me – and indeed was – a vast space, trolleys loaded with textiles were wheeled across the warehouse's wooden floors to be piled onto lifts that were still operated in those days by hand, and on which I used to ride up and down while the cloth was being packed in cases ready to be sent off on the horse-drawn trucks which still rumbled over the cobbled streets. In my father's office I would meet his clients from Brazil or North America or West Africa, or his fellow

Lebanese merchants, and in the warehouse chat or play games with the Lancashire workmen who numbered about twenty in the days of my father's greatest prosperity before the crash of 1929. In the 1890s, when my father had arrived in Manchester to work in the firm of a first cousin already successfully established there, Manchester was still the chief supplier of cotton and woollen goods to the Ottoman Empire and North Africa, and merchants from Beirut, Damascus, Baghdad, Alexandria and Cairo, Istanbul and Morocco set up their export businesses there; alone of all these oriental merchants the Moroccans kept to their traditional dress, and I remember with what wonder I used to see them in their burnouses and slippers walking in the rainy streets. But after 1929, when my father like so many others lost his money on orders placed with manufacturers in Lancashire and Yorkshire which his clients in Brazil could not take up, his business shrank and changed direction, as Manchester itself lost most of its pre-eminence in the markets of the East to the growing competition of Italy and Japan. But West Africa was being opened up to commerce by the adventurous spirit and enterprise of Lebanese traders, mostly from south Lebanon, and my father had designed and printed for this new market 'African prints' of astonishing colours and motifs inspired by designs from Java and Indonesia.

My father's business and social life, however, was not confined to the world of his Lebanese and Syrian customers and fellow merchants: he called himself a 'citizen of no mean city', and took pride in the city's political, cultural and educational life, and participated in some of its aspects. As a young man he had come to the centre of liberal thought and politics: statues of Cobden and Bright, the Manchester Free Trade Hall, Gladstone, the Town Hall, the Ship Canal, the opening of which he attended in 1891 when he saw Queen Victoria, the Hallé Orchestra, the Reform Club of which he was a member for many years, and where he regularly lunched and played bridge, the *Manchester Guardian* and C. P. Scott – all these visible signs and symbols of Victorian Manchester's greatness were vivid in his memory and were communicated to me. When later in his life – in 1946 – he became Honorary

Consul of Lebanon in Manchester and northern England, he delighted in the official status which this gave him, the opportunity to participate in the city's life, and to enter the town hall, which to him was the highest symbol of Manchester's greatness, as the representative of the country of his birth.

Much of this pride in and enjoyment of Manchester life was passed on to us children. From its public libraries I had access to the books which fed my voracious appetite for reading, the Hallé Orchestra and the yearly performance of *The Messiah* at the Free Trade Hall opened up the world of music, the Reform Club, where my father would take me often to lunch, gave me an insight into the characters of the merchants and bankers who were the backbone of Manchester's civic life – into that mixture of shrewdness, humour, common sense and concern for the problems of the world which distinguished the people of Lancashire: for Manchester was a metropolis which, because of its commerce with the outside world, escaped the provincialism of most other English cities, and felt it had missions beyond its central purpose of making money.

That there was another, darker side to the prosperous city within whose comfortable bourne we lived I became well aware at an early age. Our English nurse, Miss Ray, who remained with our family for forty years, came from Hereford from a social class which had been submerged in the early nineteenth century by industrial England, and earlier on by the encroachment of the landed gentry on the small land-holders who had been England's backbone in Tudor and Elizabethan times. She herself had found employment in the house of some member of the landed gentry before she came to us, but other members of her family had been less fortunate. A brother, gassed in the First World War, was unemployed for many years, and a sister in poor health lived in a dismal back street of Rusholme, then one of the more depressed areas of Manchester. Miss Ray would sometimes take me to visit her and the German lady who, impoverished herself, shared the mean cottage in which they lived. I well remember that there was almost nothing in the house, and that the greatest struggle of their lives was to keep themselves warm by the one coal fire, and on the cups of tea which were their main sustenance. I well remember too the feeling of guilt these visits gave me, that we should be living in comfort and ease while in these dark and primitive houses, not only in the far-off lands of Africa and China that we were shown on lantern slides in Sunday school, where Scottish missionaries ministered to the poor heathen natives, lived people here in Manchester. I can remember too the sight of women and girls barefooted in the back streets of Manchester, not like the privileged young people of today who walk unshod in the streets to demonstrate their 'freedom' from the trammels of civilization, but because they could not afford the money to buy shoes.

Thus were stirred in me the first intimations of a social conscience which, had I lived all my life in England, would probably have taken me into some sector of left-wing politics, perhaps the most radical, which in those days was the Communist Party. I was indeed tempted in that direction by an early feeling for the underdog, planted in me perhaps by the revolutionary ideas preached by Peter the sailor in his letters from Africa, and by the persuasive oratory of a Communist speaker in one of Manchester's public parks where I used to go unbeknown to my family, to listen to this new religion so much more intelligible than the sermons of our Presbyterian pastor. The Russian Revolution was recent, Trotsky was still active, and his *History of the Revolution* excited me as few other books have ever done. His picture, along with that of Lenin, I put up in our kitchen where it long hung to the complete indifference of my parents, and to the wonder of Hannah, our English cook.

At the age of fourteen I was sent, like my brothers, to a public school in London chosen by my father because it was not a Church of England institution, but one founded at the beginning of the nineteenth century for the children of 'dissenters'. I believe we were fortunate in my father's choice of Mill Hill School for our secondary education. It did not have the rigid and ridiculous conventions of many of the older – and even some of the newer – public schools, and there was an atmosphere of tolerance and respect for the individual created by a liberal tradition among its headmasters and masters, among whom had been Sir James Murray, originator of the *Oxford English Dictionary*, and in my day Maurice Jacks, son of a famous theologian and himself a civilized and humanistic man. There was little bullying of younger boys, a mild and harmless fagging system, and no excessive idealization of sport or contempt for literary or scholarly interests. It was my first experience of living in a purely English society, and I was, I think, happy with my friends and with the life of the school. I liked my teachers, among whom were A. D. Whitehorn (father of Katharine), an excellent classical scholar and a man of broad culture, Mr Mclelland, who succeeded in teaching me French, Mr A. J. Williams and Mr J. P. Taylor, teachers of history who influenced me towards making that my major subject in the four years I spent after obtaining the School Certificate at the end of my first year. These four years in which I studied a wide variety of subjects for the Higher Certificate, including musical theory and composition, gave me the chance not only to read widely, but also to satisfy my passion for music, which I studied under Mr Cane, who had been a student of Parry, and whose musical masters were German and Elgar; and with Charles Super, first flautist of the London Symphony Orchestra. The small orchestra of which I was a member played symphonies by Mendelssohn and Haydn and works by German and Elgar, and I acquired an extensive knowledge of the repertoire of the flute. At a certain point I announced to my parents my decision that I wished to become a professional flautist, and suggested that they should allow me to leave Mill Hill and enter a school of music – an idea which found no favour in their eyes.

It was the tolerant climate of Mill Hill, I believe, which reduced considerably the attractions of radicalism which flourished in some other public schools and which spilled over into Oxford where I was later to meet it in various forms. There was no need to revolt at Mill Hill because the spirit of dissent, inherited from its founders' charter, was part of its tradition: eccentricities of behaviour or views were not persecuted, nonconformism even encouraged. My first acquaintance with ideas and movements of revolt which were brewing in other institutions came with the arrival at school of a student – I think it was John Bunting – who was in touch with Esmond Romilly and other members of the group who were then challenging the conventions of Eton and Harrow, and groping towards an upper-class radicalism which was really a return to the older traditions of revolt which have often characterized the privileged sections of British society. I read with curiosity the school literature this group were putting out, and found in it a clear reflection of a book which had already impressed me and which still seems to me to be the classical expression of revolt against British society pushed to the ridiculous extreme, *Erewhon* by Samuel Butler. I was far more influenced by the books of Anatole France in their English translation by J. L. May, who, I discovered, lived not far from Mill Hill, and who was the first 'man of letters' I was to meet.

My early fascination with the Russian Revolution, and the slight contacts I had had in Manchester with the Communist Party there, which had actually led me to attend a meeting of the Young Communist League in, I believe, Birmingham, did not develop into a deeper involvement while I was at Mill Hill. That they did not do so was the result of several factors. One was a conversation with Amin Kisbany, my father's friend and our childhood 'godfather' as it were, during a visit he made to me on a Saturday afternoon when we were allowed out of school to visit a neighbouring tea-shop. I revealed to him that I was reading Marx and Lenin – cheap editions of whose works were then available in certain bookshops in Manchester – and that I felt attracted towards Communism. I did not believe in God, and found the Marxist theory of history a much more satisfactory explanation of events than Presbyterian theology – what did he advise me to do? Should I join the Communist Party? His reply was to compliment me on the motives which had brought me to my present position: concern for the poor and the underdogs of this world, a vision of a more just society. At my age these were noble sentiments, but – and it was this 'but' which shattered me – these sentiments were those of youth, they would pass when I grew older. It was as though an older man, talking to a youth smitten with the first pangs of what he believed to be eternal love, revealed to him that his sentiments found their origin not in the object of his affections, but in his own youthful immaturity: Communism, like love, was a state of the glands, not a response to an objective reality. From that moment onwards I felt a doubt in the validity of my ideas which restrained me from putting into practice what both Christianity and Marxism taught, that to believe is to act.

Another reason for my distancing myself from any involvement with Communist activity was the contradiction I early discovered between what Marx had taught and what Lenin and his successors practised. What I liked in Marx was his vision of society without the state, and the idea of the state 'withering away', but as I became more aware of what was actually happening in Russia, and learnt of the triumph of Stalin over my childhood hero Trotsky, I became more attracted to anarchism, first of all to the writings and personality of Bakunin, later on of Kropotkin. If the goal of revolution was the abolition of the state, what would be the point of abolishing one kind of state only to replace it with another? There was perhaps a streak of extremism in my temperament which made the ideas of Bakunin particularly attractive to me. I liked the thought of a violent and apocalyptic revolution and the free society which would follow, though I did not at all place it within the context of the England in which I was living: it was to be somewhere else, in some not clearly defined country, and most probably in Russia, towards which my early reading of Alexander Herzen and my fascination with the lives of the Russian social revolutionaries such as Vera Zasulich had drawn me. Later on the combined influence of Tolstoy, Kropotkin and above all William Morris steered me to a milder vision of the stateless society, and the doctrine of organized non-violence which was then being put into practice in India by Mahatma Gandhi and his followers seemed to me to be the true way.

I never imagined at that time that one day I would experience at first hand the withering away of the state, but when I lived through that experience in Lebanon between 1975 and 1982 I was confirmed in my youthful belief that anarchy is preferable to despotism, although the conditions of insecurity, terror and violence in which we survived bore no relation to the Utopian visions of Kropotkin or Morris, but were in fact a faithful reproduction of Hobbes's description of man's life in a state of nature – 'nasty, brutish and short'.

That I did not, at Mill Hill or later at Oxford, become involved seriously in any political activity was above all due to the attraction of Arab politics, and especially of the Palestinian problem, of which I became more and more conscious. The seeds of this attraction had been sown, I think, in an event in our family life which occurred when I was very small. There was one day an unusual commotion in the house, especially in the kitchen, where my mother's friends from the Lebanese community had assembled and were busy preparing large quantities of food. Amin Kisbany was to bring to lunch the Emir Zaid, youngest son of Sherif Hussein and brother of Faisal of Iraq and Abdullah of Transjordan, and my father had invited to our house those members of the community who were in sympathy with the Arab cause. I was too young to attend the lunch, but I was allowed to shake the hand of the Emir, who, if my memory is correct, was wearing the gold and white headdress of a Sherifian noble,[7] and of whose short and swarthy figure I retain a dim memory, to be revived in later years when I knew him as Ambassador of Iraq to the Court of St James's.

There were other visitors to our house from the East who brought with them intimations of problems and passions then only dimly perceived but later on to be made clear to me. One such was Selim Bey Salam, a leading Muslim notable from Beirut who had supported the Arab kingdom of Faisal, and whose son Saeb[8] was to play – and still plays – a decisive role in the reconciliation of Arab sympathy with Lebanese loyalty; and in the late twenties and early thirties delegations of Arabs from Palestine came frequently to London, where my father would sometimes go to meet them, or bring them to Manchester. Among these visitors was Jamal Husseini, cousin of the Mufti of Jerusalem,[9] and himself a member of the Higher Arab Committee.

I was already at Oxford when the Arab revolution broke out in Palestine in 1936, the most serious challenge as yet to British rule and to Zionism. It coincided with the outbreak of the

Spanish Civil War, and it aroused in me the same passionate feelings as did the republican cause in Spain among my contemporaries at Oxford. Although I also sympathized with that cause, my feelings were mixed, perhaps confused, by the fact that the spearhead of General Franco's forces were the Moroccan soldiers from Spain's North African territories. I had been earlier fired with enthusiasm for the Moroccan resistance to Spain led by Abdulkerim al Khattabi, and so my attitude towards the Civil War was ambiguous. On the one hand my sympathies were with the republicans, and in particular with the anarchists, but on the other hand the fact that Moroccans were fighting on European soil appeared to me – romantically rather than realistically – as a delayed revenge for the expulsion of the Arabs from Spain in the fifteenth century. For the cause of the Arabs of Palestine there was no such ambiguity or reservation in my mind: I saw it as the uncomplicated struggle of an oppressed people against an imperialist power, and Zionism, of which I knew little, seemed to me of secondary importance, providing the motive for the Arab revolt, but not its principal cause.

My interest in Arab politics while I was at Oxford was an important factor in my search for identity. At Mill Hill the student body had been, with very few exceptions, entirely English, but at Oxford there were students from Arab countries whom I sought out. Luli Abulhuda, Auni Dajani, Chafiq Ghazzeddin, George Mur came from Egypt, Palestine and Lebanon, and together we founded the first Arab Club in Oxford, though the range of our activities was limited to drinking Turkish coffee in each other's rooms.

I did indeed in my last year at Oxford receive a visit from a Palestinian from the Husseini family, Musa Abdullah, who tried to persuade me to go with him to Germany where there was to be a meeting of Arab nationalists all involved in one way or another with the Arab revolt against Great Britain then taking place in Palestine. Tempted as I was by the prospect of meeting men many of whom I knew by name and whom I thought of as the authentic heirs of the Arab revolt of Sherif Hussein, I fortunately preferred the intellectual and aesthetic pleasures of which I had had a foretaste in France, as I shall relate. Musa Husseini was to remain in Germany during the war, where he was closely associated with the Mufti of Jerusalem, Haj Amin al Husseini, and his end was dramatic: he was accused of complicity in the assassination of King Abdullah of Jordan in 1951, tried, and executed by the Jordanian authorities.

I was fortunate, in the three years which I spent at Magdalen reading politics, philosophy and economics, in my tutors and in the friendships which I made inside and outside the college. Both my philosophy tutors – now dead – were in their different ways remarkable. T. D. Weldon, whose output of publications was small and whose diffidence concerning his own talents sprang from a certain cynicism about the world around him, took me through the English empiricists to Kant and Hegel, passing through Rousseau; he had not yet been affected by the contemporary obsession at Oxford with logical positivism, and still believed that metaphysics had meaning. But in order to give me the opportunity of studying with someone more in touch with the new fad for analysis of which A. J. Ayer was the prophet, himself the main exponent of the work of Wittgenstein, Weldon recommended me to go to his colleague J. L. Austin to study logic. I was his student for two or three terms, but never penetrated the almost inhuman reserve with which he faced the world. He had carried the analysis of propositions, and indeed of words, so far that nothing remained of metaphysics, and little of classical logic: by the destruction of metaphysical speculation he had succeeded, for himself at least, in separating reason from life, and perhaps there lay under that cold and apparently austere exterior rivers of feeling freed from the restraints of ethics or religion whose propositions he had demolished to his own satisfaction. But he made me conscious of the importance of exactitude in speech and writing, and of the study of the meaning of meaning, and though what he had to teach was negative, and demolished more than it constructed, he sharpened my mind on the whetstone of his own, and awoke in me a critical sense without infecting me permanently with the extremism of his devastating methodology.

The most stimulating intellectual contact, however, and the

one which had the most lasting impact on me was that which I received from the lectures and the conversation of Isaiah Berlin. I do not think anyone who heard his lectures on Marx could have been insensible to that torrential flow of ideas and the long melodic line of his sentences which like a Bellini aria carried one along to a conclusion that one hoped would never arrive, so enchanting were the lights it shone on obscure and unknown corners in the history of ideas. It was indeed as a historian of ideas that he excelled and stimulated his listeners to follow the paths he showed them. His lectures, and the book on Karl Marx he published in 1939, while doing justice to that powerful and original mind, placed it within a well-defined historical and intellectual context and thus set limits to the claims of those who believed that Marxism was a 'final revelation' similar to that which Islam claims for the Quran, and convinced me that Marx was not a Marxist: and therefore why should I be?

Brilliant as were his lectures, Isaiah Berlin's conversation was even more stimulating. I do not remember in what circumstances I first met him, or why he, already a famous man with hundreds of friends, showed an interest in me. It was perhaps because he knew of my Lebanese origins, and of my interest in the Palestinian question, or perhaps because he sensed in me some of the problems which he himself had faced as the son of an immigrant merchant from Riga, although in his case he had been born there and had come to England with a Russian and European culture already imprinted on his mind. My visits to his rooms in New College were not frequent, though of those rooms themselves I have a distinct recollection, dominated as they were by the gigantic horn of the EMI gramophone on which he explored the lesser-known works of Verdi and Donizetti; but each visit excited me as though some strong injection had been administered to my mind, so full was his conversation of ideas, questions, speculations, similes, paradoxes. He did not intimidate me, as a less sensitive or considerate man might have done, nor did I feel that he was ever showing off: on the contrary, he would draw out from his interlocutor an idea and, like Bach with Frederick the Great, embroider on that theme a set of variations which one did not suspect the idea was capable of sustaining.

Although he was closely linked to the current schools of thought at Oxford which were strongly influenced by positivism and analysis, and contributed to their search for meaning in words and propositions, he himself had inherited from his Russian and Jewish background a humanistic outlook which drew on Russian, German, French, Italian and Jewish sources as well as English: and although he was, I believe, both intellectually and socially at home, or at least at ease, in England, he was really a European in the best sense of the word, and was my first contact with what I only dimly perceived was a world of culture and civilization outside the narrow confines of what I had met as yet in Manchester, Mill Hill, or even Magdalen. I remember with what excitement I discovered, at his suggestion, the essays of Sainte-Beuve which opened up a whole world of speculation and criticism of which I had been completely unaware.

That he was a Zionist I knew, but in those pre-war days the problem of Arab-Jewish relations had not reached that stage of acerbation which the creation of Israel in 1948 produced, nor had the persecution of the Jews in Europe – although it had already begun – reached the climax of the Holocaust, pushing Berlin like many other Jewish intellectuals, who might otherwise have been happy with a Jewish homeland in Palestine shared with its Arab population, to the belief that nothing less than a Jewish state could solve the problem of Jews within European and Western society. It was only much later that I came to appreciate the reasons for which a man like him, accepted and honoured in English society as he is, would not only sympathize with, but actually participate in the foundation of a Jewish state: as friend and adviser to Chaim Weizmann and other Jewish leaders, he was closely associated with the early years of Israel's existence. But my respect and friendship for him were never altered by my own involvement in Palestinian and Arab politics.

At the end of my second year at Oxford my intellectual and cultural horizons were to be widened by an extraordinary opportunity which came to me and my closest friend at that time, John Russell, now equally known on both sides of the Atlantic as art critic and historian. One day at the end of the summer term we happened to see a notice on the board at the porter's lodge, or main gate, of Magdalen: a small typewritten letter saying that any students who would like to spend some time in a 'foyer' for intellectuals and writers outside Paris were welcome to write to a M. Champigneulle at the Abbey of Royaumont. We did so, and in due course received a letter of welcome telling us how to get there.

Today the Abbey of Royaumont, near the forest of Chantilly, has become well known as the scene of concerts and conferences, but in 1937 it had only just been restored by its owner, Félix Gouin,[10] an enlightened and generous patron of culture. The Abbey had been founded by Louis IX, leader of a lost Crusade which foundered finally in Tunis, and had been closed and partially demolished at the Revolution. From its ruins Félix Gouin salvaged an elegant house for himself, a chapel and refectory, and a series of monastic rooms furnished sparsely but adequately for the visitors he hoped to attract, and the arches and buttresses of its still-ruined church towered romantically over the cloistered garden. I can still recollect our astonishment and pleasure, and still smell the perfume of the garden's scented hedges when we arrived by taxi from Paris. I remember too that at our first dinner that night, at the hospitable table presided over by Champigneulle himself and his beautiful and mysterious wife, we were given creamed spinach with nutmeg to follow the meat course – a surprising novelty to my provincial and untutored taste – and I can never eat that dish without a recollection of my first initiation into the cuisine and culture of France.

It was the wish of M. Champigneulle that, while no restrictions were placed on what his guests – for that we were, although we paid a nominal weekly alimony – might do during the day, we should meet each other at dinner and contribute to the social and intellectual intercourse which he sought to promote. It was an easy and a rewarding obligation, for there were guests with whom we soon established a close relationship: Champigneulle had a wide variety of friends from French artistic and intellectual circles, and attracted to Royaumont some already famous, others to become so later on. Among the first was a Professor of Philosophy at the Sorbonne, Jean Wahl,[11] a prolific writer and a generous conversationalist. He was intrigued, I think, by the two students from Oxford on whom he could test his own views and theories about English philosophy and literature. He was in philosophy an enemy of the positivism which flourished in Oxford, and considered himself to be in the line of Kant, Hegel, and in more recent times Kierkegaard and Heidegger; in English literature his particular admiration went to the works of Edgar Allan Poe and to Oscar Wilde, whose *Ballad of Reading Gaol* he believed to be one of the great works of modern literature – he was astonished at the little regard with which it was held in England – and of living writers he admired above all Virginia Woolf and Henry Greene. To this tiny, ugly, atrociously dressed man, whose conversation, like his writings, was full of Hegelian contradictions which he sought to resolve, delighting as he did in paradoxes and enigmas, I owe an enormous debt of gratitude, not only for his friendship, but also for the chance he gave us to accompany him to Pontigny, the 'high place' of French culture in the 1920s and 1930s.

Among other guests at Royaumont were Jules Supervielle, the poet, who first gave me the taste for French poetry, Daniel Halévy, historian of French socialism, Daniel Lesur, composer and musician, and two very young violinists: one Polish, and already becoming known – Henri Szeryng, with whom I remember playing the trio sonata from Bach's *Musical Offering*, and *Le Tombeau de Couperin*; and the other, a girl from Vienna with whom I quickly fell in love. Liselotte Marcus was a pupil of Huberman and might, had she pursued her musical career, have achieved fame; she was Jewish, and terrified of the storm which she saw coming: she told me that her fiancé in Vienna wanted desperately to leave, but needed help, somewhere to go, could I help him come to England? It was the first time I had met someone from that soon-to-be submerged world of Jewish Vienna and come into contact with the reality of anti-Semitism. I was able eventually to help her friend come, with his mother and brother, to Oxford, where they found a home in the house of Maurice Bowra, Warden of Wadham

College. It was one of the great pleasures of my last year at Oxford to visit the Grafe family in that extraordinary kitchen where Mrs Grafe had installed the library they had somehow managed to bring with them from Vienna, to eat the Viennese pastry which she used to make for Bowra but kept a part for me, and to get from her lively and witty conversation some inkling into the life of a world about to be destroyed.

At the end of two weeks at Royaumont Jean Wahl asked John Russell and myself if we would care to accompany him to Pontigny: we had no idea where Pontigny was, or what went on there, or what it represented in the intellectual life of the times, but, our appetites already whetted by our stay at Royaumont, we agreed. Pontigny in Burgundy, like Royaumont, was a medieval abbey, but of the Cistercian order – to which its stark white church bore witness. It was the property of Paul Desjardins, a man who figures in many *mémoires* of the literary and intellectual history of France in the first half of the twentieth century, but who wrote little himself, and whose great contribution was that of an *animateur* who brought together for the *décades* at Pontigny the flower of French culture. The *décades*, which in reality lasted one week, took place three times a year in summer, and each one was devoted to a subject to be discussed without any formal agenda or programme, and in an atmosphere of complete freedom. There was no obligation to contribute to the discussions, and indeed I would have been completely intimidated by the persons there had I had to reveal both the poverty of my French and the gap which existed between the narrow horizons of my ideas and culture, and the width and range of the intellects there assembled. But at table, in the elegant salons and the beautiful gardens which Desjardins and his wife placed at the disposal of their guests, we met and talked with some of the most famous and interesting figures of France.

I remember meeting Clara Malraux, for whose husband André I had already conceived a deep admiration from reading *Les Conquérants*; Bernard Groethuysen, half Dutch and half Russian, but living in Paris for much of his life, and following in the traditions of scepticism and rationalism of French thought since Diderot and the Encyclopaedists; Henri

Focillon, whose works on Gothic art and the artistic history of medieval France are still the classics in that field; Vladimir Jankelevitch and the two girls from Algeria who were his companions, still one of the most penetrating intellects of France, teaching and writing at the Sorbonne; and Nicolas Berdyaev, the unorthodox Orthodox thinker exiled from the Soviet Union to France. By 1938 Pontigny, to which I returned in 1939, the last year of its existence, had already become famous outside France, and there were guests from Europe, the USA and even Japan, some old, some young, among whom I found friends, though none of them I met again. But of the figures and the faces at Pontigny I vividly recall that of Paul Desjardins himself, tall, slightly *distrait*, but always gracious and brilliant in conversation; Mme Desjardins, a shorter, stockier figure who ruled where her husband reigned; the slim, birdlike, trousered Clara Malraux; Groethuysen, whose facial tic disturbed me at meals; Berdyaev, whose white hair sticking out from the sides of his velvet cap confirmed his prophetic soul; the cloaked figure of André Gide, one of the pillars of Pontigny, to whom I dared not talk, much as I wished to; and the white shoulders of Mme Forte from Algiers which, forty-four years later, still haunt my dreams.

Berdyaev, in his autobiographical book *Dream and Reality*,[12] has left a description of the *décades* of Pontigny which corresponds very much to what I remember:

The range of subjects was very wide indeed: romanticism; toleration and the totalitarian state; asceticism; the function of writers and intellectuals in modern society; and solitude, are some of those I remember.... Despite the multifariousness of the participants the atmosphere had a natural and friendly character and the intellectual level of the discussions was very high. There was even a note of elegance, largely due, no doubt, to the invariable presence of a number of beautiful and smartly-dressed women. The food and wines were excellent....

But to this picture of the world of Pontigny Berdyaev could not resist adding this – from him – damning comment: 'The whole set-up was typical of the prosperous and cultured French bourgeoisie.'

II
Return to the Sources

A favourite question of my father on all occasions when he believed some decision had to be made by me was: 'What is the next step?' I never liked this question, which seemed to pin me down, to force me to choose, to envisage an order and a progression in my life which by instinct, habit and a deliberate attitude of mind I sought to avoid. I had indeed never, except for my brief decision at school to become a professional flautist, thought about a 'career': in fact I positively disliked the idea, and wanted to be free to follow wherever chance or my intuition might take me. This attitude was certainly not based on any expectation that my father might be able to support me, but I was completely regardless of how I would 'earn my living' or what my 'future' might be: these seemed to me unnecessary and unpleasing questions. I think that in this carefree attitude I must have been influenced by the example of Amin Kisbany whose varied and nomadic life between Morocco and Baghdad was to my father the very epitome of unwisdom, but to me far more attractive than life in an office in Manchester.

Perhaps the reason why I had avoided thinking seriously about my future, or 'the future' in general, was the shadow of the coming war of which I and my fellow students were all conscious. We were not like those generations of students and young men before 1914 who had rarely sensed the coming storm and, if they did, never envisaged its full horror or the extent of its duration. We had read the lives of Rupert Brooke, Wilfred Owen, and all the other poets, writers, artists, and simply talented or even ordinary young men whom friends or parents or schools had commemorated in books as brief as their short span, and although we were not anxious to throw away our lives as many had done in 1914 and after, we were all of us, I think, conscious that our 'future' might not exist – better then not to think about it. In fact, when I look at the names of my friends at Mill Hill and Oxford who never returned home, the list is painfully long.

There were, however, people in the establishment, perhaps in the War Office itself, who had thought about the indiscriminate way in which the educated young men of England had been sent to die in France in the First World War, and wished to avoid a repetition of that waste. So when war broke out in September 1939 committees were set up before which the students could appear to see how best they could be used. Appearance before these committees was voluntary, so I decided that it was wiser to present myself to one which sat in Oxford, rather than run the risk of the conscription which was bound to follow later.

Of that committee I only remember that Professor Gibb, an orientalist who held the chair of Arabic, was a member. I do not think the committee regarded me as very promising material for the army. At Mill Hill I had preferred to become a boy scout rather than join the Officers' Training Corps because I was a pacifist, and although at Oxford I had, for some reason which I am now unable to remember, joined the Revolver Club, my weedy physique and unmartial appearance did not convince the officer on the committee that I was indispensable to England's war effort. The war had not yet begun seriously, no one knew or foresaw on what battlefields it would be fought, and the committee readily agreed to Gibb's suggestion that I go to the East to learn Arabic; he knew of my background, and was to recruit my brother Albert into his own section of the Royal Institute of International Affairs which did research and prepared papers on Near Eastern affairs, and no doubt felt that it was in some such activity that I could eventually be useful.

So, armed with a letter from Gibb, I set out on my own towards Beirut where at all events, had there been no war, I had hoped to go to discover the land from where I felt I came. Passing through Paris to see some of the friends I had made at Royaumont and Pontigny, I found a city dark and quiet: the black-out was in force, and a mood of pessimism and doubt already infused my friends. I took the train to Venice – for Italy had not yet joined the war – and from there embarked on the *Marco Polo*. Of those four or five days spent on the sea certain memories remain fixed in my mind. One is of a Lebanese musician returning to die in his village, his throat bandaged, his voice only a croak – for he had cancer – and in his arms an *'oud*, or Arabic lute, on which he played his last melancholy farewell to Europe; another is of a frail Jewish girl called Ruth Segal going from South Africa to live in Palestine; another of our arrival in Alexandria and the extraordinary scenes of chaos on its quays as the Egyptian porters fought each other for the disembarking passengers' effects, my first impression of the East.

So my return to Lebanon, or rather my first visit – for my parents had never taken me there in childhood – had a double sense. On the one hand it came about as a result of the outbreak of war, and of my desire to play, as all my friends were planning to do, some role, as yet undefined; on the other hand it was a journey back into time, to discover for myself the landscape of my parents' home and the society in which they had grown up. There was therefore from the beginning an ambiguity about my attitude which found its reflection in the attitudes even of some members of my own family towards me: was I coming as an Englishman looking for ways to serve the country of his birth, or was I a Lebanese looking for his roots? The truth was that I was both, but this was not easy for everyone to believe. It took me many years before I could resolve the duality in my own mind, and reconcile the loyalties of my divided self.

But these questions did not at first cloud the excitement I felt at my first visit to my parents' homes. In Manchester my father would often describe to me the view from the house he had built for his mother overlooking the western slopes of Mount Hermon: how the sun would rise each morning from behind its ranges covered in winter with snow, and how at sunset the mountain would turn purple in several shades, and the moon rise gigantic over its top. He would tell me of an ancient market held on Tuesdays where the villagers from the foothills of

Hermon would gather by a ruined caravanserai to sell and buy their cattle, mules, horses and donkeys and the produce of their land, and how as a boy he would eat there freshly killed meat served on stone tables under a bower of leaves and branches, and ice-cream made with snow brought down from the mountain caves where it was stored to last all summer.

I had never known my grandparents, nor my father's five older sisters, nor more than one or two of my mother's thirteen brothers and sisters, and only a few who came to visit us in Manchester of the hundreds of cousins still living in Lebanon or scattered around Brazil and North America, and yet I knew that my parents had maintained close contact with them all, and that we had an extended family in every sense of the word. My first visit to these scenes of which in Manchester I had been able to form only a hazy picture, and to the family in whose hearts I had a place as the youngest son of Fadlo and Soumaya, who themselves, over many years of philanthropy and love, had acquired a legendary status in their villages, was inevitably a momentous event in my life.

It was one of those days at the beginning of winter in Lebanon when torrential rains and violent thunderstorms break the long spell of summer heat that I chose to go up to Marjayoun from Beirut, where I had been staying with my second sister. As I approached the town, thick mists hid from me the castle of Beaufort which hangs over a precipice above the Litani river foaming beneath, and the storm grew more violent: peals of thunder echoed between the hills lit up by fantastic streaks of lightning. The chauffeur who had brought me in his car took me to our house, but there was no one there, nor at the neighbours: the whole quarter was deserted. The chauffeur then invited me to his house, and there a lady who spoke a little English told me, 'Adiba is dead.' As Adiba was the name of the cousin who looked after our house and with whom I was to stay, I was momentarily overcome by dismay – how would I cope with this situation, having no Arabic, and knowing nobody? But then another cousin, who had been in America and spoke English, came along and told me that the Adiba who had died – another cousin – had been killed in an accident in New York, and that the whole family, and most of the town, were assembled in the house of the dead one's mother, my father's second sister.

So I met all my father's family at once: my five aunts, the youngest of whom was seventy-five, their children, grandchildren, great-grandchildren, and great-great-grandchildren.[1] It is the custom in the villages of Lebanon that when a death occurs the womenfolk assemble in one room, the men in another, so I found my aged aunts, dressed in the black they had worn since they had been widowed many years before – as were most of the other ladies in that room – and sitting in a circle, looking like an assembly of crows. I was embraced, touched, examined all over by my aunts whose pleasure at seeing the youngest son of their beloved brother displaced, at least temporarily, their grief for the daughter whose mother had not seen her since she had left for America forty years ago, and who was only a distant memory: so must the living take the place of the dead. As my ignorance of Arabic permitted no conversation, my aunts' attempts at communication were limited to one often-repeated phrase, which later I understood to mean 'May you bury me.'

This was for me the beginning of a long process of reintegration into a family and a community of whose habits, ways of thinking and culture I had almost no inkling except what traits they shared with my father, which, after fifty years of separation, were not many. What they all had in common was a total devotion to each other, and on the part of my aunts limitless admiration and love for my father amounting to adoration, so that I had to live up to their expectations of what the son of their brother must be. My appearance, my every gesture and movement were watched and interpreted; one consequence was that I could not refuse the food which was heaped on my plate, because I was told that one should eat as much as one loves, and this was the only way I could reciprocate some of the affection they were showing me. On more than one occasion, unable to refuse two invitations to the same meal, I ate twice over, and it was not surprising that I soon developed jaundice.

My first visit to Marjayoun, and subsequent ones in which I immersed myself in the daily life of the town and in the tragedies and comedies of my new-found family, and learnt slowly to understand the language of which the sounds but not the sense were familiar to me from Manchester, satisfied my longing to see for myself the places which had so often been described to me by my parents. I could sit on the balcony of our house in the rocking-chair of my grandmother and look as she had, and my father too, at the daily ritual of the sun's appearance over the top of Hermon; I could visit my mother's house in the village not far away and visualize the life of that large family ruled by my grandfather whose grave still lies in its now-deserted garden. And I could go on a Tuesday – as I still do – to Souk al Khan, the outdoor market for the villages of Wadi Teym, the Arqoub and Marjayoun,[2] and eat grilled meat on the very same stones my father used a hundred years ago, and the ice-cream of Hasbaya made from goats' milk. In the way of life, the habits and attitudes of my father's town, Jedeidet, my mother's village Ibl as-Saqi, and Hasbaya, the town where one of my aunts lived, I was able to get an insight into not only the complex and varied life of Lebanon, but also the history of the whole area in which it is situated, between the Mediterranean and the mountains which to the east and south lead to the deserts of Arabia. This introduction into the human and physical geography of my parents' homes was to teach me a great deal about myself.

Not long after I had come to Lebanon I decided that I would like to go farther back in time and space, and visit the area from which the Hourani family had come to Marjayoun. My researches into the family history had convinced me that its presence in Lebanon was of comparatively recent origin: the fact that we had only a generic, not a specific, family name showed that we did not belong to one of the older families of Marjayoun – the Ablas, Jabaras, Farhas, Nedas, Nafis, Farhoods, Ghulmiyyas, Boyouds, Razzouks – but that probably our forefathers had come from the Hauran a few generations back, and had not yet acquired a real family name, only an indication of origin. There were family traditions, too, which related events and names of specific people who had made the move from Hauran to Marjayoun, and in my father's lineage I could not go back further than the name of his grandfather. Perhaps in the Hauran itself I would find traces of our origins. In this belief I was encouraged by a cousin, Isa Hourani, who often visited Hauran and the Jaulan in Syria to buy wheat, and who proposed to take me there in the spring.

Our destination was the town of Ezra'a in the middle of Hauran, from where he told me we came. Ezra'a, whose Greek and Syriac name was Zorara, has the oldest existing church still in use, perhaps in the whole world, a Roman temple converted to Christian use when Christianity under the Emperor Constantine became the official religion. Many of its houses still inhabited today are Roman in origin, and still have their original doors of the black volcanic stone which covers large parts of the area. To such a house my cousin took me to meet the owner, Salim Nasrullah, who said he was a relative of ours and offered to take us to the house, now abandoned, from which, according to him, our family came. It was the same kind of Roman house of black basalt with a stone door; our family, he told us, belonged to a wider group or tribe of the name of Qandil, in its Arabic meaning a lantern, or light. Of our origin in southern Yemen he could tell us nothing except what legend recounted; but it is a curious fact, which seems to confirm the myth of our Yemeni origin, that to this day the people of Marjayoun are referred to by their neighbours as the 'Hadharmi' or Hadramautis, the area of Yemen from where still come the most successful traders of Arabia.

So I had discovered a place of origin, a town, a house, and a family name more distinctive than the vague 'Hourani', and, more important, an idea of the conditions in which my forefathers lived and the reasons for their emigration. The vast plain of the Hauran, today divided between Syria and Jordan, was called, like 'Africa',[3] the granary of Rome, and has continued to be the great wheat-producing area until present times. When there was sufficient rainfall in autumn and winter there was food enough for the whole year, but when the rains failed, as they still often do, the threat of starvation moved some of the population into Lebanon, whose rainfall was more generous and regular. Equally important with the weather was the political situation in Damascus which determined the state of security on the borderlands between the desert and the sown. When authority there was weak, the agriculturalists and traders of the Hauran were subject to the depredations of the nomadic and semi-nomadic Bedouin for whom raiding the towns and villages of the settled folk was an essential part of their constant struggle to survive. By virtue of their relations with the Bedu, whether as traders or as victims, the people of the Hauran acquired some of the characteristics of the tribes: a speech in vocabulary, accent and imagery close to theirs, a similar respect for the conventions of hospitality and 'honour' which regulated the life of the desert, and an attitude to life derived from the particular form which Muslim society took among the nomads as opposed to that of the city-dwellers – and which made it more egalitarian, more free in the relations between men and women, more conscious of the transitory nature of man's life on earth and of its precariousness, and therefore more resilient and adaptable to changes of fortune.

Although they were Christians, and had been so before Islam came northwards into Syria, the people of Hauran who came to Marjayoun remained conscious of their Arab origins, and, as the possibilities of intermarriage with other groups were limited, had preserved a racial purity greater than that of most Muslim communities, mixed as these were with Turkish, Persian and many other ethnic groups. Their way of thinking, their speech, and their social customs were deeply tinged with the Bedouin and Muslim environment from which they came: they did not look west, to Beirut or to Europe, as did the Maronites and other Christian communities of Mount Lebanon, but east and south, to Damascus, Palestine and Arabia, and even as far as Egypt, where their trade in wheat and other foodstuffs took them.

The distinctive character of Marjayoun society made its people objects of a mixture of envy and ridicule among the other Christian and Muslim villages in south Lebanon. The men of Marjayoun did not work the land with their hands, but employed outsiders, for they had inherited the desert scorn for the cultivator and manual labour; nor would they be seen carrying bags or lifting weights. Unlike the villagers whose womenfolk worked in the fields and carried out the menial tasks of the household, the women of Marjayoun enjoyed equality with their men, and often dominated them, and when they could afford them they employed servants to do the housework and the shopping in the market-place where their social position did not permit them to be seen. As trading, and in some cases money-lending, were more profitable activities than agriculture, the people of Marjayoun enjoyed a prosperity which contrasted in its external evidence – in their houses, furniture, clothes, and the generous hospitality with which both friends and strangers were received – with the frequent poverty and more thrifty habits of the villagers.

It was from this background that my father's father came, but he had died when my father was an infant so that he was brought up by his mother, who came from Ibl as-Saqi, from where my mother also came. Nothing could have been more different than the habits, ways of thinking, and even speech of Jedeidet and Ibl. The people of Jedeidet, from long association with the Bedu, spoke like them and pronounced the Arabic consonant *qaf* as *gaf*, while the people of Ibl used the *qaf*, as did the Druze villagers who lived together with them.[4] Ibl lived by agriculture, not commerce, but its horizons were not those of an isolated village community. American missionaries had come early to the area,[5] and my mother's family belonged to those early Protestants who supplied several pastors, hymn-writers and literary figures to the life of Lebanon and Egypt, where one of them – Shaheen Makarios – achieved fame and married into the literary and journalistic circle of Lebanese and Syrian Cairene society which flourished in the late nineteenth and early twentieth centuries. There was a strong artistic tradition in the village of music, story-telling and craftsmanship, and many of my mother's and other families both in Brazil, where most of them went, and in Lebanon, won distinction as writers, painters and musicians.

My immersion in the life of these two places and of the area of south Lebanon in which they were situated enabled me to understand more clearly than ever would have been possible in England the character and temperament of my parents, and especially of my father, formed as it was in the mould of two different outlooks on life and social habit. It was from his mother that he had inherited his love of learning, and it was she who confided him to the American missionaries and teachers after his father's early death; from the side of his father's family and community where he grew up he had inherited his leaning towards commerce and, having experienced poverty in his childhood, a healthy respect for the importance of money. But though he was successful in his business in Manchester up to a point, and was able to maintain the standards of a respectable middle-class Manchester family, with a house in Didsbury and children who went to public school and Oxford, his natural inclinations, had he been able to follow them, would probably have led him into academic life. Thus, although he would have liked at least one of his children to follow him into business – and it was me he had most in mind – he encouraged us in our pronounced leanings towards learning, and in the case of my two elder brothers towards the steady careers which academic life offers. It was from my mother that I probably inherited my love of music, my aesthetic sensibility, widened in later life by the Turkish and Iranian tastes of my mother-in-law and wife, and a strong propensity to dreaming and fantasy which my Uncle Munah had encouraged.

But while I was thus pursuing my search for roots, and trying to understand where I came from and why I was what I was, all the while learning Arabic which was the purpose of my stay in Lebanon, the war in Europe took an unexpected and dramatic turn in the spring and summer of 1940, recalling me to the fact that my duty as a citizen of Great Britain had greater claims than the pursuit of my private pilgrimage. The advance of the German armies through Europe brought me back to the reality of the war which had receded from my mind. It also gave me the occasion to experience at first hand the deep divisions which the war was creating within Lebanese and Arab society between those who, by sympathy or education or interest, identified themselves with Great Britain and France, and those who for one reason or another longed for Germany's victory. These divisions were clearly reflected in the small society of Marjayoun, into whose warm protective womb I had returned as though in reverse of the normal process of human birth.

I well remember how, on the day the news reached us that

the German army had entered Paris, members of the Farha family, notables of the town allied by sympathy and interest to France, wept openly, while the local Communists and Arab nationalists, thirsty for the downfall of 'Western imperialism' which they hoped would bring about, among other benefits, the end of Zionism in Palestine, rejoiced. Shrewder and more far-sighted than these dignitaries and intellectuals of the mountains was a visitor who happened to be in the town on the same day. The Emir Faour al Faour was the hereditary head of a semi-nomadic tribe, Arab al Fadl, whose territory was the Jaulan in Syria, a fabled land where flocks of sheep and herds of cattle roamed among the lush spring grasses. His family, descended from Hashem, the great-grandfather of Mohammed, were the last descendants of the Abbasid dynasty and were thus related to both the Hashemites and the royal Sherifian family of Morocco. Though the Emir himself, like most of his people, was illiterate, his mind was a vast storehouse of genealogical and historical information about the Arabs and the tribes which were still at that time an active force in the life of the Arabian peninsula. He also enjoyed total recall, and could relate every incident of his childhood and youth spent between Damascus and Arabia before and during the First World War, and of the role his father and grandfather had played between the Turkish authorities on the one side and his cousin the Sherif of Mecca in revolt against the Turks on the other.

On his visits to Marjayoun, which were always unannounced and unpredictable, he would stay with my father's cousin, my Uncle Said, next door to our house. I would hear the sound of horses – for he preferred to travel on horseback – entering the cobbled pathway to the house next door, and all night the grunting of the camels that he sometimes brought with him; and no matter at what hour he arrived, my uncle's wife would cook a whole sheep slaughtered to offer the Emir. My uncle had once taken me to visit the Emir at his 'palace' in Jaulan, named Wasit after one of the capitals of the Abbasids in Iraq, though its rough walls and primitive furnishings had nothing of the splendour of its patronym. The occasion of that visit was the funeral of his aged uncle, Zaal Salloum, and I there witnessed a scene out of the dim past of the Arabs. Vast tents had been set up outside the house, and the whole tribe of the Fadl, who numbered twenty thousand, had come to offer their condolences to the Emir, who sat in regal splendour surrounded by his sons and brothers; sword dances by his ragged tribesmen preceded the repast of fifty sheep or more served on the largest copper trays I have ever seen laid on the ground for everyone to eat his fill, for death among the Arabs is to be celebrated, not mourned, when it takes the very aged.

That day when Paris fell the Emir gave his audience in Marjayoun a political lesson: England was not defeated and would fight on from its island-fortress until America came to its aid, for he had a deep belief in the greatness of England, inherited perhaps from his memories of the other war. In later years his belief in England's power and England's justice was to be badly shaken by events in Palestine in 1948 in which he lost vast lands, but in 1940 England still ruled the waves, and Faour, with more insight than most of the politicians and statesmen of the Near East, foresaw that Germany, with all its military might, could not easily cross the Channel and occupy London as it had just occupied Paris. Were his words perhaps uttered to give me comfort – for he perceived my anguish, though I had tried to conceal it – or did he prophetically see, with his Bedouin mind untrammelled by the handicaps of a formal education, more clearly into the future than did I?

My own feelings as the news of the rapid advance of the German armies reached me were mixed. There was fear that horrors such as had befallen Antwerp might be repeated on Manchester, that my family would have to flee our home, that I might not ever see them again; but there was also a fear that I was missing the chance to participate in great events and might be doomed to watch as a spectator in a distant land as history was being made: while all my friends were involved, I was sitting in a village in the mountains of Lebanon learning Arabic, and eating figs and grapes! In normal times I could have afforded, at my age, to spend a few years in quest of roots and origins, but these were not normal times, and though I had a teaching post at the American University of Beirut I knew that unless I participated in some form of national service I would lose my self-respect for ever, and reproach myself not only for cowardice, but also for missing history.

So after an agonizing year in which I taught at the university and continued to learn Arabic, I decided to leave Lebanon and go not to England, which at the time was almost impossible, but to Egypt, where in Cairo the British army and Government had concentrated their forces to resist the long-expected push of the Axis forces. But before I could make any plan of action, circumstances took charge of my exit from Lebanon. As a British subject living under the French mandatory authorities, who had remained loyal to the regime of General Pétain, I had to register periodically with the Lebanese Sûreté Générale, itself controlled and watched carefully by the French, and it was from there that I would have to get the exit visa necessary to leave the country. When I went to the offices of the Sûreté the person in charge, a Lebanese of the Hadjitouma family, took me into his office and told me that in a few days all British subjects in Lebanon would be arrested and interned as the French knew that the British forces in Palestine, together with some of the Free French forces, were about to invade Lebanon.[6] He advised me to leave immediately, and knowing my connection with Marjayoun, told me to go there and leave across the frontier as best I could. Before leaving Beirut I visited the British Consul and obtained from him a letter introducing me to the authorities in Palestine.

Next day I left for Marjayoun. There was no question of crossing the frontier in a regular way, as I had no exit visa and my name was on the list of persons to be arrested, and in addition there was a regiment of Senegalese troops waiting for any infiltrators from Palestine. I decided to leave that night and cross the frontier illegally; the commander of the 'Chasseurs Libanais', a troop of cavalry dressed in a mixture of Caucasian and Ruritanian uniforms who patrolled the frontiers at night, was Francis Francis, a friend from the neighbouring village of Qleia and a frequent visitor to the house of Raif and Zakia Abla, my close friends in Marjayoun, with whom I spent many evenings, and that night I asked him to give instructions to his troop to look after me.

I could not go alone, however, because I did not know the

best way to slip across the frontier, but my cousin Isa Hourani shared my own taste for adventure. He had spent the early part of his life in Oklahoma and Texas, but shortly after the end of the First World War had received a message that his mother, my eldest aunt, was dying; he hurried back to Lebanon, bringing with him the evidence of his success in the New World in the form not of one but of two cars, only to find that his mother had recovered – she lived another thirty years. Deciding to elope with a girl from the town, he had the misfortune to knock down and kill a man from a neighbouring village as he was proceeding on his honeymoon. His later life became progressively more difficult as children arrived, and he was never able to return to his beloved Kansas, so that he fretted away the rest of his dull life in Marjayoun, and was only too happy to accompany me on my night journey.

We set off at about one hour past midnight, and walked down into the valley which gives its name to the area – 'the valley of springs' – where Saladin and his army had once camped before attacking Beaufort Castle; it was summer and the wild flowers, grass and the sown crops of wheat and barley were as high as our heads, and provided us with cover enough. In spring and early summer blankets of mist and dew float down the valley, and that night we walked enveloped in such a cloud, as if Nature herself wished to protect us. Halfway on our journey we heard shots and cries; daylight was not far off and, as we were discussing whether to return or continue, two of the 'Chasseurs Libanais' appeared on their horses. They had instructions from Francis Francis to guard us from the Senagalese soldiers who were likely to fire on anything that moved, and they accompanied us to the frontier where they showed us how to enter Metulla, the first village in Palestine, by the back way.

The letter from the Consul in Beirut allowed me to enter Palestine without a problem; the frontier official contacted Jerusalem and informed whatever authority controlled the movement of persons entering the country of my arrival. He advised me to go to see an officer at army headquarters in Jerusalem, who informed me that he was looking for interpreters to accompany the British forces which were about to invade Lebanon and Syria. I volunteered for the job, though my knowledge of Arabic was still inadequate, but though I was sent to accompany part of the invasion forces crossing from Transjordan into Syria, I do not believe my services were ever called upon. Of that episode in my life I have little recollection except of the extreme discomfort in which I lived and was shifted around in a truck somewhere in the desert between Irbid and Palmyra. I was still a civilian, and acquired an insight into the unenviable status of those who, while suffering all the inconveniences of military life, did not enjoy its compensations, and I decided that I must go down to Egypt to join the army.

I had been fortunate to meet in Jerusalem an officer in the British forces who was to become one of my closest and dearest friends. Ernest Altounyan was not like anyone else. The son of a famous Armenian doctor in Aleppo and of an English mother, he had long ago settled any identity problem he may have had in his youth. He had been educated at Rugby and Cambridge, had mixed with the so-called Bloomsbury set, served in the First World War and been wounded and decorated. He had met T. E. Lawrence when he was working near Aleppo before the First World War, and they remained friends until his death in 1935: this friendship Altounyan recorded in a volume of sonnets.[7] And he had married the daughter of Ruskin's secretary and inherited his house by Lake Coniston.

To Ernest Altounyan, at least when I knew him, there was no conflict between his Armenian and Near Eastern origin and his integration into English society. He regarded himself as entirely English, and though he lived and worked in Aleppo in the hospital his father had built and made famous, he tried to reproduce within its solid stone-built walls an Englishman's life. A daily cold shower was a habit he had acquired at Rugby; no Syrian collation of olives and cheese, but bacon, tea and marmalade graced the breakfast table; and Dora Altounyan drew and painted the wild flowers of the Syrian desert, and sat by the fire knitting of an evening exactly as she did in Coniston. But through that outward copy of an Englishman peeped the soul of an Armenian: an irrepressible sense of fun and fantasy, a deep understanding of the foibles and failings of his fellow men, a warmth and humanity still remembered in Aleppo where he stayed until he was shamefully expropriated by the independent Syrian regime which he had helped to bring into existence.

When the Second World War broke out, Ernest Altounyan was back in the British army, this time as a major, then colonel, attached in theory to the Medical Corps, but in fact an aide to various generals at General Headquarters in Cairo who valued his contacts and insights into Syrian political and social life and were intrigued by the many varied facets of his character. He was a welcome visitor in their offices, where he would arrive unannounced from Baghdad, Damascus, Jerusalem or Beirut and enter with a salute startling in the flamboyance of its operatic style.

I believe that it was through Altounyan that I went to call on one of his friends at GHQ when I arrived in Cairo, to consult him about what I should do. Brigadier Iltyd Clayton, a veteran Near Easterner who had served in the campaigns in Egypt, Palestine and Iraq in the First World War and was the brother of Gilbert Clayton (who had been one of the main architects of the Arab rising against the Turks, and of the post-war settlement which had established Faisal as King in Iraq and Abdullah in Transjordan) occupied a special and privileged place in the political and military set-up in Cairo. From his small office at GHQ staffed only by his secretary, the powerful Mrs Girgis, he provided the filter through which came all political information from different parts of the Arab world, to be distilled and transmitted to London both directly and through the Minister of State's office in Cairo. His views and his advice counted more in both London and Cairo than perhaps any other official's, based as they were on an unequalled experience of Arab affairs and acquaintance with Arab personalities, and on his own wise judgement in which he combined a sense of practicality with a philosophic attitude to life, and a respect for the intellect and intellectuals not always to be found among high-ranking officers.

Clayton immediately understood my situation: my desire not to 'miss out' on the great historical events then taking place in the Middle East, and my anxiety not to seem to avoid paying the debt I felt I owed to the country and society in which I had been raised. It was the summer of 1941, the German armies were close by in Libya and threatening Egypt, Iraq and Iran were in turmoil, and it was still uncertain that the British forces in the Middle East could resist a two-pronged Axis assault from the west and the north. Clayton advised me not to try to return to England but to stay in Cairo and to join the army, in which he promised he would find me a position suitable to my abilities. On his recommendation I was granted a commission in the army with the rank of first lieutenant without having gone through any military training, and I was attached to an office at GHQ in Cairo where my work was research and analysis of current political events.

It was not a brilliant outfit, and I do not believe its reports or views influenced any important decision-makers, military or political; its head was a man who, having found himself in this comfortable corner of Cairo, did not intend losing it by taking up controversial positions or in any way 'rocking the boat', a favourite phrase in our office. I was bored by the routine of the office, where I was regarded as an 'outsider' who somehow did not fit into any category easily labelled, except to one officer with a Rhodesian background, my superior, who quickly classified me among the 'wogs' of whom Cairo was so regrettably full, and did not give me access to documents he regarded as too secret for my suspected eyes. But my compensation was in the relations I enjoyed with Clayton, in whose office I was always welcome, and who discussed the most important matters of the day, asked my advice and sometimes requested written memoranda so that I felt that my decision to join the army and stay in Cairo had not been a mistake. He regarded me as a young and very junior protégé, useful to him because of my friendships and contacts among the many Arab political personalities who came to Cairo to advance the various causes they were advocating: Lebanese and Syrian nationalists, Palestinian leaders, Iraqi statesmen, North African political refugees, pan-Arab agitators. Unlike my own outfit to which I was formally attached, and which frowned on my frequent absences from the office and my associations with the 'locals' and the 'wogs', Clayton encouraged me to participate in the social and intellectual life of Cairo.

I had inherited many of the friendships and relationships of my parents among the Egyptian-Lebanese and Syrian community in Cairo, so that many doors were open to me. The war years were the Indian summer of the Anglo-Levantine society which had flowered after 1882, the year of the British occupation of Egypt. It was a society composed of the Egyptian-Ottoman aristocracy who after the end of the Ottoman Empire had made Cairo their new Istanbul; of the wealthy Lebanese and Syrian families who had made their money in commerce and industry, or who had held high positions in the Anglo-Egyptian and Anglo-Sudanese civil services, or had become prominent as journalists, writers and publishers: and of the British officers, diplomats and visiting dignitaries who flocked to Cairo for one reason or another. Like all closed societies, it had its own houses and clubs, its favourite hosts and hostesses: Princess Shevikar in her fabulous palace, filled with Bohemian crystal chandeliers, Baykoz opalines, Yildiz gilded silverware; Lady Shoucair in her Garden-city mansion with its Persian carpets, Venetian velvets and Chinese porcelain; Faris Nimr Pasha and his lively, hospitable and eccentric daughters in the garden of their house in Maadi; the Mohammed Ali Club in whose silent salons and recherché restaurant British generals lunched with Egyptian pashas and Lebanese-Egyptian *bon viveurs*; and the Gezira Club, where I would meet my British friends from GHQ, the Middle East Supply Centre, and other wartime offices, along with the Lebanese and Syrian ladies who played bridge there every afternoon, and some of the few Egyptians privileged to join that last symbol of an era that was ending.

In Cairo there occurred one of the strangest, and saddest, incidents of my life. I had formed a close friendship with an Egyptian scholar, Abdurrahman Badawi, who taught philosophy at one of Cairo's universities, and whose prolific output of books on all aspects of Islamic and Arabic thought, and particularly their connections with Greek scientific and philosophical ideas, have done much to widen the horizons and enlighten the minds of the Arab reading public. Among his close friends was a colleague at the university who had come as a refugee from Austria: Paul Kraus was Jewish, and an oriental scholar whose special field of interest were the esoteric and heterodox movements of Fatimism and Ismaelism and the Carmathian revolutions which had played an obscure but important role in Islamic, Arabic and Iranian history. He had worked in Europe with Louis Massignon on the life and thought of al-Hallaj, the twelfth-century mystic martyred in Baghdad for views held to be heretical by the orthodox interpreters of Islam, and he had been given a small post at the University of Cairo through Massignon's friendship with Taha Hussein. I met Kraus through Badawi, and there immediately developed a close friendship between us; though I could not enter his world of scholarship, he initiated me into some of the most obscure and fascinating episodes in Arab and Iranian history. He had the same large and tragic eyes, the same wistful but humorous and humanistic character and temperament as I had found in Inno Grafe. Kraus I think on his side was fascinated by such insights as I could give him into the contemporary political scene in Cairo and the Levant, and perhaps also by my vivid imaginings of a new Arab state and society.

I knew of, but did not attempt to probe, his connections with Palestine. He told me that he had spent some time in a kibbutz, and it was there that he had met his first wife, by whom he had a daughter. His wife had died recently and, as he was going to Palestine to make arrangements for his child to go to his wife's family in New York and to get remarried himself, he offered to lend my brother Albert, then also in Cairo, and myself his apartment in Zamalek, where we were looked after by an admirable Nubian servant. On his return to Cairo Paul Kraus asked us to stay on and live with him in the apartment until his new wife joined him.

Our life followed a regular pattern in which we met together daily for lunch at home. One day my brother and I returned at the usual time and waited for Kraus to appear, but he did not. I noticed that one of the two bathrooms was locked but thought it might have got stuck, and anyway we did not use it, but as it got later and later we became anxious. I decided to push out the key of the door which was inside, looked through the keyhole, and saw Paul Kraus hanging from a cord suspended from the flush. I can still see in my mind's eye the sunken, agonized face of my friend, the thin and pitiful body from which that brilliant mind had fled, and I still reproach myself that I had not imagined or pierced the despondency that must have lain beneath that quiet façade. I had felt that something had happened during his last visit to Palestine: he had lost much of the liveliness and humour which I had so much enjoyed when first we met, and when we would sit up till the early hours of the morning talking of my mad dreams of the future, and his extraordinary insights into the past. But as we never discussed personal matters, I knew as little of his private life as he of mine.

To the Egyptian police whom we called to the apartment we could give little information, and Taha Hussein, whose name we gave to them as the person closest to him in Cairo, came to the apartment, though he did not attend the funeral: a sad, pathetic affair to which came the very few friends he had, among whom was Aubrey Eban and myself who joined in carrying the coffin of our mutual friend to his grave in the Jewish cemetery.

But to the story of Paul Kraus there still remains, in my mind at least, a mystery. It looked like a story of a Jewish refugee from Europe, uprooted from his native city and intellectual milieu, and forced to live in an environment in which he had few friends to share his ideas and anxieties, but an event occurred a little later which suggested to me that perhaps there was another hidden aspect to his suicide.

In November 1944 Lord Moyne, representative of the British Government in Cairo as Minister of State, was assassinated by members of the Zionist 'Stern Gang' who were arrested, tried and executed. I was told by someone, whom I do not now recollect, that among the papers of the assassins the police had found a list of 'safe' houses where if they escaped they could take refuge, and that among these addresses was that of Paul Kraus's apartment where we had lived.

It was, and still is, difficult for me to believe that the gentle

Kraus had any connection with the determined terrorists who had killed Lord Moyne, but the thought remains in my mind that it may have been just that contrast between a natural gentleness and the desperate plight of the Jews in Europe, which drove some of them, with whom he may have had connections of friendship or collaboration at an earlier period in his life, to terrorism, and which brought him to suicide, that final escape from the necessity of making impossible choices.

The pleasures of my social life in Cairo were to be disturbed, although only temporarily, by an episode which at the time seemed to me disastrous, but which I now find comic. Periodically someone in London – maybe Winston Churchill himself – would decide that the officers at GHQ in Cairo were enjoying themselves too much, and issue orders that everyone, regardless of rank or position, should do a spell of active service, though these orders were to my knowledge never put into execution. After one such message from London someone in Cairo must have looked into my file, and discovered not only that I had seen no active service, but that I had not even had any military training. This serious weakness in the ranks of the British army had to be quickly corrected: orders came that I should proceed immediately to a camp in Palestine to undergo a period of training along with soldiers aspiring to be officers. I did not like the idea but could do nothing about it. My own outfit at GHQ did not view my absence with any serious concern, and although I informed him of my departure I was ashamed to ask Clayton to intervene.

The shock of moving from the comforts of Cairo, where I had been living in some style at the old Shepheard's Hotel, to a training camp in an isolated area of Palestine, was considerable, and my discomfort was the greater because, whereas I had no experience of real military life, my fellow trainees were mostly toughened soldiers from the ranks who had had battle experience. I did not know the most elementary things, such as how to handle a rifle, and my sessions at the firing range might have ended in disaster had not a friendly instructor realized my plight and sent me off on invented missions. On the parade ground my situation was much more dramatic: I had not the faintest idea of what to do when the parade sergeant barked out his orders, familiar to the others but to me totally unintelligible, so that very soon I had accumulated a horrendous number of punishment drills, only outnumbered by those of a fellow sufferer, an English poet.

My relations with the sergeant, though consistently bad on the parade ground, improved somewhat at other levels after a small incident. Inside the camp I had no right to wear the insignia of my officer's rank and was treated on the same basis as the other inmates aspiring to the rank I had already attained, but outside I could and indeed had to wear my cap and jacket with their officer's badge. One day, returning from a visit to the family of two of my students in Beirut who lived in the walled city of Acre, not far from the camp, I met my sergeant, who did not salute me. I saw my chance and stopped him: 'Don't you know that officers should be saluted by their subordinates?' I asked the man who only the day before had been calling me, on the parade ground, 'hopeless', 'unfit to be in the army', 'ought to be court martialled', 'stupid', and was now all apologies and sweetness. 'I ought to report you,' I told him in a magnanimous gesture, 'but this time I won't.' From that time onward, though he continued to pile up extra drills on me, he was more cautious in the expression of his disgust.

From his point of view he was quite right to despair of both the poet and myself, for the visit of an important general was to take place soon, and there was to be a parade at which we would all be inspected. The prospect of this impending visit haunted me like the recurrent dream of a friend in later life, Dale Macadoo, in which he found himself on the platform at Carnegie Hall scheduled to play a concerto which he was incapable of doing. I was certain that on the fatal day I would make some terrible blunder, and be disgraced, or be retained for ever in the accursed place trying to work off all the punishment drills which would never cease accumulating. But once again Fortune, which has played a big role in my life, intervened. The general arrived; there was great activity in the camp, close inspections of our boots and belts, and the parade was fixed for the next afternoon. About nine o'clock in the morning I was summoned by my sergeant to the general's office: I was certain that my record had been reported and that

I was to receive some unpleasant announcement. The general received me with visible signs of irritation on his face. 'Hourani,' he said, 'I have received a request from the office of Brigadier Clayton in Cairo to send you back there. I am reluctant to release you because I understand your performance here has not been satisfactory, but I have no choice – you may leave immediately.' I rushed back to my room, packed my bag, obtained a travel order, and before anything could happen to change the decision, or to delay it until after the dreaded parade, I was out of the camp, standing on the road to get a lift to Haifa, and then by the first train to Cairo. Thus ended my first and only period of training in the martial arts.

When I came to be demobilized in 1946, I was sent back to England until my papers came, and spent some weeks in a splendid though dilapidated seventeenth-century palazzo in Yorkshire. There I had time to reflect on my army days, and it was with some regrets that I envisaged my return to civilian life. I had grown used to the advantages and compensations of army life, and its disadvantages and risks had been minimal for me; I had met many congenial fellow officers and colleagues and made many friends in Cairo, of whose social life I had been a small part, and I had enjoyed the lack of financial care that my pay – which I believe never exceeded sixty or seventy pounds a month – gave me, and the way in which the army looked after one's material problems. So when my demobilization orders finally came and I could return home to Manchester at last, after an absence of seven years, my pleasure at being free was tempered because, except for rare moments such as those spent in the camp in Palestine, I had never felt really 'unfree' in my army life, and had succeeded in doing what I really wanted to do.

Looking back now, forty years later, at my decision to join the British army, I realize that my motives were personal as well as patriotic. I certainly believed that England's survival was crucial to the survival of Western civilization and was worth fighting for if fighting had been demanded of me, but I also wanted to prove to myself that I was loyal to the country and the people to whom I owed my education. That I had this feeling was proof that I had a problem of identity, for to someone entirely English the question of loyalty would not have arisen. I did not wish to feel that I was an alien in England, as I would have done had I avoided some form of national service, but on the contrary felt that, once I had done what I believed to be my duty, I would feel more free to explore the side of myself which belonged to another world, the 'distant land' of my childhood dreams.

I realized at the time that my service in the British army would be seen by many people I already knew, and was likely to meet in the future in the Arab countries, as proof of what they perhaps already thought, that I was a British 'agent' or even a 'spy', but, I argued to myself – and I believe I was right – those people who so regarded me would do so whether I had been in the army or not; on the contrary, had I, a British subject born and brought up in England, as everyone knew and I never tried to conceal, *not* openly and unashamedly worn the uniform of the British army, their suspicions that I was an agent in disguise would have been confirmed. I could not win either way, and I decided that what counted was my own opinion of myself, and my knowledge of my own motives, and this has ever since regulated my attitude to the opinion of others about my actions and my views.

Thus the transition from being a British officer in Cairo to becoming a member of an office set up by the newly created Arab League to make propaganda for the Arab cause in Palestine and elsewhere – which was to be 'the next step' in my life – while it must have seemed suspect to many people, to me represented a vital step towards recovering part of my lost or still unfound identity. I was fortunate that the friend who organized the Arab Offices in Jerusalem, London and Washington realized that I would find the transition less difficult, less embarrassing for me to make in Washington than in London. In Washington I was able to add to the advantages of my English education, my experiences in Cairo, my friendships and contacts in the Arab world, a new dimension: I discovered America, and this gave me a new insight into the problems of identity, of roots, and a broader vision of the human condition than I had acquired within the narrower confines of my life so far.

III
Discovery of America

Among the members of the Arab delegation from Palestine which took part in the St James's Conference called by the British Government in 1939 to try to reconcile the conflicting engagements it had made to the Arabs and the Jews was Musa Alami. He was a member of an old Jerusalem family who had come to Palestine from Xauen in Morocco to fight the Crusaders, and who were the traditional custodians of a Holy Place in Jerusalem; as a young boy he had worked in the office of the Turkish censorship during the First World War, and had afterwards gone to Cambridge, where he studied law. He then entered the administration of the Palestine Government, becoming the senior Arab official, and, through both his intellectual abilities and the warmth and charm which he shared with his wife Saadia,[1] achieved great influence among British officialdom and among the leaders of the Arab resistance to British policy. While he was in England in 1939 as a member of the Palestinian delegation to the St James's Conference he visited Oxford, and I was introduced to him, perhaps – although I am not sure – through my father's friend Jamal Husseini, who was his brother-in-law. Of that meeting I do not have a precise recollection, but it was four years later to bear fruit in a friendship and collaboration which have extended over many years.

Musa Alami held in the leadership of the Palestinian Arabs a very special place. By the marriage of his sister to Jamal Husseini he was allied to one of the closest collaborators of Haj Amin Husseini, Mufti of Jerusalem, the unchallenged leader of the Palestinian Arab movement, but his own allegiance to the leader was tempered by a number of factors. He did not approve of or like the methods by which Haj Amin controlled the movement, which included intimidation and assassination, having a healthy and well-founded desire not to become one of the Mufti's victims. He had links of friendship with many senior British officials as well as with some Jewish and Zionist personalities in Palestine; he was completely devoid of any anti-Jewish or anti-Semitic feelings, and frequently recalled that, like many of the children of old Arab families in Jerusalem, including Haj Amin himself, he had had a Jewish wet nurse; and he was by nature a diplomat, preferring the negotiating table to the battlefield. Most important of all, he had never been tempted by the rise of national socialist Germany or by the seemingly irresistible might of the Axis powers to throw in his lot with them at a critical moment of the Second World War; he was in Baghdad in 1940 and 1941, along with the Mufti and other Palestinian leaders, but did not follow them in their support of the Iraqi leader Rashid Ali's desperate adventure which ended in failure, nor in their flight to Berlin.

So in 1943, when the tide of war seemed to be slowly turning against the Axis, and Egypt had become the centre of British military and political control of the whole Middle East, Musa Alami came to Cairo to take up again the threads of his many connections and friendships among British and Arab officials. The Mufti was in Berlin, Jamal Husseini deported to the Seychelles by the British authorities, and Musa represented a Palestinian leadership acceptable to the British, and welcomed by the Egyptians and the Syrian, Lebanese, Iraqi and other Arab leaders who also gravitated towards Cairo. It was, I believe, in the house of Faris Nimr Pasha,[2] one of whose daughters was married to George Antonius,[3] a close friend and collaborator of Musa, that we met again, and instantly became close friends.

In Cairo in 1943 there were several centres of power and decision. One was the office of the British Ambassador, Sir Miles Lampson, a powerful and domineering personality; another the office of the Minister of State, Lord Moyne, to be assassinated in 1944; another the Middle East Supply Centre, headed by Commander Jackson, which exerted an economic and financial control over the entire Middle East, between Libya in the west and Iran in the east; and the headquarters of the British military forces, GHQME. At these headquarters there were several sections providing political intelligence and analysis and even advice both to the military leaders and to the Government in London; among these the most influential and respected was that of Brigadier Clayton. It was to his office that many important Arab visitors came, either to understand British policy on one or other Middle East problem, to present their own views, or to ask for favours. Because of my own connection with Clayton, I was to provide the link with several of these Arab visitors. To the events leading to the independence of Lebanon and Syria, the creation of the Arab League, and the evolution of the Palestinian problem, I was an inside witness, and sometimes participant.

In the absence of the Mufti in Germany, and the impossibility of his playing any effective or acceptable role in the foreseeable future, Musa Alami aspired to remodel the Palestinian Arab leadership to conform to what he perceived would be the situation when the war was over. He was not motivated in this by any desire to take over the leadership himself, because he disliked the limelight and preferred to work behind the scenes, to influence decisions without assuming public responsibility for them. His plan was to bring back his brother-in-law Jamal Husseini from his exile in the Seychelles to assume this leadership, and he enlisted my assistance in convincing Clayton, with whom he was to form a close friendship, that the return of Jamal would make it easier for the British in Palestine to find an *interlocuteur valable* among the Arabs: Jamal, he argued, was not really an extremist, but had been pushed by the Mufti to take up positions in which he did not fully concur, and his exile in Rhodesia and the Seychelles had saved him from contamination with national socialist ideas and practices such as made the Mufti's return to political influence no longer conceivable. I believe I contributed considerably to convincing Clayton that a new Arab leadership in Palestine was desirable, that Musa was the most intelligent and reasonable element, and that Jamal Husseini, if he were brought back, could be rehabilitated and become the figurehead behind which Musa would be the effective power. Jamal Husseini was released and brought first to Cairo, then to Palestine, but although he returned to political activity there, he was never able to recover the influence he had enjoyed in the days of Haj Amin, and after 1948 left for Saudi Arabia, there to begin another career and another life.

Musa Alami, on the other hand, was to play an important and indeed crucial role in the coming years: in the formation of the Arab League, in the effort to make the Arab cause in Palestine better known in the West, and in the events preceding and following the partition of Palestine. In these events I was closely associated with him, both as a friend and collaborator; this association was to change the course of my life, to involve me in important moments of history, and to give me an inside view of modern Arab history. I must therefore briefly relate the circumstances in which this came about.

Nuri Pasha Said was for many years a leading figure in the Government of Iraq. As a young officer in the Ottoman army he and a group of friends had decided to work for the establishment of an Arab state which would bring together the Arab provinces of the Ottoman Empire. He had joined the Arab revolt led by Sherif Hussein of Mecca against the Turks in the First World War, and when the Arab kingdom established briefly in Damascus by Faisal, son of Sherif Hussein, had collapsed, Nuri Said returned to his native Iraq and was one of the closest collaborators of Faisal, who had become King in that country. The creation of a number of states under British and French control in place of the Arab state never dimmed Nuri Said's vision of Arab unity, and when British forces in 1941 effectively ended French rule over Lebanon and Syria, the moment seemed to him ripe to revive the idea. In his *Blue Book* he set forth his proposal for the consideration of the British Government. It found a favourable echo in London, and Eden, Foreign Minister in Churchill's wartime Government, issued a statement encouraging the idea of some form of Arab unity.

Musa Alami was an intimate friend of Nuri Said, and shared his vision of an Arab union; he believed that such a union would provide the framework within which the Palestinian problem could best be solved. Within a larger entity than

Palestine the Arabs would no longer fear that they would be outnumbered by Jewish immigrants, and the Jews would have the 'National Home' promised them by the Balfour Declaration in the form of one or two Jewish 'cantons'; both Alami and Nuri Said also envisaged a similar canton for the Christians of Lebanon. Clayton, with whom both of them discussed their ideas at length, was convinced that this formula might work: it seemed to him that this would be the opportunity to return to the idea of an Arab state which had been abandoned by the British Government at the Versailles and Lausanne conferences. But there were serious difficulties in the way of bringing about such a state in the form which Nuri Said had proposed. In the first place, Nuri Said's original idea was to start with a union of the so-called 'Fertile Crescent', which would have excluded Egypt. This would have given a preponderant influence to Iraq, and after the events in that country in 1941 and the deep-rooted anti-British sentiments which they had revealed, both Churchill and Eden were chary about making Baghdad the centre of a new Arab entity over which they might lose control. In the second place, the British Ambassador in Egypt did not like the idea of the creation of a new entity which would take away from Cairo the central role it had played in Middle East affairs since the beginning of the war. But thirdly, and most important, Churchill, whose connections and sympathies with the Zionist movement went back many years, was unwilling to close the doors to the possibility of the eventual creation of a Jewish state in Palestine, and was opposed to the confinement of the 'National Home' to a canton or two. A further difficulty was that the Christians of Lebanon did not accept being reduced to a canton of an Arab state.

So the idea of an Arab state was abandoned in favour of an Arab League of States, which came into existence as a result of a series of compromises between different centres of power in the Near East, and between different branches of the British Government. Nuri Said came to insist on the inclusion of Egypt in the League; the Lebanese Government, newly independent, agreed to join on condition that its sovereignty was safeguarded; and although Palestine was not yet an independent state, a representative of the Arabs of Palestine was invited to take part in the first conference at Alexandria which drew up the Charter of the League. Palestinian representation was accepted on the basis of equality with other members: that Palestine, although not a state, was allowed to join the League was due to Musa Alami's persuasive insistence.

The presence of Musa Alami in Cairo in the period of the League's gestation, the role he had played in formulating its aims, and his position in Palestine, all made him the obvious choice to represent the Palestinian Arabs. Their six parties for once agreed on the choice of Musa to go to Alexandria, later to Cairo, where he signed the Charter of the League on behalf of Palestine.

The 'Alexandria Protocol', which had laid the bases of the future Charter of the League, was drafted by the delegates of the Arab governments of Egypt, Iraq, Lebanon, Syria, Transjordan, Saudi Arabia and Yemen, and by Musa Alami, but with the participation from behind the scenes of Clayton. Except for the Egyptians, who preferred to deal with the British Embassy, the delegates would go to Clayton's office in secret of each other, some to consult, some to discuss, and others to receive instructions. I was the amused observer of many of these comings and goings, as well as the recipient of confidences from some of the delegates whom I knew personally.

I did my best to persuade Clayton that Musa would be the best choice as Secretary-General of the new organization; the fact that he did not represent a government would be an advantage and, since one of the main objectives of the League was to find a solution to the Palestine problem, as Secretary-General he would be in a stronger position to influence the League's decisions than he would be as a mere representative. I was afraid too that the six Palestinian parties which had chosen him as their representative would soon change their minds and begin intriguing to remove him. But although Clayton was, I believe, at first convinced, he had lost some of his influence once the League was formed. His friendships were mainly with the Iraqi, Lebanese and Syrian delegates, and of course with Musa Alami, but the Egyptian delegates, and especially the Egyptian Prime Minister Nokrashi Pasha, soon began to ensure that the role of Egypt in the League should correspond to what they believed was Egypt's rightful place as the largest and the oldest Arab state. The Egyptian candidate for Secretary-General was Abdurrahman Azzam, a colourful personality who as a young man had fought against the Italians in Libya before the First World War. He had close ties with nationalist movements in North Africa and other parts of the Arab world, and although Musa Alami also had close personal relations with the governments and leaders of the countries of the Fertile Crescent, they finally preferred Azzam, who, in addition to being an Arab nationalist, rare among Egyptians at the time, believed also in a form of Islamic nationalism quite foreign to the sophisticated, Westernized, liberal background of Alami.

Among the reasons for the failure of the Arab League to fulfil the hopes and goals of its founders, to help in the solution of the Palestinian problem along the lines laid down by the Palestinian Arab leadership, or to become in any way an effective instrument of Arab interests, the choice of Azzam Pasha as Secretary-General was, I have always believed, one of the most important. Azzam's personal charm, which appealed to Westerners fascinated by his stories of the Libyan resistance to Italy, was not matched by political experience or organizational ability. He was essentially a poet: the Arab League was a romantic dream through which, Quixote-like, he could relive his early days of adventure in the Libyan deserts. He was unable to envisage, or to create, the institutions without which the League was doomed to remain more of an idea than a reality. The secretariat was soon filled by Egyptians and Arab officials sent there by their governments either because they wished to get rid of them, or to do a favour to this and that leader, and their laziness was only matched by their incompetence. No succeeding Secretary-General has been able or willing to deal with this problem, and indeed it has become worse, and has reached its apotheosis at the present time.

Musa Alami obtained from the Arab League two important decisions: the first was to set up an organization to promote Arab causes, and principally that of the Palestinian Arabs, in the Western world; the second to establish a fund to be used to purchase land from Arab owners in Palestine who for one reason or another wished to sell, to prevent it falling into the hands of the Zionist land-purchasing agency, and to help Arab landowners to improve their agricultural methods. The Council of the League entrusted both of these projects to Musa Alami.

In the organization and choice of personnel for the Arab Offices, as the first of these projects was called, both my brother Albert and I played an important role. We had between us a wide circle of friends and acquaintances in the Arab countries, in Great Britain and the USA, and our Anglo-Saxon education enabled us to judge what kinds of person could be effective spokesmen for the Arab cause, and be socially acceptable and presentable in the capitals where they would work, principally London and Washington. We succeeded in gathering around Musa Alami a group of remarkable men and women, many of whom were to achieve prominence both during their period of work in the Arab Offices and later on.

Among these officials of the Arab Offices were Edward Atiyah, a Lebanese who had been educated at Oxford and who had spent years as an official of the Government of Sudan, and who was a forceful speaker and writer; Ahmed Shukairi, a Palestinian who was later to become the first head of the Palestine Liberation Organization; Jamal Nasir, a Palestinian who became Justice Minister of Jordan; Khulusi Khairi, a Palestinian who later became Foreign Minister in the short-lived Iraqi-Jordanian union in 1958; Bedia Afnan, an Iraqi whose husband had been the representative of Iraq at the Court of St James's in the early thirties, and was later to serve for many years as Iraq's representative on the fourth committee of the General Assembly of the United Nations; Charles Issawi, Lebanese-Egyptian economist and historian, now famous as a writer on the economic history of the Middle East; Wasfi Tal, a Jordanian who became Prime Minister of Jordan; Burhan Dajani, a Palestinian who for many years has been the moving spirit of the organization of Arab Chambers of Commerce; Walid Khalidi, a Palestinian who later on was to contribute significantly to recording and explaining various phases of the Palestinian struggle, and to play an important role as publicist and advocate of the Palestinian cause; and Najla Izzeddin, a Lebanese scholar educated at Vassar. My brother Albert was the principal researcher and writer at the Arab Office in Jerusalem, and I became director of the Office in Washington.

So in the autumn of 1946 I left for Washington by plane from Jerusalem. At Rome a short, stocky man with a fiery complexion and long white hair which stood out from the sides of his head joined the plane and sat down in the seat next to me. I recognized him as David Ben Gurion,[4] whom I had met at the wedding in Cairo of Aubrey Eban. Ben Gurion was curious to know who I was and why I was going to America. I told him that I was working with Musa Alami, whom he knew. 'Oh,' he said, 'I thought you were a halutz,' or young Jewish pioneer: coming from him, this was probably a compliment, perhaps prompted by the mess of untidy black hair which was one of my characteristics in those days, and which I imagined was shared by young halutzim – though I had never met any. When I told him that my parents came from Marjayoun he became excited: 'Marjayoun is part of Eretz Israel' (the land of Israel), he exclaimed. This story, which I related to Alfred Abusamra, the editor of a local newspaper in Marjayoun, was used by him on many occasions as evidence of Israel's ambitions to annex that area, but I myself never took it for more than a quip intended to provoke me, and later experience convinced me that, if that had really been Israel's intention, they have had many opportunities to do so, but never taken them. I was to meet Ben Gurion only once again, in 1947 when he invited me to breakfast at the Plaza Hotel, along with Moshe Shertok, to try to persuade me to establish a connection for them with the Arab delegations in New York, and to help persuade the Arabs that it was better to come to terms with them directly rather than place their faith in the United Nations.

I remained in Washington from 1946 until 1948, with intermittent periods spent in Jerusalem. The first time I returned to Washington after a brief visit to Jerusalem was the occasion of an incident of which I have still a very clear and painful recollection. I had thought that the visa I had obtained from the American Consulate in Jerusalem for my first visit would be valid for a second one, but when I arrived at New York the immigration authorities denied me entry: my explanations were not accepted, and I was sent to Ellis Island. I was desperate, and had visions of being kept in that enormous hall, along with hundreds of would-be immigrants waiting for entry into the Promised Land, for days and days, or of having to return ignominiously to Jerusalem or London. Then I had an inspiration. I knew from Cairo a man whose family had played an important role in the life of my own family in Lebanon, William Eddy, whose grandfather, a missionary in south Lebanon, had converted my grandfather to Protestantism; Colonel Eddy, as he now was, was head of some important branch of intelligence in Washington, and was a close adviser on Arab affairs to President Roosevelt and later Truman. Maybe I would find him in his office, maybe he could save me from the clutches of the immigration department; I was allowed to make a telephone call, and although I did not find Bill Eddy in his office, I explained my case to his secretary. I did not really expect that he would be able to do anything for me, the next day was a Saturday, and I was almost reconciled to the idea that I would have to spend the weekend in that vast and gloomy prison-like place, sleeping as best I could, like the hopeless people I saw around me, with my head on my suitcase, hungry, unshaven; I could see in my imagination all the generations who had passed through Ellis Island on their way to liberty – for the myth of America was vivid in my mind from the stories I had heard all my life from cousins and friends who had passed that way – and, had the circumstances been less annoying, I might have enjoyed seeing the fabled Ellis Island before it was abolished for ever. But God is great: my name was called out by the immigration officer, word had come from Washington that I was to be admitted, and so I was perhaps the first man ever to enter legally into America without a visa!

The years I spent in Washington were among the most exciting and fruitful of my life. The ideas and the personalities of the great Roosevelt era were still around; it was an era of optimism and enthusiasm, generated by the tremendous effort which had enabled the United States to mobilize all its resources in the space of three years in what seemed at the time to be the final battle against the forces of evil. The United Nations had just come into being, and seemed to represent a new hope for mankind. Arab embassies had opened with new faces and new ideas, and we in the Arab Office felt that we were part of a new phase in Arab history in which all the Arab countries would emerge into independence. Moreover relations between the Arabs and the Zionists had not reached that pitch of bitterness and hostility which in later years were to make relations between Arabs and Jews difficult if not impossible, so that we could still meet Zionists and carry on our disputes and dialogue in a civilized and generally peaceful climate.

That climate we in the Arab Office were anxious to maintain. We did not favour the aggressive attitude which later generations of Arab propagandists and publicists were to assume, and we were careful not to associate with the fringe groups of American political life – whether of the right or the left – although some of them were anxious to get in touch with us and to demonstrate their 'sympathy' for our cause. In spite of this we incurred the suspicion of the Jewish B'nai B'rith organization – the Anti-Defamation League – which denounced us to the FBI and provoked a search of our offices by inspectors who came to examine our books and papers. What B'nai B'rith was trying to pin on us was some connection with right-wing anti-Semitic groups in America, and to establish a link between us and the Mufti of Jerusalem, whose activities in Germany during the war were a favourite theme of the more rabid Zionist press. No such link existed; on the contrary, the Mufti, who had returned from Germany via France to Cairo, had already begun to intrigue against Musa Alami and the Arab Offices with Azzam Pasha and certain Arab nationalist circles in Egypt and elsewhere. I believe I convinced the inspectors of the FBI not only of our innocence of the charges against us, but also of the Palestinian cause.

The Jewish community in the United States, although still traumatized by the events in Europe in which their co-religionists were almost exterminated, had not yet been fully mobilized in support of the Zionist cause as it was to be later in support of the state of Israel, and there were Jewish Americans who would come to us and offer their services of one sort or another to help us publicize our point of view. There was, for example, Ben Freedman, a wealthy manufacturer of a well-known brand of soap who appeared to us to be a genuine supporter of the Arab cause in Palestine. We persuaded him, along with Garland Hopkins, a Methodist pastor, and Kermit Roosevelt, whom I had first met in Cairo and whose political and social position in Washington was of invaluable service to us, to form a committee for 'Peace and Justice in the Holy Land', the forerunner of many other such committees set up for good – and sometimes bad – causes. Our soap-manufacturing friend would pay from his own pocket for the full-page advertisements we placed in various American publications to counter the newspaper campaigns then rampant to persuade the American public that a Jewish state in Palestine was an American national interest. It was only on closer contact with him that I came to realize that he was less motivated by a love for the Arabs than by an obsessive hatred of Russian and Polish Jews; he himself was of German origin, and had brought with him from Europe an ancient prejudice which was in fact a form of racism. He claimed that the Russian and Polish Jews were not racially Jews at all, but descendants of a Tartar tribe, the Khazars, who had been converted to Judaism in the eighth century – a theory to be taken up and expanded by Arthur Koestler in his book *The Thirteenth Tribe*. That he himself, as a German Jew, was probably not a descendant of the twelve tribes of Israel did not matter to him. He succeeded in convincing some of the Arab delegates, who in 1947 were fighting the idea of a Jewish state at the United Nations, that this was a valid anti-Zionist argument, and the Syrian delegate, Faris al Khouri, at that time Foreign Minister of his country, made a long and learned speech in one of the sessions of the General Assembly arguing that, since most of the Jews weren't really Jews at all, they had no right to a state: at which point Chaim Weizmann, who more than anyone else could be called the real father, or progenitor, of Zionism, got up to say that he had always thought of himself as a Jew until corrected by the honourable delegate of Syria.

The search of the Arab Office by the FBI gave us a considerable amount of publicity, and resulted in an increase in our contacts with schools, universities, churches and the press, which we realized were just as important in the formation of American public opinion as our contacts with the administration. We were invited to take part in debates, lectures and radio discussions throughout the country; of these there is one I remember in particular, in which I was pitted against the combined forces of Moshe Shertok and Nahum Goldmann, then, as he was to remain for many years, President of the World Zionist Federation. They were speaking in the name of powerful organizations, and were men of long experience in politics; I was a brash young man, confident that I was speaking in the name of fifty or however many million Arabs we claimed there were in the world at that time, and looking back at it now I am amazed that I had the courage – or perhaps it was less courage than bravado – to take them on in public debate. But I liked Goldmann, and I think he liked me: I felt he was a deeply sincere man whose motives were humanitarian more than they were political. He believed in the Jewish state not because he wanted power, or to play a role in world politics, but because the sufferings of the Jewish communities in Europe during the war had convinced him that this was the only possible solution. His later career, and the articles and statements he was to make shortly before his death in 1982, confirmed my earlier view of him as a man who, while he was certainly a Zionist, regretted that the Jewish state was created at the expense of the Palestinian Arabs.

Shertok,[5] whom I met on a number of other occasions, was a different kind of man: he was highly intelligent, and within the logic of Zionism was consistent and sincere, but I felt that his personal relations with the Palestinian Arabs among whom he had passed his childhood were based on a certain contempt for their political abilities combined with a resentment of what he felt to be his own exclusion from their society. After the creation of the state of Israel in 1948 I met him only once, when he was out of office. We were together members of a conference called on the island of Rhodes by the Congress for

Cultural Freedom, and I found that much of the apparent arrogance of his earlier manners had disappeared, and that he foresaw, with some sadness, the night shadows which were falling on Arab-Jewish relations.

In those years in Washington, between 1946 and 1948, it was not difficult for an office working on behalf of Arab causes in general, the Palestinian cause in particular, to establish contacts on all levels of government and public opinion. The State Department was anxious to talk to representatives of Arab points of view, and our Office was not tainted by any of the associations which in later years and more recently have poisoned the relations between official Washington and Palestinian spokesmen. The fact that we were not all Palestinians, but came from Iraq, Lebanon, and in my case from a British background, gave us a very special status in Washington, for we had the entrée and enjoyed the support of all the Arab embassies whose governments, in those early days of independence, were not yet divided by the mutual rivalries, antipathies and antagonisms which have sometimes prevailed more recently. In those days it was remarkably easy to make friends in government offices: there were no closed doors, no security checks, no locked files, and I remember that I often walked down the corridors of the old White House building, which then housed the State Department, looking for whomever I could find to visit. As there was no hierarchy in the Arab Office such as existed in diplomatic missions, we were not restricted to our equivalents in the State Department hierarchy, and we could make friends with the highest and the lowest officials with the same facility. So Loy Henderson or Bob Satterswaithe[6] would come to dinner, or invite me to lunch in the Department or at the Metropolitan Club with the same characteristically American simplicity and friendship that we maintained with quite junior officials or with friends of my own age.

Looking back at our efforts in Washington to present a reasonable case for an independent Palestinian state which at that time would have included a population two-thirds Arab and one-third Jewish, it is clear to me that we were in fact following the only realistic method of conducting propaganda which later generations of Arab propagandists have abandoned for more aggressive, more brazen methods which tend to produce exactly the opposite effect to that intended. We were trying to make friends, not to create enemies, and friendship is a mutual relationship which demands on both sides a will to like and be liked. I loved America and the Americans I was meeting; I found them open, friendly, spontaneous, generous, hospitable, and I suppose that the people I met socially, or whom I addressed at conferences and lectures, must have felt this, and reacted reciprocally. Later Arab propagandists regarded America as the enemy, every American as pro-Israeli, and every Jew a Zionist, and with this attitude it is not surprising that they have had no impact on either public opinion or official policy, and that such support for the Palestinian cause as exists today is the product only of commercial or financial interest, or of anti-Israeli feeling, or of the efforts of American Jews who feel that Israel, in its own interests, should be more understanding and flexible in its treatment of the Palestinians.

That we failed to achieve our major political objective was the result of factors completely outside our control. The Arab Offices depended for their success on a unified, consistent and effective policy from the Arab governments in the face of the mounting pressure in the USA, Great Britain and many other countries for the creation of a Jewish state in Palestine. Our task was to try to prevent that happening, and our major argument was that such a state would not be accepted by the Arabs of Palestine, who constituted two thirds of the population, nor by the surrounding Arab states or the wider Arab world, and that if it were to be created it would face a united Arab opposition which would quickly destroy it. What we proposed as a valid alternative was an Arab state in which the Jews would have equal political rights, though not sovereignty, guaranteed by a constitution establishing a democratic system of government. This proposal for a 'democratic Palestinian State' was to be revived much later by the Palestine Liberation Organization as its official policy when circumstances had changed radically, and it was no longer a practical solution, but at the time it was a reasonable idea.

Unfortunately our efforts in the Arab Offices, whether in Washington, London or Jerusalem, were weakened in their effectiveness by the situation which revealed itself not long after their creation. Azzam Pasha was not happy that the Office enjoyed an autonomous status under the direction of Musa Alami, and that he had no say either in the nomination of its personnel or in the formulation of its policies, and he worked assiduously to limit and finally put an end to our activities through cutting off the financial support pledged by the members of the Arab League at its early meetings in 1944 and 1945. In this he was successful: apart from an initial small contribution from the governments of Egypt and Syria, the only government which gave substantial financial support was Iraq. In his efforts to cut off the lifeline of money, Azzam was assisted by the Mufti of Jerusalem who, after his return to Cairo in 1946, immediately began to try to recapture his previous position as sole leader and spokesman of the Palestinian Arabs. Musa Alami and the Arab Offices represented a challenge to this, and had to be demolished in one way or another. Ignoring the fact that his own pro-German attitude and his open collaboration with the leaders of the national socialist regime in Germany during the war – he counted Himmler as his special friend, and received double rations for himself and his entourage – had grievously harmed the cause of the Palestinians in Western eyes, the Mufti attacked Musa Alami on the grounds that he was pro-British. To his way of thinking – and regrettably of many Arab leaders today – to be on good terms with those you are trying to convince is equivalent to collaboration with them; the only patriotic or 'national' attitude is to cultivate the enemy of your enemies in the hope that they will fight the battle you are unable or unwilling to fight yourself. This mentality Azzam shared with the Mufti, and though he was not willing to go to the same lengths of intimidation, he used his position as Secretary-General of the Arab League to destroy the Arab Offices at the very moment when, in 1948, they were most needed.

But of course the major failure was that of the Arab governments themselves to prevent the establishment of the Jewish state. It is not my purpose in this book to trace the sequence of errors, miscalculations and weaknesses of both the Arab governments and the Palestinian leaders which led to the creation of Israel in 1948. Looking back at the history of Palestine and of the Zionist movement, it may be that what happened was inevitable: that the odds against the Arabs were too great, and that what appeared to be a struggle between the Arab and the Jewish inhabitants of Palestine was in reality a struggle between a small, poor and relatively uneducated and unsophisticated community, and a movement of which the Jewish immigrants were the pioneers, but behind whom were ranged some of the most powerful, sophisticated, intelligent and cohesive Jewish communities in the world. But it still seemed to us in the Arab Offices between 1946 and 1948 that there could be an accommodation between the two communities within the framework of a united Palestinian state, and that the relative weakness of the Arab community could be compensated by bringing into the picture the Arab League and the Arab governments.

We were encouraged in this belief by the evolution of British policy towards Palestine. The defeat of Winston Churchill in the election of 1945 brought the Labour Party into power, and in the new government Ernest Bevin became Foreign Secretary. Bevin had as his close adviser Harold Beeley,[7] who, without being anti-Zionist, anticipated the growing importance of the Arab countries in the post-war world, and urged on him a more balanced view of British interests in Palestine and elsewhere than Churchill's openly pro-Zionist sympathies had imposed on British policy; and Bevin himself, influenced partly by his own natural sympathy for the 'underdogs' of this world, partly by the presence in the Labour Party of pro-Zionists such as Richard Crossman and Harold Wilson who supported Zionism for intellectual and personal motives with which Bevin had no sympathy, was anxious to find a solution to the Palestinian problem and to place Great Britain's relations with the Arab world on a new and happier basis. Musa Alami himself had established a close and warm relationship with Ernest Bevin, who had considerable respect for his judgement and wisdom.

The first warning that we were being perhaps over-optimistic came with the appointment of an Anglo-American Committee of Inquiry, which was an indication of the growing pressure on the British Government from Washington to find a solution to the problems created by the German persecution of Jews in Europe, and of the changing balance of power between London and Washington. The appointment of the Committee was in itself a sign that the British Government, faced by the irreconcilability of its promises and commitments to the Arabs and the Jews, was seeking to share its responsibility for the future of Palestine with the American Government. The introduction of the Americans into the problem was bound to increase rather than diminish Zionist influence because the Jewish communities in the United States were more powerful than those in Great Britain, and the American Government by its very nature was more susceptible to the pressure of sections of public opinion than was the British. The very composition of the Committee reflected this: while some of its members were either new to the problem, or emotionally or politically uncommitted to either side, others were openly and unashamedly sympathetic to the Zionist point of view. Richard Crossman, for example, did not conceal his sympathies and attachments, and an American, Bartley Crum, was even more openly biased, though perhaps his motives were less intellectual than those of Crossman.

In anticipation of the Anglo-American Committee's visit to Jerusalem to hear evidence from a number of different organizations and spokesmen of Arabs and Jews, the Jerusalem Arab Office produced a vast documentation of every aspect of the problem of Palestine under the supervision and with the active participation of my brother Albert, who also appeared before the Committee to give evidence on behalf of the Office. There were other Arab organizations, such as the Arab Higher Committee, which presented evidence, and I myself wrote part of the evidence given by Jamal Husseini on behalf of that Committee, although I did not share his 'optimism' that once the British authorities left Palestine the Arabs would be able, in one way or another, to come to terms with the Jews. But by general consent, and in the opinion of the chairman of the Committee, Albert's evidence was the ablest, the most convincing and the best presented of all the statements made from the Arab point of view.

The Anglo-American Committee's report rejected both the Arabs' demand for a Palestinian state in which they would have been a majority and the Jewish Agency's demand for a Jewish state in part of Palestine, but it did go a considerable way towards meeting the Zionists' point of view: it recommended the ending of British restrictions on Jewish immigration and the admission of 100,000 Jewish immigrants immediately, and the continuation of British mandatory government until some later time, thus reinforcing the Jewish population of Palestine and opening the door to an eventual partition of the country. The arguments in favour of partition had been presented in a serious form by a Royal Commission under Lord Peel in 1937, but were not accepted by the British Government. Under the pressure of the Arab governments and of the Arab uprising in Palestine, the Government published a White Paper in 1939 which, had it been implemented, would have led to the Palestinian state for which we in the Arab Office were working. The Anglo-American Committee's report effectively put an end to the White Paper, which had been rejected by both the Palestinian Arab Higher Committee and the Jewish Agency, and opened the door to the next scene which was the British Government's decision to throw the problem of Palestine into the lap of the United Nations. In May 1947 the General Assembly set up a Special Committee on Palestine – UNSCOP – to investigate the situation and to recommend solutions.

Angered by the conclusions of the Anglo-American Committee's report, and confident in the support which they believed the Arab League and governments would give to the Palestinian cause, the Arab Higher Committee under orders from the Mufti decided to boycott the new UN committee, as did the Arab governments and the Arab League. This decision was seen by Musa Alami as a mistake. To assume beforehand that the new committee would be prejudiced in favour of the Zionist point of view and to refuse to talk with it would mean that the Zionists would have the field to themselves, and the Arab case would go by default. On the other hand, to go against the decision of the Higher Committee and against the decision of the Arab governments and the Arab League was difficult, and might even be dangerous. He asked me to join him in Geneva, and there we decided on a compromise: we would not ask to appear before UNSCOP, but we would prepare a document and place it in their hands. There were advantages in this stratagem: it would be the only document presenting the Arab point of view, and would not therefore reflect the divisions and dissensions within the Palestinian camp or among the members of the Arab League, and instead of the incoherent or extreme language which others might have used, ours would be a reasonable and well-documented presentation. We decided to prepare and print a book in Geneva, a convenient place to meet privately with officials of the United Nations whom we knew without attracting the publicity that could not have been avoided in Jerusalem or elsewhere.

The book, which we entitled *The Future of Palestine*, was very largely based on material written by my brother or embodied as evidence in the documents presented to the Anglo-American Committee, edited and prepared for the press by myself. As a presentation of the Arab case against partition, it was certainly the best written and the most forceful, and though its arguments were not to be accepted, its description of the probable consequences of partition were prophetic in all but one respect – we did not foresee the fiasco of the Arabs' attempts to prevent it, nor the tragic consequences for the Palestinian people of that fiasco.

Twenty-three years later I decided that *The Future of Palestine* was still a valid analysis of the effects of the partition of the country on the Near East, and that the position taken up in those days by Musa Alami, and by the Arab Office, needed a reaffirmation of his and our place in the history of the Palestine problem, and I therefore published a new edition of the book at my own expense, together with a preface by Musa Alami drafted by myself with his approval.

The partition of Palestine was recommended by the General Assembly of the United Nations on 29 November 1947. I was present, along with Musa Alami and other colleagues, during the debates which preceded that resolution, and worked closely with the Arab delegations, who included among their numbers Emir Faisal Abdulaziz – later King Faisal of Saudi Arabia; Camille Chamoun of Lebanon, later to become President of his country; Charles Malik, Ambassador of Lebanon and later President of the General Assembly, Foreign Minister of Lebanon, and one of the authors of the Declaration of Human Rights; Fadel Jamali, Foreign Minister of Iraq; and Faris al Khouri, Foreign Minister of Syria. Our attempts to defeat the resolution were unsuccessful: both the Americans and the Russians were in favour of it and worked hard, by fair means and foul, to ensure that their client-states voted for it. In the history of the twentieth century that day, 29 November, must surely take its place as one of the most momentous in its consequences, not only for the Arabs and Jews living in Palestine, but for the Middle East and indeed for the whole world: its repercussions are still with us today.

As I sat with my colleagues in the Arab Office and friends from the Arab delegations while the final stages of the General Assembly's discussions were being held, an atmosphere of almost unbearable tension built up. We were all conscious, I think, that history was being made, but until the final vote was taken the outcome was uncertain. When it was announced, the scene which followed has been for ever engraved on my memory: the jubilation of the Zionist delegation and the emotional congratulations they received from both the American and the Russian delegates, and the slow march of the Arab delegations led by Emir Faisal as they walked out of the General Assembly in protest both at the decision and at the way it had been taken.

In so far as our mission in the USA had been to prevent partition, we had failed: the thoughts of the Arab governments and the Palestinian leaders turned from diplomacy to war. What they had been unable to achieve in New York they believed they could achieve on the battlefield, and they announced their determination to frustrate the General Assembly's resolution by force. There seemed to be little for us to do in Washington, funds were running short, and the Arab League was not disposed to maintain offices over which it had no control. The London Office, on the other hand, was nearer to the centre of decision-making, and the British Government had announced that it would withdraw from Palestine on 15 May 1948, so that it seemed more logical to concentrate our efforts there and in the Arab countries near Palestine.

Musa Alami himself still believed that a political rather than a military solution could be found, and he moved untiringly between Jerusalem, Amman, Cairo, Damascus, Riyadh and Baghdad trying to bring about some consensus of policy and coordination of action which might yet prevent the implementation of the partition resolution. I accompanied him on some of these visits; in Baghdad in particular we found that there was a seriousness of purpose and a willingness to make sacrifices which we felt might either influence the British Government to renounce its immediate abandonment of Palestine to the fortunes of war, or, if war was inevitable, ensure that the Arabs won it. But as the fateful day of 15 May approached, chaos grew in Palestine, and the British authorities seemed to have only one preoccupation – to get out. The Arab governments, though vociferous in the declaration of their intentions, were less energetic in planning their actions. They did not believe that the British would leave Palestine, and Azzam Pasha proclaimed publicly not only that they would not leave, but that, if they did, they would return a few days later.

A week before 15 May I met Musa Alami in Amman. The Philadelphia Hotel, at that time the best in town, housed politicians from Palestine, journalists from all over the world, and officers from various Arab armies. A few days before their armies were due to enter Palestine, the Arab governments finally got round to appointing a commander-in-chief: he was an Iraqi, General Nureddin Mahmud, and I well remember the optimism which his nomination generated, for had it not been a general from Iraq, Nureddin al Zanki, who had led the army of Saladin to the liberation of Jerusalem? This was the same optimism which had moved Jamal Husseini to prophesy that the Arabs would sweep the Jews into the sea with their brooms! But Musa Alami and I had reasons to question that optimism: not only did we realize that there was no possibility of the newly appointed commander-in-chief being able to coordinate the military operations about to be launched from Egyptian, Syrian, Lebanese and Transjordanian territory, but he had no military maps of Palestine to guide his own Iraqi troops; knowing of Musa Alami's contacts with British officials, the General asked him to obtain some, which he did.

So I was a witness from close-up of the military and political fiasco of Arab attempts to prevent partition and the establishment of the state of Israel which was proclaimed on 15 May, as well as of the impact of these events on the Arab population of Palestine, who streamed in hundreds of thousands into the neighbouring countries, and especially into Lebanon, which opened its doors without reservation. Marjayoun in particular, on the frontiers between Palestine and Lebanon, received thousands of refugees, some of whom camped in the centre of the town and in surrounding fields and olive groves, others in the homes of the inhabitants, many of whom had properties in Palestine and looked after the Ghawarneh peasants who had worked their land in Huleh.[8]

At the end of the fighting in Palestine, and with the conclusion of armistice agreements between the Arab governments and Israel in 1949, *de facto* frontiers had come into existence between Israel and the territory still held by the Arabs. In this division of territory part of Jerusalem remained in Arab hands, including the walled city containing most, though not all, of the Holy Places, as did the area to the east of the city down to the Ghor Valley, where around the town of Jericho hundreds of thousands of refugees from other areas of Palestine were encamped. On top of the political problem of Palestine there was now a humanitarian one. Musa Alami, who had lost his family house in Jerusalem, but kept a small property at Jericho, now turned his mind to this new problem. He still had some funds from those he had received from the Government of Iraq to set up the rural organization he had proposed to the Arab League, and he decided to undertake a bold and apparently foolhardy project in the Jordan Valley.

Musa had for a long time believed that underneath the Jordan Valley as it fell down to the Dead Sea, the lowest place on earth, there must be vast accumulations of water formed by the rains and melting snows from the mountains of Lebanon and further north in Syria. Between Jericho and the Dead Sea was a large area completely devoid of cultivation or human habitation, and classified by the mandatory authority and later by the Government of Jordan as 'dead land'. From the Jordan authorities he obtained a grant of several hundred thousand dunams[9] on which to set up a project for the refugees and their children, which he named the Arab Development Society. Against the advice of all the 'experts' he began to dig for water, found it, and on the land slowly and painfully reclaimed began to build a village, to plant cereals, vegetables and fruits, and to create a school for orphaned children. It was, and still is, a pioneering project, providing a demonstration of an alternative to the soul-destroying refugee camps which the United Nations set up in former Palestine, now divided between Israel and Jordan, and in the surrounding Arab countries, as well as giving a lesson to the other Palestinian leaders and intellectuals who abandoned the land of Palestine to seek refuge in more comfortable places – a lesson which, unfortunately, few of them learnt.

The creation of the farm and the school in Jericho tempted me strongly to throw in my lot with the Palestinians whose cause had aroused my early idealism and absorbed much of my efforts at a more mature age. I had been influenced by the history of the young people in pre-revolutionary Russia who had gone 'among the people', and was also impressed, and somewhat envious in my heart, of the young Jewish pioneers, the 'halutzim', who were building a new society in Palestine. I had witnessed in Beirut, Damascus, Baghdad and Amman the flood of Palestinian politicians, professional people, landowners, middle-class merchants and academic persons who had left Palestine in the vain hope of a swift return, and I realized even then that it was the Palestinian people, and above all the peasants and small farmers, who were being left behind. I had to make a choice – to go down to Jericho, work with Musa Alami, whose marriage had broken up and who needed friends around him, and realize my romantic yearnings for a life reduced to its most primitive forms – for in Jericho there was nothing but heat and hard labour – or to return to the more comfortable world of my family in Manchester and in my rediscovered country, Lebanon. I chose the latter course for reasons which at the time were not completely convincing to myself, but which time revealed to be wise. While I was completely convinced of the justice of the Palestinian cause, had worked wholeheartedly for it, and had achieved among the Palestinians a certain prestige and recognition, I was *not* a Palestinian: I had no roots in that country or society, and my main connection was my friendship and collaboration with Musa Alami, who believed in the sincerity of my devotion to 'the cause'. But there were others among the Palestinians who regarded me as an outsider who for one motive or another had ingratiated himself into *their* cause. In the suspicious atmosphere which the total disruption of Palestinian society in 1948 and 1949 had brought about, my position in a Palestinian refugee community would have been difficult. In addition, as I had no independent income of my own, I would have been dependent on the generosity of Musa Alami and, although I knew that generosity to be great, I was reluctant to become a dependant of anyone. So I decided not to go down to Jericho, but to help the project as much as I could by accompanying Musa on some of his journeys to the United States and Europe in search of help, and by publicizing its achievements and its aspirations in the Western press.[10]

I am proud to have been associated with the beginnings of the only serious effort to rescue something out of the catastrophe which had struck the Palestinians. In the conditions prevailing inside Palestine and in the Arab countries I did not then see that much could be done by political activity, but I believed that it was our duty, as members of a group of people who had failed to prevent the catastrophe, to do what we could to alleviate its consequences. And I admired, as I still do, the courage and humanity of Musa Alami, who alone among the Palestinian leaders stayed on to serve the people and their land, without whom there can be no 'return' and no 'liberation'.

IV
Wars of the Middle East

The end of my work with the Arab Office and of my close collaboration with Musa Alami did not end my involvement in the Palestinian question nor in its consequences for Lebanon and indeed the whole world – for who has been able to avoid its impact, in one way or another, upon the history of our times? While I have not made of Palestine my profession, as have some, I have on all occasions when it has seemed possible tried to contribute to a solution, or at least a settlement of its central problem: the relations between two peoples, two communities each claiming the same piece of earth, and each, within the logic of its own thinking, right. That I now believe that all we can hope for is a settlement, not a solution, is the product of my mature judgement, based on my later experiences, that matters have gone too far for there to be, at least in our times, a solution: I cannot envisage 'final solutions' without feeling the horror that phrase evokes in every decent mind. But settlements – that essentially Mancunian, liberal word, with all that it implies of compromise, of give and take, of contract between debtor and creditor – are always possible, provided they contain within their terms the embryo of eventual solutions.

In 1949 the Arab Office closed, and still resisting the 'next step' my father would have liked me to take – return to Manchester and the family business – I decided to try my hand at journalism. I was asked by Tom Little, a friend who had collaborated closely with the London Office, and who was now head of the Arab News Agency, to cover the special session of the General Assembly called to decide on the future of the former Italian colonies in Africa. My friendships and connections with the Arab delegations to the United Nations and the Arab embassies in Washington made it easy for me to know what was going on behind the scenes and to write the reports the agency requested, but I was soon recruited to participate in the debates themselves, not as speaker, but as ghost-writer. I had a friend in one of the Arab delegations whose name, since he is still alive and flourishing, I do not wish to divulge, and who, profiting from the absence of the head of the delegation, wished to make his mark as an orator and statesman, though he did not have the necessary command of English nor the ability to draft a convincing political document. At his request I wrote for him a long and eloquent speech in which I put myself in his Arab shoes, and indulged to the full my own natural inclinations towards flamboyant phrases normally restrained by the reserve and understatement of my Oxford training. It was my first taste of the pleasures – and pains – of ghost-writing. The speech made a sensation: the *New York Times* devoted a column to quoting its fiery denunciations of colonialism, and my friend, who had rarely been known to open his mouth, became instantly famous. The only problem was that, having established his reputation as a speaker, he could not lapse into his former silence, so that I had to write other speeches and interventions for him, including one on the Palestinian problem. After a while his colleagues, most of whom were also my friends, began to suspect what was going on, and mischievously reported it to the head of the delegation when he returned to New York. My friend soon after came to complain to me: 'Imagine,' he said, 'so-and-so says that you are writing my speeches!' I pretended to share his indignation and assured him that it was a horrible lie, invented by his colleagues because they were jealous of his talent as a speaker. For him this was the beginning of a long and successful career: he became the permanent delegate of his Government, convinced by now of his fitness for the position by the brilliant speeches he had made, and later on an important official of the United Nations, where he was no longer required to make speeches. On the occasions when I now meet him I never fail to congratulate him on those brilliant performances, and he never gives me credit for them.

Having enjoyed working at the United Nations, and the

many pleasures of living in New York, I stayed on between the special session and the regular session of the General Assembly in September 1949. My friendship with Charles Malik, which had started with my first period of teaching at the American University of Beirut, when I lived above his room and taught logic as his assistant, brought me into the Lebanese delegation as an adviser. Malik combined his position as Ambassador to Washington with that of chief delegate of his country to the United Nations. He had spent part of the year in Paris and Geneva at meetings of the United Nations dealing with the many and complicated problems to which the partition of Palestine had given rise, and principally the problems of the Palestinian refugees and of the status of Jerusalem. Charles asked me to join his staff to help in the vast amount of research and discussion which went into his speeches: with us was another friend from the American University of Beirut, Fayez Sayegh, himself a Palestinian with an encyclopaedic knowledge of every phase of the problems, and a sharp logical mind, but also a streak of intransigence and bitterness which with time, and frustration as the faith he had put in the capacity or the willingness of the Arab regimes to solve the Palestinian question in the way he wanted faded away, overshadowed his other more human qualities.

Charles Malik himself was, and still is, one of the most brilliant minds of his time. A scientist and mathematician by training, he had turned to philosophy and studied under Heidegger at Freiburg and Whitehead at Harvard: he combined these two dominant influences over his philosophical thinking with a deep interest in Christian theology and, from the point of view of his own position within the Orthodox community, a vision of the role of the Christians of the Near East within the ecumenical unity of the universal Church. From his position as Professor of Philosophy at the American University of Beirut he had been chosen by the newly independent Government of Lebanon to head the first Lebanese Embassy in Washington, and to represent his country at the United Nations: he was elected President of the General Assembly in 1958, and as a member of the committee which drafted the Universal Declaration of Human Rights he played a key role in the formulation of both its substance and its wording.

Those who had known him in Beirut were not astonished at the transformation of the teacher into the diplomat and the statesman. His powerful intellect enabled him easily to master the rules of diplomacy, and his years at Harvard, with its long tradition of involvement in American public life and its intimate connections with the highest level of government as well as the intellectual world, had prepared him for the role of statesman, and imposed on his natural exuberance an Anglo-Saxon pragmatism and clarity of language which did not conceal or distort the profundity of what he was saying. The deeper issues of the Palestinian question, the stages by which Israel from dream became reality built not on the goodwill or acquiescence of its neighbours, and in defiance of the international community's wishes with respect to Jerusalem and Nazareth, have never been better set forth than in the speeches of Charles Malik in the year 1949, in the drafting of some of which I had a small share as friend and confidant.

At the end of the session I returned to London by boat. As the United Nations paid the passage of some members of each delegation, and as I was officially inscribed on the list of delegates, I decided to take the most agreeable way back to England, which was to travel first-class on the *France*, a luxurious French liner since put out of service. For five days, after the hectic life of New York, I enjoyed the tranquillity and isolation of a sea journey, and above all the extraordinary meals which the French kitchens provided: it was possible to order any dish however rare or costly, and I remember with what delight I watched the nightly production of giant *pièces-montées*, of pigs made out of *pâté de foie*, of mountains of meringues and profiteroles. It took me several days of dieting in Manchester to recover from that orgy, but I was dismayed a few days later to receive a letter from the secretariat of the United Nations demanding payment for my passage, on the ground that the request for my transport had not been received from Beirut! The sum involved was over £500, for that time a colossal amount, and for me ruinous: I never replied to that demand, and have no qualms of guilt for my default.

My experiences in the Arab Offices in Washington, London and Jerusalem left me in a mood of disillusion and frustration. I could not see how an Arab world, which in the wake of the disasters of 1948 and 1949 was sinking deeper into instability and chaos, as one regime after another collapsed, and military *coups d'état* substituted young officers for the older and more experienced statesmen held guilty for the loss of Palestine, could seriously face the challenges which the young state of Israel presented. But I could not see, either among the older or the new leaders of the Near East, any one or any party or group in power who had the capacity to understand the seriousness of the new situation created by the rise of Israel, or the ability to redress it. In 1949 Musa Alami had published a booklet in Arabic in which he analysed this new situation, went deeply into the causes of the Arab catastrophe, and proposed ways to redress it: it was a call for both political action and change in the social and economic systems of the Arab countries, radical but not Marxist, and based on the belief that some form of Arab unity was necessary. I translated the article into English and had it published in the *Middle East Journal* in Washington;[1] but although it aroused considerable interest in the Western world, I do not believe it had a serious impact on Arab thinking.

In a later chapter I shall tell of the circumstances of my first meeting and the course of my lifelong friendship with Habib Bourguiba. Although Tunisia was his main concern, the question of Palestine played an important role in his thinking, and, once he came to power, he was to exercise a considerable influence in the way the Arab attitude towards the problem evolved. In some of the stages of his Palestinian policies I was myself involved.

During his short stay in Washington at the end of 1946, Bourguiba wrote at my request a short exposition of his views on the Palestinian question for the bulletin on Arab affairs which we published in the Arab Office. From that article one phrase in particular not only stuck in my own mind, but also was eventually to germinate a new way of thinking among the Palestinian leadership in much later years. The phrase was to the effect that the Jews in Palestine should be 'de-Zionized'.

Bourguiba's argument was that the problem of Palestine was the same kind of problem as he and the nationalist movements in the other countries of the Maghrib[2] were facing: namely, a colonial problem between indigenous populations on the one side, and settlers from outside on the other. Today this is a commonplace of Arab and Palestinian thought and propaganda, but in the thirties and forties it was only the Communists and Marxists who viewed the problem in this light. The theory then prevalent was that the struggle in Palestine was between Arab nationalism and British imperialism, of which Zionism was regarded as an extension. There was, of course, an element of truth in this. One of the main motives behind the British Government's support for the Jewish 'National Home' was the intention to take control over Palestine as an important link in its strategic lifeline to the Indian sub-continent, and it was also already known in London before 1914 that there might be vast reserves of oil in the Near East. But the Arab leadership did not think in Marxist terms: they were more impressed by the ideas of extreme right-wing and anti-Communist authors and marginal political movements who saw in Zionism a gigantic conspiracy of 'world Jewry' to seize the Holy Land from the Muslims and Christians who formed the majority of its population and to turn it into a Jewish state. They did not read Lenin's *Imperialism, the Last Stage of Capitalism*, but *The Protocols of the Elders of Zion*. The idea contained in Bourguiba's embryonic phrase, 'the de-Zionization of the Jews', was quite new, and conflicted with the current idea that every Jew was a Zionist, and that there was no possibility of understanding, and no common interests, between Arabs and Jews. It took the Palestinian leadership many years before it came round to the idea that not all Jews need be Zionists, and even today the tentative and hesitating contacts between Palestinian activists and non-Zionist Jews are viewed with suspicion and even hostility.

Bourguiba was a nationalist, not a Marxist, and his policy of trying to win over to his side a section of opinion among those whom he was opposing was tactical and eventually succeeded because he was able to put himself into the position of his adversaries, and understand their way of thinking and their motives. Dialogue, to his way of thinking, was just as important as confrontation, and each had its place and its time.

This way of thinking, and this approach to political action, combined with the disillusion I felt with the leaders and the regimes who had brought about the catastrophe in Palestine, provided me with the main inspiration of my thinking and writing in the years between 1949 and my eventual move to Tunisia in 1956. In 1950 I married Furugh, the daughter of Hussein and Bedia Afnan,[2] who had been the close friends of Amin Kisbany in Baghdad, and, faced at last with the problem of supporting a family, and not just my vagrant self, I thought that perhaps I should 'settle down'. The war years, of which my time in Washington and New York had been a kind of prolongation, were over, and my father, who had been deeply affected by the death of my mother, which occurred while I was in Cairo, still harboured the hope that I might join him in his office. Partly out of a feeling of guilt that I had left him waiting for so long, partly out of expediency, because I had no job, no savings, and a wife, I decided to give business a trial. But by now my father's business had shrunk to almost nothing, and he found it difficult to change the habits of sixty years which made his daily routine in the office immutable, and my own functions minimal. I found myself doing very little except lunching with the fast-dwindling members of the Lebanese and Syrian business community who provided a link with my recent experiences in the East and in Arab affairs as well as with my earlier oriental childhood. The climate of Manchester, from which I had been absent for so many years, began to depress me as I remembered the lush springs and hot summers of Lebanon, the delights of Damascus and Aleppo, the sounds and smells of the East. I decided to accept an offer which came to me from the American University of Beirut to return as a teacher with the status of associate professor. This was a definite 'step' such as my father, though reluctant to see me leave him, could understand, and he found consolation in the thought that I would follow my brothers in a steady and serious academic career at his old university. There I might have remained until today had not the seeds of adventure been sown in me from childhood, whetted by my first taste of politics in Cairo, Jerusalem and Washington, and fertilized by my friendship with Bourguiba in whom I recognized a total disdain for the practical concerns of life similar to my own.

At the American University of Beirut the principal subject which I taught, and on which I reflected, was the history of political ideas. Although I gave no courses on the contemporary Arab world, most of what I taught had some relevance to the problems of the day. In the fifties the Palestinian question did not yet play the dominant role it later on assumed in the minds of the student and teaching body of the university: there were other issues just as burning, such as the best form of government for the Arab countries, and the role and qualities of the 'Arab leader' eagerly awaited. The parliamentary systems which some of these countries such as Iraq, Syria, Lebanon and Egypt had inherited from the days when they were under British and French domination were breaking down, partly under the pressure of new ideologies, partly because of the emergence of a politicized class of officers in the new armies. Discontent with the outcome of the 'war' in Palestine was the occasion for the overthrow of the regime in Syria, and the beginning of a series of *coups d'état* to be imitated in nearly all the other Arab countries except Lebanon. My lectures, whether on Plato, Aristotle, the seventeenth-century English revolution, Hobbes, Hume, Rousseau, Marx, or John Stuart Mill, revolved around the questions of liberty and constitutionalism, the necessity of curbing authority, and the peaceful passage of power – all of them burning questions of the hour. Among my students were some who were to become important figures in their countries as ministers, ambassadors, and high officials, others, like George Habash, to take the path of opposition and violence. I was active in writing articles, lecturing, and taking part in university affairs which, on a small scale, provided the theatre for my political instincts. I had time also to form my own ideas about government, society, freedom, power in the Arab countries. But I was not altogether happy at the distance which academic life put between me and active involvement in public affairs, and when the opportunity came for me to escape, I took it without much hesitation: I hankered after a role which would put me at the heart of events. Thus when I went to Tunisia, as I shall later tell, it was my hope that from there might come the solution of the Palestinian problem which had occupied so much of my earlier life.

If, after almost a century of French colonialism – in the case of Algeria after an even longer period – the North Africans were to succeed in recovering their political identity and in their countries, this would, I hoped, help the Palestinians in their own struggle to recoup the losses they had incurred in 1948. I also believed that the North African states, once they acquired independence, would set up regimes more imbued with the liberalism and constitutional ideas of Western democracy than those of the Arab East, and thus acquire a greater influence and a greater weight on the international scene which would be exercised in favour of the Palestinians. Time was to reveal that these ideas were only partially true: I had not anticipated the direction which Egypt under Jamal Abdul Nasser could give to Arab nationalism, nor the divisive and disruptive impact of his personality on Arab society and on inter-Arab relations. All this became clear to me when Bourguiba attempted to promote his ideas about the Palestinian problem in an Arab world not yet ready to listen to them.

I had gone to Tunisia in 1956 and as an adviser to President Bourguiba participated in the gigantic efforts which the new regime had made to lay the foundations of a modern progressive state. There was not much time to think about the problem of Palestine, faced as we were by more immediate and pressing problems, among which the most important was the Algerian revolution whose forces were on Tunisian territory, and whose leaders' presence in Tunis posed daily problems for the Tunisian Government. In addition, Bourguiba's distrust of President Nasser did not encourage him to become involved too closely in the increasing turmoil of the Mashriq.[3] But in January 1964, on the occasion of an Arab summit meeting in Cairo, he returned to his old thesis, the germ of which had been contained in the article he had written for me in Washington in 1946: the problem of Palestine was not between the Arab states and Israel, but a colonial one between the indigenous population and the colonizers, and therefore the Palestinians still on the soil of Palestine must liberate themselves by a struggle waged from inside their territory, not from outside. Although Bourguiba agreed to the creation of the Palestine Liberation Organization decided upon by the Arab governments meeting in Cairo, it was not long before he clashed with the leadership of the new organization.[4] Never shirking confrontation, President Bourguiba decided to bring his ideas directly before the Palestinian people and public opinion in the Mashriq.

The occasion came at the beginning of 1965 when Bourguiba decided to go on official visits to Egypt, Jordan, Lebanon and Syria. Someone in his entourage or among his close collaborators who disliked my closeness to the seat of power suggested to Bourguiba that my presence in Cairo would not be welcome, although whatever unpopularity I might have acquired in that capital was because of my association with him, and in consequence he asked me to join the official party in Jordan after the visit to Egypt was over. In Jordan the Prime Minister was Wasfi Tal who had been my close friend in Beirut when I was teaching at the American University in 1940, and who, like me, though for different motives, had joined the British army during the war. He came from Irbid in Jordan, where his father was a well-known poet. He was a dreamer, but of politics and power, and although he was later to fall out with most of his early fellow Arab nationalists who then flourished at the American University, he and I remained friends: but that friendship was interrupted by a series of events in which I was unwittingly involved.

Wasfi had joined the British army during the war because he believed that this was an opportunity to prepare for the military showdown with the Zionists in Palestine which he saw was coming. Young Jews were flocking to the army to acquire the military training which they later used against the British, but the Arab population kept away, believing that any form of 'collaboration' with the British Government was treason, and Wasfi was much criticized among his friends for his decision. When he left the army in 1945, Musa Alami was looking for young men to join his staff in the Arab Offices, and I suggested the names of two of my own close friends from my American University days: Burhan Dajani and Wasfi Tal. Wasfi became in a short time Musa's personal assistant, but in the period between 1948 and 1949 when their world crumbled around them, a crisis developed in Musa's private life, his marriage broke up, and his wife left him to marry Wasfi.

The simultaneous loss of his country, his wife, and most of his property was a bitter blow under which most men would have collapsed. Only his devotion to the children whom he decided to save from the refugee camps, and to the families of his servants and retainers, kept up his morale. But his friends found themselves forced to choose between the two former partners, and although I had been closely attached to his wife, as had all of his friends, I found it impossible to continue seeing both of them, and so I did not meet her or Wasfi Tal for many years.

But in March 1965 Wasfi was Prime Minister of Jordan, and as a member of President Bourguiba's delegation I was happy to renew my friendship with him and his wife. He had won the confidence of King Hussein who appreciated his remarkable qualities of integrity, hard work, and clear-headedness which made him the most successful Jordanian prime minister of recent times.[5] And Musa Alami was down in Jericho where by now his project had grown in size and in fame, and was internationally recognized and supported by a variety of foundations, organizations and friends who admired, as I did, his obstinate courage. I felt it important to arrange a meeting between President Bourguiba and Musa Alami who had met through my friendship with both of them before Bourguiba became President of Tunisia and Musa had gone down to Jericho: I wanted Bourguiba to see for himself the conditions in which the refugees were living, and to hear from the one leader who had remained on Palestinian soil the authentic voice of Palestinian nationalism.

Among the engagements organized for President Bourguiba and his delegation during the official visit to Amman was a briefing session conducted by the Prime Minister and the Chief of Staff of the Jordanian armed forces to inform Bourguiba of the military capacity of Jordan in the event of war with Israel.

From that session Bourguiba emerged profoundly pessimistic: the presentation of the military situation by the Jordanians convinced him that Jordan could sustain a confrontation with Israel only for a very few days, and not long enough for the Arab governments to send the help which the Jordanians – but not Bourguiba – believed they would offer. If confrontation would be disastrous, an alternative had to be found, and with the clarity of his Descartian mind Bourguiba saw that it could only be found by accepting some form of partition of Palestine between the state of Israel and the Arabs. This meant a reversal of the position of the Arab governments and the Palestinians which rejected partition in all its forms. Bourguiba saw clearly that the only way to prevent the expansion of Israel from the *de facto* frontiers it had won in warfare in 1948 was to return to the boundaries proposed by the United Nations General Assembly in 1947.

Today, when the organization which claims to be the sole legitimate representative of the Palestinian people is prepared to accept any portion of Palestinian territory Israel might relinquish and to set up a Palestinian state on it, Bourguiba's arguments in 1965 do not seem revolutionary or even controversial, but in the climate of the times they were profoundly shocking to the Arab governments and the Palestinians as a whole. I did not agree with Bourguiba on his attitude towards the legitimacy of Jordan's *de facto* sovereignty over the West Bank, and doubted the wisdom of undermining Jordan's position before being certain that Palestinian sovereignty would take its place; and while I could see that the advantages of calling for a return to the frontiers of the partition plan of 1947 were tactical, I could also see the difficulty of implementing it; but I did agree with Bourguiba that something had to be done to make the Arab governments and the Palestinians aware that they were in danger of losing what remained of Palestine in Arab hands if they could not find some way to contain Israel within internationally recognized frontiers, and that the only real option was not the military confrontation of which they dreamed, but negotiation.

The opportunity to administer the shock which Bourguiba by now was determined to give the Arab governments, the

Palestinians, and above all President Nasser, was provided by the visit to Musa Alami's project in Jericho which I had arranged for the President on 3 March 1965, during which he saw not only the school and model village on the project but also the refugee camps in nearby Jericho. After the lunch offered by Musa to his Tunisian guests and the Jordanian and Palestinian ministers and personalities who accompanied them, Bourguiba addressed a vast crowd of Palestinian refugees. In this historic speech he developed once again the thesis which had brought him into conflict with President Nasser and the leadership of the Palestine Liberation Organization: the Arab-Israeli conflict was between the colonized and the colonizers, not between the Arab states and Israel, and the Palestinians living under Israeli control should organize themselves and follow the strategy which had led the Tunisian movement under his leadership to independence. He attacked the policy of 'all or nothing' which had brought them to their present plight. 'It is extremely easy', he cried, 'to make inflammatory and grandiloquent speeches, but one should not accuse of defeatism or submission an Arab leader who proposes partial or provisional solutions if these are necessary steps towards the final objective.' He had, of course, himself in mind, and knew that his proposal that the Arabs should accept the 1947 partition plan as the lesser evil would bring on his head a storm of recriminations, especially from those Arab leaders and governments who regarded his initiative as a direct challenge to their own positions. In another speech in Jerusalem he developed the same ideas.

The first reaction to Bourguiba's speeches in Jericho and Jerusalem from the Arab press in Amman, Beirut, Cairo, Damascus and Baghdad was one of astonishment and hostility, but the full fury of Arab and Palestinian opinion came during Bourguiba's official visit to Lebanon on which I also accompanied him. Provoked by the negative and hostile reaction to his ideas, Bourguiba did not retreat but pursued them still further. I had rarely seen him in a more excited and combative mood than on one occasion for which I provided the scenario. I had suggested that he should meet Saeb Salam, then, as he still is, the leading Lebanese Muslim statesman, but the meeting was a disaster: a word – I believe it was 'submission' or 'surrender' (in Arabic, *istislam*) – spoken by Saeb with no intent to provoke, produced the most violent reaction I had ever seen from Bourguiba. All the pent-up anger and tensions which he had so far managed to suppress in the face of the attacks to which he had been subjected now burst out against Saeb, who maintained his habitual calm, while I looked on in embarrassed silence.

In a more controlled form Bourguiba's anger and combativeness was to be publicly displayed at a lecture before the 'Cénacle du Liban', an organization which provided a forum for visiting and Lebanese intellectuals to discuss issues of the day. At the meeting organized in a large cinema in Beirut, at which were present all the prominent political and intellectual figures of Lebanese life, Bourguiba delivered a passionate attack on current ideas and practices of Arab nationalism which delighted many of his Christian Lebanese audience, but infuriated the followers of the many ideological movements then flourishing in Lebanon. The result was an even more violent reaction than that provoked by the speeches he had given in Jericho and Jerusalem: the local and Arab press denounced him as a traitor, and threats against his life were received by the Tunisian delegation. I myself came in for my share of the insults, especially from the Egyptian-inspired press in Beirut and Damascus which was delighted to find in my person the villain of the piece. We left Beirut precipitously, and Bourguiba was never to return there.

The violent reaction to Bourguiba's proposals to return to the 1947 partition plan, and to seek a negotiated settlement rather than a military solution, was not entirely due to the content of his proposals, but more to the challenge they represented to the leadership of President Nasser. A large part of Nasser's popularity and prestige in the Arab world, and among the Palestinians both inside and outside Palestine, was due to the belief that under his leadership the United Arab Republic would defeat Israel militarily, and Bourguiba's position was in contradiction to this vision of the solution to the Palestinian problem. His direct appeal to the Palestinians still on the soil of Palestine also represented a challenge to

Ahmed Shukairi, head of the PLO, and to the governments which supported him, who for their own reasons preferred to see Palestinian resistance organized from their own territories, and therefore susceptible to their control, rather than in Palestine itself. In a meeting called by President Nasser in Cairo in April 1965 attended by representatives of most Arab governments with the intention of taking some common action against Tunisia, Shukairi declared, 'Bourguiba is a traitor, and therefore I demand a punishment for the Tunisian President commensurate with the gravity of his crime', which was equivalent to demanding his assassination.

The views expressed by Bourguiba on his visit to the Near East in 1965, and in Tunisia following his return, were to be proved prophetic in 1967 when, in the 'Six Days War', Israel inflicted a resounding defeat on the Egyptian, Jordanian and Syrian armies, and took over the entire territory of Palestine as well as occupying Sinai from Egypt and the 'Golan Heights' from Syria.[6] I had by then left Tunisia for reasons which I recount later, and of the genesis of that war, and the scenario of its outbreak, I had an inside view.

The circumstances of my departure from Tunisia, which I had not planned or made provision for, left me and my family in considerable financial and personal difficulty, which, had it not been for the kindness and generosity of certain friends, among whom I must name Leo d'Erlanger,[7] might have caused us serious problems. I decided then that I would no longer work for governments, but try to maintain my independence of judgement and freedom of action by earning my living as a freelance writer and consultant. My friends and contacts acquired through my years in Washington, New York, London, Paris, Cairo, Beirut, and other Arab capitals were many, and I conceived the idea of producing a bulletin for private subscribers in which I would analyse current events in the Arab countries from my own, perhaps original, perspective.

Among the many friends I had made in the course of my activities as founder and director of the International Cultural Centre in Tunisia was the late Julius Fleischmann,[8] who had made a generous donation to the Centre, and who had placed his apartment in New York at my disposal on more than one occasion. At the end of May 1967 I decided to go to New York to stay there while I sought support for the bulletin I planned to publish, and on the plane which carried me there I met again a friend I had known in my Cairo years, whose wedding I had attended, and with whom I had been one of the solitary mourners at the funeral of our common friend Paul Kraus. It was Aubrey, now, since the creation of Israel, Abba Eban. I had met him once or twice in secret in New York while I was still in Tunisia – for in those days a mere handshake with an important Israeli, if seen in public or photographed, could end the career of an Arab official, or at least cause a scandal – but now that I was a free agent I felt at liberty to sit with him in the first-class cabin in which he sat in solitary splendour. Eban was then Foreign Minister, and was on his way to Washington on a mission which was to play a decisive role in the frantic days which preceded the Six Days War.

The Israeli Government was sending Eban to Washington in order to decide how best to face the crisis which had developed with the Egyptian Government. President Nasser, confident in his own armed forces and in what he believed to be widespread international support, had asked for and obtained the withdrawal of the United Nations forces which had provided a barrier between Egypt and Israel since 1956, and had gone on to announce that he had closed the Gulf of Akaba to Israeli shipping. This latter action, had it been true, would have deprived Israel of access to the Red Sea, but it was not actually true: it was a move in a game of poker which Nasser was trying to play to see how far he could go with Israel without actually declaring war. Eban's mission to Washington was to find out what the American Government's reaction would be if Israel attacked Egypt: would it repeat the policy of President Eisenhower in 1956 which had forced Israel to relinquish the territory it had occupied in the Suez affair? From my conversation with Eban it was easy for me to see that Israel and Egypt were on the brink of war, and that whatever President Nasser's intentions might be, Israel now had sufficient pretexts to attack. If in Washington Eban was not told that Israel should not attack, this would be interpreted by the Israelis to mean that Washington would not intervene if the Israeli strike were to be successful: the Israelis knew, on the other hand, that the Americans would come to their rescue if there was any serious danger of their being defeated.

When I arrived in New York and Washington I gave my friends among the Arab delegations to the United Nations and the embassies my interpretation of events, and hoped they would convey some idea of the gravity of the situation to their governments, but no one was prepared to listen seriously. They were thrilled at what they saw to be Nasser's determination to finish once and for all with Israel, and the thought of war did not frighten but rather excited them with its prospect of the victory they were sure would follow.

On the morning of 6 June I heard the news early in the morning that war had broken out. I hurried to the United Nations where the Arab delegations were meeting. The mood was one of jubilation, the Egyptian delegation had received news from Egypt that the Egyptian airforce had inflicted a crushing blow on the Israelis, and Dr Izzet Tannous, who represented the Arab Higher Committee at the UN, where he had the status of observer, told me, 'This is the happiest day of my life.' I could not share the enthusiasm of the Arab delegates. I did not believe the Israelis would have attacked unless they were certain of a quick and decisive victory, and I had learnt from my experience in 1948 that the communiqués of Arab governments should be treated with caution when they claim victories, and only be taken seriously when they admit defeats – which they rarely do. Moreover I was sure that even if the Egyptians had succeeded in dealing Israel a severe blow, the USA and the Western world as a whole would not permit a decisive defeat of Israel.

As the morning progressed the jubilation of the Arab delegates began to diminish noticeably, and by one o'clock it was clear that it was the Egyptian airforce which had been almost entirely destroyed on the ground, and that a massive Israeli onslaught on Egypt was under way. The remaining days of the Six Days War confirmed my worst fears, and I decided that I would put down on paper all the thoughts about the Palestine problem, the attitudes and actions of the Arab governments, and the future of the Arab world which had been brewing in my mind for some years but which, because of my official position in Tunisia, I had refrained from publishing.

The abandonment of the Palestinian people by their leaders in 1948; the lessons of the Algerian revolution; the conflict between Nasser and Bourguiba; the creation of a Palestinian 'resistance' movement in the image of the Arab regimes which brought it into being; the role of the Arab governments on the international scene – my reflections on these matters formulated themselves in my mind into a point of view which I knew would not be popular with the governments and movements which it attacked, but would find an echo in the minds of many people throughout the Arab world who wanted someone to express in clear and unambiguous language thoughts which they could not, or dared not, utter themselves.

In Paris, Geneva, and Provence I wrote a long article born of my feelings of anger and frustration at the incompetence, misjudgements and demagogy of some of the Arab governments and leaders, and sent it to the editor of the *Nahar* Arabic daily published in Beirut, then perhaps the most widely-read and respected newspaper in the Arab world. It was published in the form of a supplement to the paper, and although the censorship then in force in Lebanon cut out large sections in deference to the Arab regimes which I criticized in no uncertain terms, it created a sensation, and the large white spaces only provoked curiosity to know what had been cut out – a curiosity to be satisfied a few days later by the editor, Ghassan Tueni, who defied the censor and reprinted the article in full. At the same time I circulated the English version of the article in Beirut privately among friends under the title 'Torero or Bull?' extracted from a sentence in which I claimed that the Arab leaders – and I meant primarily Nasser – could not decide what role they were trying to play. The article, under the title of 'The Moment of Truth' – again taken from the bull-ring – was published in November 1967 by the English literary and political monthly *Encounter*, and was subsequently translated and published in German, French, Spanish and Hebrew, and eventually found its way into a number of source-books on Middle East affairs.[9]

The reactions to the article in the Arab countries were various. In the columns of the more rabid Arab nationalist press of Beirut and Damascus I was vilified as a traitor, an advocate of peace with Israel, a Bourguibist, British agent, and – ultimate honour – caricatured to look like an Israeli! In Egypt the article was not reproduced, but I learnt that it had been read in official circles, and although displeasing to the unthinking followers of President Nasser, found an echo in later years when Nasserism had died, and the more realistic and intelligent policies of President Sadat had taken its place. Among the Palestinians it was appreciated by many of the intellectuals, whose thoughts it expressed, but who, because of my association with Bourguiba and my consequent disfavour in Arab nationalist circles, would have preferred that it had been written by someone else, as I was told by one of them.

Re-reading the article today, after fifteen years, it is not easy to understand the controversy and indignation it aroused, as many of the ideas I expressed have now become part of the official thinking of some Arab regimes, and even of the mainstream of thought in the Palestine Liberation Organization. It is only the extremes of Arab opinion, for whom any form of compromise with the existence of Israel is anathema, who still reject the 'containment' of Israel which I advocated and still hanker after the 'conquest' which I argued was impossible, at least in any foreseeable future. The germ of the 'democratic Palestinian state' which is now the official policy of the PLO – though recently it has receded into the background in favour of a more realistic acceptance of a Palestinian state on any part of Palestine which can be recovered – was also contained in the alternative I suggested in the event of there being no return to the situation before 6 June 1967. The dilemma which I pointed out would be created for Israel by the occupation of the whole of Palestine, and the inclusion within the bounds of its responsibilities of a large Arab population which would eventually dilute the 'Jewishness' of Israel unless they could somehow be made to disappear, is now accepted by many Israeli and Zionist thinkers as a genuine problem, though one to which no solution has yet been found.

The *Encounter* article, however, does not represent an accurate picture of my views today: in fifteen years many things have changed both in the situation and in my thinking – I no longer believe, for example, that there are any circumstances in which the Jews in Israel would prefer to live in an Arab state rather than in their own – but at the time the article was published it was, I believe, a step towards a greater understanding of the issues involved in the Arab-Israeli conflict.[10]

In the autumn of 1967 I returned to New York and joined the delegation of Lebanon to the United Nations, then headed by George Hakim,[11] in the capacity of adviser, and I sat in on the long debates and negotiations which culminated in the passage of resolution 242 of the Security Council voted on 22 November 1967. This resolution, which in general terms linked recognition by the Arab states of Israel's right to exist within secure and recognized frontiers with the withdrawal of Israel's armed forces 'from territories occupied in the recent conflict', has become the basic policy of the American Government and most Western governments towards the Arab-Israeli conflict, but I have never believed that it has contributed substantially towards a solution: the ambiguity of 'territories occupied' and 'the territories occupied' which was the reason for its acceptance by the Security Council, is not a real one, but only semantic, and does not exist in the French version because the French mind, unlike the Anglo-Saxon, cannot accept contradictions in thought, and therefore not in language either. Nor do I believe that acceptance or refusal of resolution 242 should be made a condition for a negotiated settlement of the conflict between the Palestinians and the Israelis, which can only come about when both parties recognize their mutual rights to statehood, and negotiate between themselves on the form in which they agree to live together in the same land and under the same sky.

The following year, 1968, I wrote another article which aroused considerable interest and controversy, especially among the Palestinians now under Israeli rule. The origin of this article was a suggestion made by Musa Alami in a memorandum he submitted to the Secretary-General of the

United Nations, U Thant, to place the territories occupied by Israel in 1967 – that is the West Bank and Gaza – under an international trusteeship, and to appoint a High Commissioner who would organize a plebiscite among all the Palestinians who returned to Palestine for the consultation. The plebiscite would ask them if they wished to form an independent state or if they wished to enter into federal or confederal relations with any neighbouring state. I presented the proposal in an unsigned article which the London *Times* published on 17 May, in which I elaborated on the suggestion of an international trusteeship as a way of reconstituting the Palestinian Arab community on Palestinian soil, and thus returning to the idea of partition which the 1967 war had pre-empted. I argued that this would be in the interests not only of the Palestinians but also of the Israelis, who, if they were at peace with the Palestinians, need no longer be at war with the Arab countries. I further proposed that Jordanian sovereignty over the West Bank should be 'frozen' until the Palestinians decided in the plebiscite what relations they wished to establish with their neighbours.

The article, which was in no way intended to challenge the authority which the Jordanian state had exercised over the West Bank since 1949 and which implicitly envisaged the possibility of federation between the two entities, was not well regarded in Amman, and *The Times* of 17 May was confiscated. The Israelis also were not happy about the article which they called 'the Alami plan', and which they believed was a British-inspired ploy to return to Palestine. But the Palestinians themselves on the West Bank and Gaza were immensely excited by the article. The fact that it had been published in *The Times* seemed to them to imply that there was British backing for the plan, which of course was not the case. Although the plan implicitly accepted the partition which the Palestinians had previously rejected, by now most of them still living in their land realized that it was an irreversible fact of life which they were prepared to accept provided it satisfied their minimum demands for a recognized national status.

Although both Washington and London received reports of the proposal's favourable reception on the West Bank, neither the American nor the British Government gave it substantial support. And the Palestinians themselves had no leadership with authority or courage enough to accept it publicly. I did in fact receive a visit from Kemal Nasser,[12] who had been a student of mine at the American University of Beirut and was now a prominent member of the Palestine Liberation Organization, who guessed my authorship of the article, and was curious to find out what lay behind it. More recently the ideas I proposed have been suggested on more than one occasion by Palestinian and other Arab leaders. Had the USA or the British Government sponsored the proposal, it might at that time have won over some of the Israeli establishment, such as General Dayan, who favoured a settlement of Israel's differences with the Palestinians after the 1967 war. But it may be too late now to revive it.

One important outcome of the Six Days War in 1967 was to create a new wave of Palestinian refugees who flooded into Jordan and Lebanon; another was the new impetus it gave to the 'resistance movement' set up by the Arab League in 1964. The revitalized leadership, now rid of the disastrous Ahmed Shukairi, set about organizing its followers into military and para-military units, some attached to the official armies of Syria, Egypt and Jordan, other autonomous under the aegis of the various parties and groups of which the Palestine Liberation Organization was constituted. In Jordan their activities –increasingly undisciplined as they became – quickly led to confrontation with the Jordanian army and state, and their expulsion from Jordan in 1970. From then onwards Lebanon, whose free society was a more propitious ground for their activities, became the main base for the political, military and informational efforts of the resistance movement. The concentration of these efforts in Lebanon was to lead to the chain of events of which the final scene has still to come. In these events I was to be closely involved, and they were to have a profound influence on my thinking not only about 'the problem of Palestine', which was becoming more and more 'the problem of the Palestinians', but also about Lebanon, and about my relations to the country which was now my permanent home.

V

AN ARAB LEADER: THE TUNISIAN EXPERIENCE

In the last three years of the Second World War Cairo became a centre of attraction to leaders of nationalist movements from all over the Arab world anxious to publicize their causes and to profit from a freedom which many of them did not enjoy in their own countries. Among these leaders was Habib Bourguiba, who, after confinement in Italy during the war, succeeded in reaching Cairo after a gruelling and hazardous journey on foot across the western desert.

I met him first on the balcony of the Hotel Intercontinental where late every afternoon politicians, writers and intellectuals from Egypt, Lebanon, Syria, Iraq, Palestine and Transjordan would meet to discuss the latest events and developments in the course of the war and in Arab politics. I was a frequent participant in these sessions, and one day Taqieddin Solh, a friend from Lebanon active in pan-Arab politics, whose father, an important official of the Ottoman administration in south Lebanon, had been a close friend of my mother's father, introduced me to a short, vivacious though in appearance fragile man called Habib Bourguiba. The name was familiar to me, but of his role in Tunisian affairs I was only vaguely aware. I was immediately impressed by his fiery eyes, the vivacity of his conversation, and the fascinating story he told of his stay in Germany and Italy from where he had recently escaped. On parting he gave me a copy of a small book he had recently published on relations between France and Tunisia, and in which there was a photograph of himself still wearing the long black beard he had grown during one of his frequent residences in French prisons. I realized that he was a very different type of leader from the Arab politicians who were frequenting Cairo.

The Iraqis, Syrians, Lebanese and Palestinians still bore the stamp of their Ottoman background: their education was Turkish, French or English, their social background that of the *effendi* or notables class. Bourguiba had none of the manners of an Ottoman gentleman of the old school: socially he came from a class of small landowners from the Tunisian Sahel, the coastal area from where the greatest resistance to the French Protectorate had come, and whose people had suffered most from the consequences of the European colonization which followed French occupation in 1881. His education was both Arabic and French, and his political ideas were formed in the image of the French liberal and mildly socialist currents with which he had come into contact during his student days in Paris in the twenties. While he was more at ease in France than any of the Near Eastern leaders felt in Europe, he was also closer to his people, a more 'popular' leader, in the true sense of the word, than any of them, and envisaged independence not just in terms of the ending of European rule, but as a real liberation of the people from what he saw as the source of their subjugation to Europe – ignorance, antiquated ideas, and the conservatism which the people of North Africa had imposed on themselves to protect their personality from the impact of European ideas and colonial domination. He was also, again unlike most Near Eastern leaders, a brilliant orator in both Arabic and French, capable of arousing the masses not by demagogy but through the intelligible presentation of sophisticated ideas.

There grew up rapidly between us a friendship, based on my side on a fascination for a new type of Arab leader with whom I had both an intellectual and an affectionate relationship, and based on his side at first on the calculation that I could be useful to the cause which was his obsession. To get Tunisia within the orbit of the Arab League, and to open up windows onto the Anglo-Saxon world was his main ambition in Cairo, and my closeness to British officials such as General Clayton who were, behind the scenes, the architects of the League, and my friendship with some of the Arab leaders who had formally established it, made me in his eyes a valuable ally.

But from that position of the 'useful contact' my relations

with Habib Bourguiba were soon to develop into those of a confidant and friend. It was his ambition in those years to establish close contact with Washington in order to enlarge the area of activity of the Tunisian nationalist movement, and to bring pressure on France from the two principal partners of the Western alliance, the United States of America and Great Britain. He had witnessed at first hand from Cairo the way in which Lebanon and Syria had achieved their independence through the pressures brought on France by the British Government and in particular by General Spears.[1] He was also aware that Great Britain was reluctant to upset the French Government further by pressuring it to relinquish its position in North Africa, and he had therefore come to the conclusion that it was to Washington that he must appeal to prevent the relapse of France's North African dominions into their former status. In addition, the United Nations had just been created, and he hoped to use his friendships with the Arab leaders he had met in Cairo and other Arab capitals to further the Tunisian and North African cause within the international organization.

When he learned that I was going to Washington as director of the Arab Office there, he decided that he would go there too and profit from the contacts I hoped I would be able to make with the State Department, the press, and other sectors of American life. So it was that early one Monday morning in November 1946 my secretary at the Office, Juliette Khouri, came into my office in a state of astonishment to announce to me that a man in pyjamas was asking to see me. It was Habib Bourguiba, who over the weekend had arrived in Washington, and knowing only the address of the Arab Office at the Wardman Park Hotel, had moved in there to wait for me to arrive on Monday morning. He was in poor condition: the fatigue of his twenty-day voyage across the Atlantic on a Dutch cargo-boat without an overcoat, and of the bitter cold of that New York winter, had told on him; he had almost no money in his pocket, and being unaware that he could sign the bill for meals taken in the hotel, he had not eaten for two days. The first thing we did was to order an enormous American breakfast.

Along with my colleagues we immediately adopted him as a member of the Arab Office, and I set about arranging meetings with the American friends and contacts we had made during the few months we had been in Washington. Among these friends were people of importance in Washington: Loy Henderson, Assistant Secretary of State for Near Eastern Affairs, who agreed to receive Bourguiba in his office at the State Department in which hung a life-size portrait of a Tunisian Bey who had concluded a Treaty of Friendship with the USA in the nineteenth century; Colonel William Eddy, head of an American intelligence agency, who had played an important role in North Africa and the Near East during the war, and whose sympathies were pro-Arab and anti-French; and Kermit Roosevelt, whom I had met in Cairo, who was close to the Secretary of State, Dean Acheson, and whose name opened many doors to us in the society of Washington and New York. The Arab Office was also in close contact with the newly established Arab embassies in Washington; Ali Jawdet, Ambassador of Iraq, Assad al-Faqih, Ambassador of Saudi Arabia, Charles Malik, Ambassador of Lebanon, Ali Fahmi, Ambassador of Egypt, and Constantin Zurayk, Ambassador of Syria, all opened the doors of their embassies to Habib Bourguiba, entertained him, and introduced him to their own friends and contacts.

Bourguiba was quick to realize that what he could reasonably hope to achieve in Washington was not any major political decision by the American Government in favour of Tunisian or North African nationalist aspirations, but a first contact with American officials and opinion-formers which might plant the seeds of a more sympathetic and understanding American attitude towards the North African leaders and their parties. Bourguiba also saw his visit to Washington and New York as a way of enhancing his own position in Tunisia among the members of his party and his colleagues, some of whom he suspected, from motives of jealousy or rivalry, did not look with a benevolent eye on his one-man adventure into the Anglo-Saxon world. A further benefit was the irritation his visit was certain to cause to the French Government, and particularly to the French officials in Tunis who had done their best to make it impossible for him to travel. In other words, the visit to the United States of America was primarily an exercise in public relations. In this exercise I was an invaluable and willing ally.

Apart from the private meetings I was able to arrange for him in a wide spectrum of Washington's official and social life, there were two public occasions which furthered the purposes for which he had come to the United States. No North African leader had ever had the opportunity to address an important American public: one obstacle was language, another the opposition which the French authorities had always made to the granting of visas by the American Government to persons they described as undesirable, or the issue of passports valid for travel outside of a very limited number of countries. Through two friends in the administration, Edwin Wright and Harry Howard, who were both sympathetic to Arab causes in general, and who had been charmed by Bourguiba, I was able to organize a public lecture in a well-known meeting-place and to distribute invitations to a wide selection of officials, journalists, Middle East experts, intelligence officers, and diplomats. I prepared a translation of Bourguiba's address, and he delivered it in French. The lecture received considerable coverage in the press, and was the subject of an official protest by the French Government to the Department of State, which politely ignored it.

The second occasion was more dramatic and was to play a more important role in the history of Franco-Tunisian relations and of the inner affairs of the Neo-Destour Party of which Bourguiba was the founder and leader. In one of his messages sent to his colleagues in Tunis, Cairo and Paris Bourguiba had rashly announced that his friend Cecil Hourani was arranging a meeting for him with Secretary of State Dean Acheson. It was true that I had asked through friends in the Department of State if such a meeting was possible, and although the request was never granted, neither was it refused. When the news of this impending meeting reached the party, it was received with scepticism and consternation by some of his colleagues, who disliked the idea of his achieving an international limelight denied to themselves. The famous meeting did take place, however, though in circumstances I had not foreseen. The occasion was a reception given by the Saudi Arabian Ambassador in Washington, Assad al-Faqih, in honour of a visiting Saudi Arabian personality, to which Bourguiba and I were invited. At the party was the Secretary of State. I had met him on a number of occasions at similar receptions, and he probably knew who I was, although in all honesty I could not claim much more. Nevertheless the presence of the two men in the same room seemed to me to be an opportunity not to be missed. Fortune came to my aid in the presence of a photographer: I pulled Bourguiba towards Dean Acheson, introduced him, and told the photographer to take a photo, which he did. When it was developed there emerged the picture of the two men smiling at each other, and Bourguiba holding a cup of tea which appeared to be on the point of crashing to the ground.

The same night telegrams were sent by Bourguiba to Tunis and Paris announcing that he had met the American Secretary of State. The reaction was predictable: the French-controlled press in Tunis denied it, but a few days later the photograph arrived, and was distributed by the party in thousands of copies. The incident, and the picture itself, still have their place in official histories of the Tunisian national movement – of such stuff is much of history composed!

In another way I was able to be of service to Bourguiba. He had arrived in New York with a very small amount of money, and a Tunisian friend there, himself earning a meagre salary at a printing press, had lent him money until the cheque promised him by the colleagues in the party should arrive.[2] This it never did, and Bourguiba found himself stranded in America, in the coldest winter for years, without a coat, without money. I obtained the authorization of the head office in Jerusalem to pay his bills at the hotel in Washington, and for his own personal needs Rafidh al Askeri, the son of the Iraqi Ambassador in Cairo who was a close friend of Bourguiba, and myself provided what we could out of our meagre salaries.

Habib Bourguiba never forgot the services I was able to render him in Washington, and throughout the years he has been President has again and again recalled them to the

Tunisian people on television and the radio, often with tears in his eyes as he talks of Cecil Hourani, the 'friend in need'. But in fact the days in Washington were only the beginning of a collaboration which was to prove crucial in my life, and of some importance to the making of the new Tunisia in which I was later privileged to participate.

The Arab Office in Washington was closed down after the United Nations General Assembly recommended the partition of Palestine in November 1947, but the Office in London continued to function until 1949, and I moved there, making frequent visits to Paris and Geneva in connection with meetings of the UN and sometimes in the company of Musa Alami, who continued his efforts to save something from the disasters which had befallen the Palestinians. I met Bourguiba again in both Paris and Geneva, and met too his French wife, Mathilde, or Sitt Mufida as she later became, and his only son Habib Junior, and there began a lifelong friendship between his family, myself, and my future wife Furugh Afnan, then studying at the Sorbonne with Louis Massignon as her supervisor. I did not know at the time that Bourguiba's marriage to his French wife, and the birth of his son, had given him a personal motive – though his national and public motives were much more important to him – for his struggle to end the French Protectorate over Tunisia, and to restore that country's sovereignty in its full meaning. For one consequence of marrying a French wife was that his children, according to the French law then in force in Tunisia, would have to be French; and as French law did not permit at that time the naming of a French child by a Muslim name, Bourguiba's son's legal name became Jean. And though he was called Habib, or Bibi, by his family and by the Tunisians generally, the fact remained that Bourguiba's son could not be Tunisian, and could not bear a Tunisian or Muslim name! 'After stealing my country, France has stolen my son!' he wrote to one of his friends. The solution of this personal problem – small in itself, but of great significance to the family – had to wait until Tunisian independence separated not only the political ties between the two countries, but also the different and often conflicting claims of the laws defining personal status.

One of my visits to Geneva in 1949 was to provide the occasion for a scenario which might have changed the course of Tunisian history. I received one day a telegram from Bourguiba, at that time in Paris, asking me to meet one of his friends by the name of Lamine Bellagha at the Hotel de la Nouvelle Gare in Geneva, where he himself had the habit of staying.[3] When I went to the meeting-place I found with Bellagha another friend, Hedi Jellouli, member of an ancient and famous Tunisian family. They explained to me that Bourguiba had asked them to organize a plan to rescue Moncef Bey, the ruler of Tunisia who had been deposed by the French for his sympathetic attitude towards the Neo-Destour Party during the German occupation of Tunisia and was confined to a house in Pau in southern France, and to bring him to Switzerland from where he would proclaim a government-in-exile. Bourguiba, who had already formed the idea that I was capable of doing anything, had suggested to his two friends that I might be able to help them. The problem was that in order to cross the frontiers between France and Switzerland he needed a passport, and also a safe place where he could go on first arriving, and from where the proclamation of the government-in-exile could be made.

At that time the newly appointed Ambassador of Lebanon, the late Jamil Mekkawi, happened to be a friend of mine from my Cairo days. He was himself an Arab nationalist, and readily agreed to my request to provide a Lebanese passport and to offer Moncef Bey refuge in the Lebanese Embassy in Berne. All was set for the adventure, but in order to ensure that it was feasible, Hedi Jellouli decided to make a trial visit to Pau, to enter the house where Moncef Bey was confined, and to come back to Geneva unobserved. The trial was successful, Moncef Bey had agreed to accompany him back, and Hedi set off again in his superb Delahaye, while I waited in my hotel room for the call which would tell me that they had arrived. I waited all day and all night, but there was no sign of the Bey: the next day a crestfallen Jellouli came to tell me that the Bey had taken fright, and refused to leave, pleading illness.

On a recent visit to Tunis in October 1982 I recalled this incident to President Bourguiba, whose memory of the distant past is now much more vivid than that of more recent events. He remembered it in every detail, but, he said, 'Thank God he refused: if Moncef Bey had accepted, we would never have been able to abolish the monarchy, and in prison he was much more useful to us as a subject of grievance against France than he would have been if he had escaped and formed a government-in-exile!'

The failure of the plot to rescue Moncef Bey did not quench, but rather whetted, my appetite for adventure. In May 1952 Bourguiba was sent by the French to his last exile, this time on the island of La Galite, far from the Tunisian coast, a bleak and isolated place famous only for its giant lobsters. In 1953 I made a brief and secret visit to Tunis to see his wife, and to find out whether it was feasible to help him to escape. It was 14 July when I arrived, and the French immigration and security officials at the airport were celebrating 1789, so that my arrival and my presence in the country escaped their attention. Most of Bourguiba's colleagues and close friends were also in prison or detention, the political atmosphere was heavy, and the final phase of the Tunisian struggle for independence was about to begin. I realized that there was nothing I could do, and left as discreetly as I had arrived.

By now Habib Bourguiba and his family had become intimate friends of my wife and myself. We had married in 1950 and shortly after met the Bourguibas in Paris. We had been given a car, a Peugeot 103, by my mother-in-law, and one day proposed a visit to Fontainebleau to Bourguiba and his wife. At some point in the journey I suggested to him that he might like to drive, and much to the horror of his wife he readily accepted. As we set off she told us the story of how he had almost been drowned in a car he was driving near Bir Bou Rekba in Tunisia, and I soon realized her anxiety, for driving did not stop the flow of words nor the gestures of his eloquent hands, and very soon we also landed in a ditch. In the following year Bourguiba suddenly arrived in Beirut, where I was beginning a new career as a teacher in the American University. He came to dinner with us, and asked me where the vegetable market of Beirut was to be found. I was surprised at his question, as the Nouria market was one of the filthiest and least hygienic places in the city, but he told me he wanted to find a Tunisian who came from Msaken near his own home town of Monastir. The next day we went there, and eventually found Khalifa, who had a small stand and was selling fruits and vegetables. His son, who married a Sudanese lady, is today one of the richest men in the Arab world.

This ability to combine his commitment to the cause of national independence with his concern for the common people of Tunisia, which I found so lacking in the leaders in the Mashriq, was one reason for which I decided, when the chance came, to throw in my lot with him and the new Tunisia. This opportunity came to me in the following way. In June 1954 a new French Government was formed by Pierre Mendès-France who reversed previous French policy and decided to come to terms with the nationalist movement. Bourguiba was released from La Galite, and a chain of events set in motion which led eventually to the offer of the status of internal autonomy, formalized in an agreement in June 1955. Though this was less than the complete independence which the Neo-Destour Party aimed at, the moral influence of Bourguiba was strong enough to convince most of his colleagues that they should accept the offer. His argument was that once France accepted the principle of Tunisian sovereignty, and once it agreed that its settlers in Tunisia would enjoy no political rights which would have given France co-sovereignty, internal autonomy would inevitably lead to independence. There were some, however, within the party who did not accept the argument, and to whom the acceptance of anything less than full independence was treason. While this argument was going on I decided to visit Bourguiba at Aix-les-Bains where he was resting for a few days. At the French border with Switzerland from where I was coming by car I was stopped by the French police, and obliged to give a written statement about the reasons for my visit: they had obviously been tipped off, or had heard my telephone conversation with Bourguiba from Geneva in which he invited me to visit him. It was only the intervention of Mohammed Masmoudi,[4] then a close collaborator and confidant of Bourguiba, which secured my release from the clutches of the French police, who were highly suspicious of a Lebanese with a British passport visiting Bourguiba. It was on that visit that he suggested that I should go to Tunisia to visit him.

In March 1956 the French Government decided that, since autonomy would obviously lead to independence, they might as well shorten the process and put on the shoulders of the Tunisians the problems of governing the country which were becoming increasingly difficult. The news of this sudden and unexpected turn in the course of France's relations with Tunisia created considerable excitement in the Arab countries, but one day late in March the BBC Arabic Service announced that Habib Bourguiba had been assassinated in Tunis, and this news was confirmed in the morning papers. I was not convinced, however, that the news was true because it was unclear in its details and I decided to try to telephone Tunis, although in those days there was no direct line, and I had no number to give the operator, only the name 'Habib Bourguiba'. To my astonishment about ten o'clock that morning the call came through, and there was Bourguiba himself on the line, assuring me that he was not dead, but that it had been a colleague who had been assassinated. He said, 'Why don't you come to Tunis?', and as our vacation was beginning I said I would, and left the next day.

The atmosphere in Tunisia was one of delirious joy. The day after my arrival Bourguiba was to go on tour through the south, and he invited me to go with him. It was a week of triumph, punctuated by speeches, banquets, popular demonstrations which were completely spontaneous, and which were my first introduction to what later on was to become a familiar routine, though the excitement and enthusiasm of those days had no equivalent in recent Tunisian history except for Bourguiba's triumphant return on 1 June 1955, a day still celebrated as Tunisia's principal anniversary. On leaving Tunis I informed Bourguiba that I would try to return and spend my sabbatical leave, due that year, in Tunisia.

On my return to Beirut, fired with enthusiasm for this new event on the Arab political scene which I believed was the beginning of the liberation of the Maghrib, and anxious to make its significance known and understood in the Near East, where Bourguiba was regarded by Arab nationalist circles as a stooge of France, and the newly won independence as fictitious, I wrote a series of articles and reports for the BBC and for local newspapers about the events that I had witnessed. I also organized the first celebration of Tunisian independence in any Arab country, which took the form of a ceremony held in the American University of Beirut attended by a large audience of teachers, students, journalists, and political personalities, among whom were Saddoq Mokaddem, later to be Tunisia's Foreign Minister and President of the National Assembly, and Dr Charles Malik, then Lebanon's and the Arab world's most distinguished diplomat and representative at the United Nations, at which I was the principal speaker. My address was a political discourse on the meaning of 'Bourguibism' as distinguished from 'Youssefism'. I contrasted the policy of Bourguiba, which consisted in taking what it is possible to get without prejudicing the future, and that of his opponent and enemy Salah Ben Youssef,[5] whose policy of 'all or nothing' was that which guided the actions and thinking of most of the parties and movements in the Arab countries, and which led – and still leads – to the many disasters which have marked the modern history of the Arabs.

So in the autumn of 1956 I set out for Tunis with my wife and infant daughter, with no idea where we would live or what kind of life lay ahead of us. In my mind was a project to write a book describing the events of which I would be the spectator, but I was soon to discover that I was not to be a spectator but to participate in them. In the late autumn, after about only two months since our arrival in Tunis, Bourguiba, now Prime Minister of the first independent Tunisian Government, was invited to Washington on an official visit. Two days before he was due to leave, he sent his Minister of Information, Bechir Ben Yahmed, to inform me that the Prime Minister would like me to accompany him, and that my wife was invited too. Although I had no clearly defined status within the delegation, I accepted because I felt that I could be of use to Bourguiba and to the delegation of which only one member could speak English, and none of whom had my experience of American politics or American ways.

As it turned out, although my wife and I were included in all the invitations and receptions which normally accompany official visits, I was not included in any of the meetings with State Department or White House officials. I felt, and my feelings were later confirmed, that my presence in the delegation was not welcomed by the newly appointed Tunisian Ambassador to Washington, Mongi Slim, who hardly knew me but was aware of my relations with Bourguiba and transferred to me the reservations he kept within his very secretive bosom about Bourguiba himself. However, I profited from my presence in Washington to renew my many contacts there among officials of the State Department, the press, and academic circles.

Two days before our visit was to end, Bourguiba called me to his room: he was in a bad mood, the visit had produced no tangible results, he had nothing to bring back to Tunis, what did I propose doing about it? Because of my close friendship with the American Ambassador to Tunisia, Lewis Jones, who was in Washington with us, Bourguiba seemed to believe at times that I also represented the American Government. I had learnt from one of my friends then in the foreign aid branch of the administration that there were large stocks of milk, butter and cheese as well as wheat which could be theoretically 'sold' to foreign governments, under programme PL480, while in reality the proceeds of the sale would be used to finance development projects. Lewis Jones, whose own position with Bourguiba would, he felt, depend to a large extent on the success of this first visit to Washington, was a willing accomplice to my plan. As time was short, we would immediately draft a letter from Bourguiba requesting cheese, milk and wheat with which to start a child-feeding programme for every child in school throughout Tunisia, and Lewis Jones would draft the reply granting the request. In spite of a last-minute delay caused by the Tunisian Ambassador who said that the letter should go through him, Bourguiba signed, and was able to return to Tunis with something in his hand.

This was an important first step towards the cooperation between the American Government and Tunisia which was to develop over the years in a spectacular way, and which was to make of Tunisia the most favoured recipient of American aid among all the Arab countries. In these first years of Tunisian independence I was to play an active role in developing these relations and in exploring, through many visits to Washington, all the many channels of aid and cooperation which the American Government and people, with their limitless generosity, offer to whoever wins their confidence and their hearts.

After the visit to Washington Bourguiba decided he would like me to join his staff. My experience of accompanying him in an unofficial and undefined capacity simply as a 'friend' had demonstrated the inconveniences and sometimes the humiliations to which this status exposed me, so I accepted his invitation to join him on condition that I received a clearly defined status and an official position. I believe that I drafted the letter he signed appointing me his Special Adviser, with the rank of Ambassador Extraordinary. I was given an office in the Prime Minister's headquarters at Dar al Bey, a complex of eighteenth- and nineteenth-century beylical palaces at the edge of the Medina of Tunis, and it was from there that I was to work for the next ten years as adviser, confidant, and friend of Habib Bourguiba. I believed – and still do – that he was the most intelligent, progressive and wise leader in the Arab world, and my judgement, although regarded by many of my friends in the Near East as subjective and even ridiculous, was to be confirmed by the success of the Tunisian regime in emerging as the most stable, and the most internationally respected Arab state.

The success of the Tunisian experiment was not an easy one. At the time it achieved independence in 1966 the Tunisian state was extremely poor: it had no important sources of mineral wealth except some deposits of phosphates, its agricultural resources were very largely in the hands of the European settlers brought in by French governments in the expectation that they would form a permanent and integral part of the country's population, commerce was controlled by France, as was the educational system, and there were very few Tunisian economic or cultural contacts with countries other than France, and to a much lesser extent with Italy. There was only a very small Tunisian middle class, and only a few educated Tunisians in the professional class, and of these many of the Jewish members, who had occupied an important place in Tunisia's cultural and professional life as well as in commerce, had left, either in 1948 after the creation of the state of Israel, or in the early days of Tunisian independence, fearing as many did – unnecessarily – that they would have no place in the new regime.[6]

I remember the indignation of Bourguiba when I reported to him a conversation I had had with the American Ambassador, Lewis Jones, very soon after our return from Washington in 1956. Jones had told me that in his opinion Tunisia was not a viable state, and I had unwisely repeated this to Bourguiba, who happened at that moment to be lying in bed: this provoked an outburst of one of those rages to which his family and entourage were quite accustomed, and which I knew by now were only made more violent by argument. I pointed out that this was Lewis Jones's opinion, not mine, and that what we had to do was to show him that he was wrong. In due time Jones was to become Tunisia's best advocate in Washington and was of considerable help in assisting the young and fragile state in its first steps to viability.

Although I could see that in the given circumstances of Tunisia at the moment of independence its viability, which I took to mean its capacity to stand on its own economic feet and to liberate itself from dependence on France, was doubtful, I believed that these circumstances were not immutable, and that Tunisia contained within its human and physical resources the possibility of change and development. It had many potential assets: its geographical position at the point where the eastern and western Mediterraneans joined gave it a strategic importance of which the great French naval base at Bizerta was the proof: culturally it provided the link between Mashriq and Maghrib, the two wings of the Arab world; it had a well-defined historical and cultural identity and was untroubled by problems of ethnic or linguistic minorities such as existed in both Algeria and Morocco: and seventy-five years of French rule had created an intelligentsia which, although opposed to France politically, was profoundly impregnated with French and Western ideas about society, government, and law.

But just as important as these factors, so it seemed to me, was the presence at the head of its Government of a leader who had forged, in twenty-five years of struggle and opposition, a cohesive party deeply rooted in the people which he could use to implement programmes of far-reaching changes in every aspect of the country's life. I had seen how in the Near East independence had not brought about these changes so necessary if the Arab countries were to enter into the modern world, and that their new ruling classes, with even the best will, did not have the ability to govern, only to rule: and how in consequence no Arab regime had survived for long the transition from dependence to independence without revolutions, *coups d'état*, and eventual dictatorships. I had been profoundly influenced, during the years in which I had taught political philosophy at the American University of Beirut, by Plato's definitions of the true and the false leader, and of the philosopher and the sophist, and I believed that Habib Bourguiba corresponded more to the Platonic vision of the 'philosopher-king' than any other Arab leader of his time.

The full story of my Tunisian experience must await a later time for publication: I still have too many bonds of affection and friendship with many actors on that scene to write with both objectivity and frankness, or to breach the confidences to which my long association have made me privy. In this book I am concerned with certain events which were important in recent Tunisian history and also influenced the evolution of my own ideas.

My role as adviser to President Bourguiba had two distinct phases. In the first it was mainly a political one, and covered the years between 1956 and 1962. In the second phase, though I still had a political role, it was curtailed by my own decision, and I concentrated my efforts in the sphere of culture. By 1962 I was beginning to feel restless: by now there had been formed, with an astonishing rapidity, a class of professional diplomats, young technocrats, and both men and women who had established widespread contacts with the Anglo-Saxon world – and indeed with every part of the world – so that I no longer felt that my own participation in this field of activity was indispensable. And I wished to leave behind me in Tunisia something which would have a less transient and ephemeral, and a more permanent mark of my passage through that land to which I had given my heart than a mere political role would leave.

The years 1956 to 1962 were the years in which the foundations of the new Tunisia were laid, and in which it faced its most serious problems and its gravest crises. When the Tunisian state achieved independence it did not automatically accede to all the institutions of a modern state, and many facets of power still remained in French hands: there was still an important naval and military base at Bizerta: large areas of the best lands were still held by French and Italian companies and individual agriculturalists: its financial institutions were linked to France, and the very foundations of economic and financial independence, such as a Central Bank, did not exist.

In addition, there had existed since 1954 a state of open revolution against France, and large numbers of Algerian refugees, political leaders, and armed men and women were on Tunisian soil. I remember how on 1 November 1956, as my wife and I were sitting in the early evening in our room at the Hotel Majestic where we had lodged on first arriving in Tunis, we heard a strange and eerie sound of men marching as if with padded shoes along the avenue leading to the centre of the city: outside our window there passed a seemingly endless stream of armed men and women carrying banners, but completely silent. I had seen many demonstrations in Cairo and Beirut, and they were always noisy and chaotic, but I had never before seen a silent one, and I realized that this silent march through the streets of Tunis which marked the second anniversary of the proclamation of the revolution was a symbol of the determination of the Algerian masses to be free, which did not need the shouting and the outward demonstration of emotions which so often in the Arab East conceal an inner weakness. I did not know then, but later came to be familiar with and to understand, the two most famous lines of Abulqassem Chabbi, the poet of Tunisian dreams: 'If a people one day wills to live, destiny will no doubt respond.'[7]

The presence on Tunisian soil of the active forces of the Algerian revolution was the source of serious problems for the new Government of Tunisia: not only were there still French forces on Tunisian soil, but the Tunisian army and security forces were still in their infancy, and could not easily cope with the problems created by the coexistence on Tunisian territory of two mutually hostile armies. The first major crisis which faced the Government arose out of the proximity of Algerian guerrilla forces stationed on the Tunisian side of the frontiers to the French army in Algeria. On 8 February 1958 I had accompanied Bourguiba on a visit to Souq al Arba in northwest Tunisia. That evening we heard on the radio the news that the French airforce had bombarded the town of Sakiet Sidi Yusuf on the Tunisian side of the frontier, and that the damage was considerable: many Tunisian civilians were reported dead and wounded. This was exactly the mistake which Bourguiba was waiting for the French to make. We returned to Tunis that night, and I remember that it was in the car in which I accompanied him, and in which was also Sitt Wassila Ben Ammar, who was later to become his second wife, that we worked out the strategy to exploit the incident to the full. Washington and London were to be drawn into the picture, and to be convinced that the presence on Tunisian soil of French forces while a revolution was going on in Algeria, and while there were considerable Algerian forces on Tunisian soil also, was no longer possible: what was at stake was Tunisian sovereignty, and a situation might arise in which France and Tunisia would be engaged in active hostilities, with consequences for the West in the Arab world which Washington and London did not wish to face. My mission was to go to the two capitals to help the Tunisian embassies achieve the maximum publicity for the Tunisian cause, and the maximum support from the two governments. In both Washington and London I had letters published in the press presenting the Tunisian case, and met a wide variety of official personalities in both capitals as well as journalists and political commentators some of whom I had known from my Arab Office days.

The outcome of our activities was the appointment of a 'good offices' delegation consisting of Harold Beeley, an old friend from London, and Robert Murphy, a distinguished American diplomat, from Washington. I played an active and I believe an effective role during their visits to Tunisia in providing them with an accurate picture of the thinking of President Bourguiba, and of his personality, and in helping Bourguiba himself to understand the subtleties of Anglo-Saxon diplomacy. The complete evacuation of French forces demanded by the Tunisian Government was obtained by Anglo-American pressure on the French Government, which fell shortly afterwards, and the evacuation of French troops from Tunisia took place in May 1958, with the exception of their base in Bizerta, which was to provide the occasion for another crisis between Tunisia and France.

The success of the Tunisian Government in exploiting the mistake of the French in bombarding Tunisian territory had consequences which indicated in Bourguiba's character an impulsiveness and a readiness to listen to the arguments of some of his collaborators whose intelligence was less than his, and whose motives he did not always fathom. In more recent times this weakness was to lead him into errors of judgement such as the union with Libya he signed in 1974 at the instigation of Mohammed Masmoudi, his Foreign Minister, a mistake which he was quick to rectify at the insistence of his Prime Minister, Hedi Nouira. But in the affair of Bizerta there was no one to tell him he was wrong except myself, and he would not listen to me.

President Bourguiba's Prime Minister, Bahi Ladgham, who held that position from 1957 until his removal in 1969, had played a leading role in the crisis of Sakiet Sidi Yusuf, and he came to believe that another crisis with France would lead to the liquidation of the remaining French military presence on Tunisian territory at Bizerta, which was the most glaring and irritating reminder that Tunisian sovereignty was not complete. In the course of time the problem of Bizerta could have found a diplomatic and peaceful solution, but the Prime Minister was in a hurry, as were some of his younger ministers. Among these was Ahmed Ben Salah, who had visions of the creation at Bizerta of a great commercial port and a free zone, and was also anxious to begin his programme for the installation of a form of cooperative socialism in the country. To this programme there were two main obstacles: the first was that a large proportion of Tunisia's best agricultural land was in foreign hands, the second that so long as Bizerta remained under French control, Tunisia's freedom to control its economic and financial destinies lived under the shadow of a permanent French veto on decisions which might run counter to French interests. The Government decided on two measures to put an end to this state of affairs.

The first was to seek a quarrel in the summer of 1961 with the French military authorities about the exact delineation of the perimeter surrounding their base at Bizerta. The Prime Minister had been encouraged by the success of a similar quarrel on a matter of much less importance. In order to enlarge a road in the district of La Marsa, of which the mayor was the Minister of the Interior, the late Taieb Mehiri, it was necessary to demolish a wall of the French Embassy garden, and to diminish the area of that garden considerably. The French Embassy was itself perhaps the most beautiful example of a former beylical palace of the late eighteenth and early nineteenth centuries, and its spacious garden provided the perfect setting for it. After months of negotiations between the Tunisian and French governments the French gave in, the new wall was built, and the palace gave directly onto the street, thereby losing much of its character. The affair of the wall was regarded by Mr Ladgham and the Minister of the Interior as a victory over the French, but in reality it was a 'victory' obtained at the expense of La Marsa, because the road did not really need to be widened.

But Bizerta was quite a different matter from La Marsa. The crisis of Sakiet Sidi Yusuf had led to the downfall of the French Government and the return to power of General de Gaulle on 13 May 1958. Between General de Gaulle and President Bourguiba there existed an uneasy relationship: the one was the big President of a big country, the other the big President of a small country, but the disparity in size and power of the two countries was discounted in Bourguiba's mind by the importance he rightly attributed to his own role outside Tunisia, and principally in the Algerian affair. He knew that he held one of the keys to the solution of this problem, as the leaders and the armed forces of the Algerian revolution were on Tunisian soil, and to a considerable extent influenced by his counsels and by the example of the success of Bourguibist policies. But to de Gaulle Habib Bourguiba was a constant challenge to his own attitude towards the leaders of the territories which France had previously controlled. He was neither an out-and-out enemy, nor a Frenchman with a darker skin, neither a Sekou Touré nor a Léopold Senghor;[8] he combined a full understanding of the political and cultural values of France with a total commitment to the interests of Tunisia, and to the values of the Arab-Muslim society of which he was a part. That Tunisia should challenge France, and that Bourguiba should match himself against de Gaulle was a situation which de Gaulle found intolerable. He refused to repeat the fiasco of the famous wall of La Marsa, and resisted by force attempts by Tunisian soldiers to alter the perimeter of Bizerta. The result was a bloody clash which began on 4 July 1961, and in which heavy losses were inflicted on the town of Bizerta and on the Tunisian military and civilian population.

This affair distressed me because I foresaw that it would lead to bloodshed on a larger scale than the Tunisians had imagined, and because I did not believe it was really necessary. Bourguiba himself, who is not by nature a bloodthirsty man, although in the last resort he has never held back from the use of violence, was both distressed and made bellicose by the battle of Bizerta: the loss of Tunisian lives moved him deeply, and while his Government was preoccupied with defending the Tunisian case diplomatically and by military confrontation, he was seeking a way out which would put an end to the bloodshed without too much loss of face. One way he found to probe this possibility was to send me to Paris, while the battle was still raging, to meet with Georges Gorse, at that time head of General de Gaulle's cabinet.

Gorse had been France's first Ambassador to independent Tunisia, and later became Ambassador to Algeria: he was married to a Lebanese lady from a well-known Cairo family, and his sympathies towards Tunisia and his knowledge of Tunisian politics made him the ideal interlocutor in this delicate mission. My task was to propose an immediate cease-fire to be followed by bilateral negotiations to settle the status of Bizerta, but it was extremely important that my *démarche* should remain secret, because it was the intention of the Prime Minister and the Foreign Minister to take the matter to the United Nations where they hoped to get a vote favourable to their demand for a French withdrawal. It would have been embarrassing to President Bourguiba had it become known that I was in Paris trying to arrange a bilateral agreement which would have made recourse to the United Nations unnecessary.

In the event fighting between the Tunisians and the French stopped suddenly, but General de Gaulle did not agree to direct negotiations: he saw no reason to do so, and he was not ready to give Bourguiba a victory for which there was no military justification. The Tunisian Government thereupon decided to take the matter to the Security Council, and to seek a resolution ordering France to withdraw from Bizerta. President Bourguiba then sent me to London, Washington and New York to help in the diplomatic manoeuvres which precede the passage of resolutions in the organs of the United Nations. It was obvious that in these negotiations the position of the Government of the United States of America would be crucial. It was improbable that Great Britain and the USA would vote for a resolution asking their ally France to withdraw from Tunisia at a moment when relations between the West and the Soviet Union were at danger-point, but, at least, we hoped that we could persuade Washington and London not to use their vote.

In London I was received by Lord Harlech, then Minister of State at the Foreign Office, and presented the Tunisian case to him: I also had a letter published in *The Times*, and made a number of important contacts among Members of Parliament, journalists, and other makers of public opinion. My visit to Washington and New York was more important, because the United States of America was clearly the leader of the Western alliance.

It was fortunate for me that the Tunisian Ambassador in Washington at that moment was Habib Bourguiba Junior. He had acquired a position in Washington's political and social life which gave him easy access to everyone, from the President downwards. His familiarity with the Washington scene, his command of English and insight into the American mentality, his sense of humour which sometimes concealed an inner fire as intense as, though more restrained than, that of his father, made him my ideal ally in the campaign to convince Washington that Tunisia was a valuable friend of the United States, of whom there were not many others in the Arab world. Moreover, because of my old and affectionate relationship with both his father and mother, I did not have with him the problem of jealousy of my role as adviser to the President which coloured and sometimes clouded my relations with some of his other ambassadors, and all of his foreign ministers, resentful as they often were – and naturally enough – of an 'Ambassador Extraordinary' who did not come under their authority and did not always go through what they regarded as 'the proper channels'.

My request for a meeting with President Kennedy was granted almost immediately, and I went to the White House with Bourguiba Junior with a memorandum I had prepared to leave behind. It was the most acute moment of the Berlin crisis, and Kennedy was faced with one of the most dangerous situations in all his period of office. He sat in his rocking chair and listened carefully to what I had to say, which was basically what I had written in the memorandum which I left with him. When I had finished he asked me to go out on the balcony with him, and told me that at any moment there might be a nuclear exchange with the Soviet Union; that otherwise he would not have hesitated to support the Tunisian resolution at the Security Council, but that he could not do so because of American relations with France, but promised that he would instruct his delegate at the United Nations to abstain from voting, which he did.

The second action of the Tunisian Government about which I had doubts as serious as those I had experienced over the Bizerta affair was its decision in May 1964 to nationalize land and property belonging to Tunisia's foreign population as well as to foreign companies. This, like the question of Bizerta, was a decision taken by the Government, and in which Bourguiba acquiesced. In his anxiety to press on with the complete control of the country's economic destinies, this was in the mind of Ahmed Ben Salah the necessary condition for the far-reaching changes he was contemplating in Tunisia's economic, social, and consequently political set-up.

It seemed to me that what Tunisia would lose by hasty and indiscriminate legislation would be more than it gained. It would gain land, houses, commercial and industrial enterprises: but it would lose the skills and services of the foreign community, which no longer posed any political threat, and undermine the international confidence which Tunisia needed to attract the foreign investment so necessary to develop her natural and human resources. I was particularly concerned for the considerable numbers of French, Italian, and Maltese small farmers and skilled craftsmen, many of whom had become completely Tunisian in all except nationality, and whose presence I believed to be an asset in preserving for Tunisia that cosmopolitan, multinational, and open society which, along with Egypt and Lebanon, distinguished it from other Arab countries.

Here again I was unsuccessful in persuading President Bourguiba that the action of his Government was neither necessary nor wise. My position was weak, because I was myself a foreigner, or at any rate not Tunisian, and open to the accusation that I was not thinking in terms of Tunisian interests. I was particularly sensitive to the criticisms and complaints to which I was exposed from some of the foreign community, and from some of the members of the privileged class of the old regime who had been pushed out of power by the Neo-Destour, who blamed me for a decision in which I had no part. I was myself outside of any Tunisian class: class-struggle was an element in the Tunisian Government's decision to nationalize foreign property, but I had no private economic interests in the country, and was there only because of my personal attachment to Bourguiba. I felt concern, but no responsibility for its decision. Perhaps, I later said to myself, I did not appreciate the depth of humiliation felt by the Tunisians during the years when they were governed by France in which they were treated as second-class citizens within their own country. Looking back at the situation, I can now understand how newly won political independence must inevitably lead to the desire to extend that independence to all spheres of a country's life: and also that what happened in Tunisia was only one part of a more general readjustment of the relations between the European and the Arab shores of the Mediterranean. Although they suffered at the time, it was perhaps better for the Europeans that they went back to Europe, and for the Tunisians that they were faced with the full responsibility for every aspect of their country's life, and for both sides that it all happened sooner rather than later.

In the long run it was the two main actors in these two crises, Ahmed Ben Salah and Bahi Ladgham, who were to be the victims of their own 'successes'.[9] The 'Tunisification' of large sectors of the country's economy, and in particular of its agriculture, posed problems which the cadres of the Tunisian administration were not ready to face. To split up the large domains of the French *colons* and to distribute them to the Tunisian peasants and small agriculturalists would have gone against the theories of Ben Salah, who wanted to introduce a socialist economy based on the Yugoslav model: but to preserve the large units of production demanded an organization and personnel which did not exist. 'Tunisification' did not lead to any real improvement in either the economy of the country or the condition of the peasants and farmers: it only provided satisfaction to the governing party, which felt it had won a victory over France.

From 'Tunisification' to 'nationalization' seemed to Ben Salah to be a natural step. If the lands and properties of the foreigners were not to be handed over to individual Tunisians, why should not everything be 'collectivized'? Ben Salah was not a Communist: his ideas were nearer to the theories of the Scandinavian cooperative movement and of Yugoslav collectivism, but his enthusiasm and energy sometimes prevented him from facing realities. Confident that he had the support of the President and his Government, he embarked on a policy which frightened the Tunisian people into believing that they were going to lose their lands, their shops, their businesses, and he brought into being a coalition of all those forces, within the party and outside it, which for one reason or another sought to bring about his downfall. The architect of that downfall was Bahi Ladgham himself, who feared the ascendancy which Ben Salah appeared to have gained over Bourguiba, and who put on Ben Salah's head the responsibility for the popular discontent which was properly that of his whole Government.

Bahi Ladgham was later to be the victim of the same kind of accusation which he had concocted against Ben Salah – of abuse of power, and plotting against the state. In both cases Bourguiba was able to dissociate himself from the actions of his closest collaborators, and the Tunisian people, whose trust in his judgement and belief in the infallibility of his policies was infinite, did not lay at his door the responsibility for the errors of his ministers.

VI
Hammamet: a Cultural Adventure

By 1962 I was beginning to feel restless in Tunis. I had never intended settling in Tunisia for good, and I was on a yearly leave of absence from the American University in Beirut, and still toyed with the idea of returning to my teaching position there. I was sensitive to the jealousies which anyone in my position was bound to arouse among those who envied my closeness to the seat of power, and my personal relations to the President and his family. As his adviser, with the status of Ambassador Extraordinary which he had given me, there was no higher rank to which I could aspire, and I did not wish to enter into competition with Tunisians in the administration. On the other hand, I did not wish to leave Bourguiba or Tunisia, to whose people, way of life, and landscape I had become deeply attached, without leaving behind me some legacy which would mark my passage through that enchanting and enchanted land.

It was this motive which led me into an experiment which had both happy and unhappy consequences for me: happy because I was successful in much of what I aimed at doing, and did create an institution and a monument to leave behind me, unhappy because the very success of my experiment aroused jealousies and animosities which were the cause of my leaving Bourguiba and Tunisia in circumstances not of my own choosing, and because these jealousies led to the demolition, though not the total destruction, of much of what I had built up in five years of hard work.

My years in academic life in Beirut had made me aware of the limitations imposed on many educational institutions by curricula which have little relevance to the societies in which they operate, or to the intellectual and spiritual needs of the students they are teaching. I believed, as I still do, that a renaissance of the Arab mind and creative spirit could not be achieved purely from within their own cultural heritage, by turning inwards and trying to find their inspiration uniquely from their own past, but that it could come only through the impact of other cultures, other civilizations, and perhaps even of other languages. And I had conceived the idea of a 'centre' which would provide just these possibilities of cultural and intellectual interaction, which would not only open windows for the Arabs on the outside world, but also provide new sources of inspiration from the still largely unexplored resources of Arab culture for those who might be attracted by it to Tunisia. I believed that Tunisia offered the ideal location for one such centre in the western Arab world, Lebanon for one in the east, and Egypt for one in the centre. These three countries were the ones which had the longest traditions of contact with the outside world, and Tunisia in particular, both because of its close ties with Europe, and the political stability of its new regime, seemed to be the best place to begin.

I was encouraged to pursue this idea by my contacts with friends in Europe and the United States of America. Denis de Rougemont,[1] director of the 'Centre Européen de la Culture' in Geneva, and Don Kingsley at the Ford Foundation in Beirut, as well as other members of the Foundation in New York, liked my idea and gave me hope that they would support it if it took concrete form. The occasion to give it this concrete form came in 1962 with the chance to acquire a unique property on the still unravaged bay of Hammamet.

The idea of the International Cultural Centre had grown from the seed planted in my mind by my experience of Royaumont and Pontigny in my student days. Both these places offered ideal settings for the intellectual exchanges and the stimulating encounters which they promoted, though without the dominating though discreet presence of Paul Desjardins and Mme Desjardins at Pontigny and the warmth and friendliness of the Champigneulles at Royaumont, neither place would have left so strong a mark on the cultural scene of their days. They did not go beyond the opportunity they offered at certain periods of the year for meetings, and a quiet atmosphere where the individual could pursue his work, but I had in mind something more ambitious, and not exclusively intellectual. For while I envisaged that purely intellectual or scholarly encounters between Arabs and outsiders would only repeat the same pattern of platitudes or dry academic discussion that characterized most such encounters, I believed that the arts, in all their forms – performing, graphic, plastic – offered a more fertile field in which to stimulate the cultural interaction I had in mind. For that I needed a site which could be used for meetings, for retreat and meditation, and for artistic activities: these need not all be in one place, because the centre I envisaged was not so much a place as an activity, a pole of attraction around which would gather many talents and many searchers for something new.

The visitor to Hammamet today will find at least thirty large hotels, a modern commercial centre, and hundreds of new houses on what were formerly groves of oranges and lemons. But the Hammamet I found in 1956 was still the jewel which had enchanted Paul Klee and Auguste Macke when they visited it together in 1914,[2] and which, according to his own testimony, was to influence profoundly Klee's conception of light and colour. Hammamet was still a medieval walled town: outside its walls the little fishing port witnessed each morning and evening the departure and return of a hundred painted boats across a gulf which, facing south and protected as no other North African bay is from the cold north wind, gives Hammamet that extraordinary luminosity, that mild and gentle climate, which in the twenties and thirties of this century attracted to it a small colony of English, French, German, American and Roumanian expatriates seeking peace, or pleasure, or a sexual facility which they did not find in their own countries. These lovers of Hammamet and what it had to offer, among whom were some famous names, such as Schiaparelli and Hoyninghen Huene,[3] built for themselves a string of astonishing houses along the gulf, inspired in part by Tunisian vernacular architecture and constructed by local builders and craftsmen.

Among these houses the most famous was that built by a Roumanian related to families who tradition said had moved from Byzantium to Roumania after the fall of Constantinople. Through an improbable marriage to a Chicago heiress George Sebastian had acquired the means to indulge his highly developed and extravagant aesthetic taste in the construction of what Frank Lloyd Wright is said to have called the most beautiful house on the Mediterranean.[4] Although much imitated in recent times in Tunisia, no architect, decorator, or landscaper has been able to rival or to excel the startling beauty of Sebastian's house and garden, with their almost total absence of colour except that given by the reflection of the blue and green sea, and filled with an emptiness which makes one aware only of light and shadow.

By 1962 Sebastian, who had come to Hammamet in the mid-twenties, had decided he would like to leave: his companion of many years, Dicky Woodruff, a painter of some talent, had died, his income had dwindled, most of his friends and enemies – in that small and closed society of the beautiful houses and beautiful people the two were indistinguishable – had died or left, and he did not much like the changes which independence had brought to Tunisia, nor the new relations between Europeans and Tunisians which now prevailed. I had seen others of the Hammamet houses fall into the clutches of the new class of entrepreneurs and hotel-keepers who were laying their hands on what was clearly the best touristic site in the country, and I was aware that the Minister of Tourism hoped to add Sebastian's house to the string of hotels he was promoting, so I decided to try to acquire it for the Tunisian state and make it the headquarters of the Centre. In this I enlisted the help of Sitt Wassila, now President Bourguiba's wife, who knew the house and appreciated its importance as part of the Tunisian architectural heritage, and who shared my enthusiasm for turning it, not into another hotel, but into a haven for artists, writers, and dreamers. Together we persuaded the President to allow me to negotiate the purchase, and Sebastian, who disliked the idea of his house becoming another hotel, but liked the idea of the Centre, agreed to sell it for 64,000 Tunisian dinars, at that time equivalent to about 200,000 dollars.

I had already set up the Centre as an independent cultural

association with a distinguished committee. Its president was Hedi Nouira, Governor of the Central Bank and later Prime Minister until his illness in 1980; I was Director, with all executive reponsibilities, including the raising of funds, and among other members of the committee were Lamine Chabbi, a former Minister of Education and the brother of the poet Abulqassem Chabbi, Hassan Husni Abdulwahhab, Tunisia's most distinguished and famous scholar and orientalist, and Mahjoub Ben Milad, philosopher and intellectual. I had succeeded in obtaining a grant from the Ford Foundation for one year to enable me to recruit staff, furnish an office, and organize at least one conference, with a promise of a further grant the following year much larger in size. My first intention had been to make the Centre a meeting-place along the lines of Royaumont and Pontigny, but I soon enlarged the scope of my ambitions. In this I was much influenced by a French friend who was teaching at the University of Tunis under loan from the Sorbonne: Jean Duvignaud was a sociologist, but his interests and his activities went far beyond the confines of his academic life. He was novelist, playwright, man of the theatre, and a prominent member of France's post-war and contemporary class of intellectuals. The house where he lived with his companion Christine in Sidi Bou Said, where my family and I also lived, became the meeting-place of a wide and vivacious group of French, Tunisian, and visiting friends from the world of politics, literature and the arts. His special interest was theatre, and he helped me to realize the potential importance of *le spectacle* in influencing the way the Tunisian people looked at themselves and at the outside world, and to see that the spoken word, the gesture, the costume, were more potent instruments of change than the written word, especially in a society where literacy was not widespread. Duvignaud saw theatre all around him – in the great demonstrations and meetings at which Bourguiba was displaying his mastery of oratory, in the life around him in Sidi Bou Said, as yet unspoilt by the tourism which has now changed its character, in the village in the Tunisian south where he and his colleagues and students were conducting a programme of research,[5] in the speech and gestures of the daily life of the Tunisian people, their costumes, the tattooed symbols on face and hands, the celebrations of birth, marriage, death, and the religious processions of the Sufi orders.

From my discussions with Duvignaud emerged the idea of the Hammamet Centre as the catalyst of this 'theatre of the people': the performing arts, theatre, dance, music, and the plastic arts would constitute the main activity of the Centre, along with the conferences and seminars which would relate to them: and from this formulation of the Centre's programme and role grew the idea of adding to the house and garden at Hammamet a theatre, or at any rate a 'theatrical space'. The city of Tunis possessed a charming baroque theatre dating from the end of the nineteenth century, which housed the Municipal Troupe. At the head of this was a remarkable man, Ali Ben Ayad, who was to become one of my dearest friends in Tunis. His one ambition in life was to create a genuine national Tunisian theatre, but at the Municipal Theatre he was limited by budget, and by the restraints which the cultural bureaucracy placed on him. If we had a theatre at Hammamet we could do things impossible in Tunis.

Although at the time when I decided that we must build a theatre we had no funds, but only a vague promise of support from the Ford Foundation, we started to make plans of the building. The first suggestion, made to me by Khaled Abdulwahhab, the son of Hassan Husni, was for a simple structure on the Greek model, a copy of an antique theatre. But we needed to find an architect, and I decided to consult André Malraux, then at the height of his reputation and power as Minister of Culture in France. Malraux received me with the greatest courtesy, and showed enthusiasm for the idea of the Centre which I expounded to him in my far from perfect French – on which, to my amazement, he actually complimented me! He advised me to consult a group of architects and designers in Paris working together in L'Atelier d'Architecture et Urbanisme.

Paul Chemetov and René Allio, whom I met at Malraux's suggestion, showed me the plans of the theatre they were designing for the Théâtre National Populaire at Villeurbane near Lyons which incorporated concepts of a theatrical space that were revolutionary at the time, although they have since become generally accepted as a valid alternative to the classical proscenium design. I liked their project and invited them to Tunisia to choose a site for the theatre at Hammamet, and to design it.

The theatre designed by Chemetov, Jean Deroche and his other colleagues, in collaboration with Allio, was indeed revolutionary and innovative: not only did it combine the plan of Greek and Elizabethan theatre design in an original way, but it also incorporated an electric installation which made it possible to obtain all the effects of interior lighting. The German firm of Siemens, whom we asked to design the lighting, told us that no precedent existed for what we wanted to do, but they made a special study of the problem, and eventually provided us with the equipment for a nominal sum. But the most original feature of the design was its provision for rooms for the artists which could be used not only for changing, but also for sleeping and recreation, which, together with a sitting space and kitchenette, made it the world's first theatrical hotel.

That the site and the orientation of the theatre which Paul Chemetov chose had attracted others in the past was proved by a remarkable discovery when we began to dig the foundations: outside the area of the artists' living quarters we had planned a small patio, and under the ground we uncovered a Roman mosaic on the floor of a room with exactly the same orientation.

When we had decided to add a theatre to the existing house at Hammamet I had planned on using part of the money which I hoped the Ford Foundation would give us for a three-year period, and which I hoped to augment from other sources: it was admittedly a gamble, and the gamble came very near to failure. I had commissioned the architects but had delayed paying them, and I had also entered into a contract with a Tunisian builder, whose workmen had begun to dig the foundations, when I received news that the Ford Foundation in New York had had a change of policy: they would no longer finance cultural projects in the Third World. This was a disaster for me, because not only had I incurred considerable expenses, but I had also announced that the theatre would be opened in July 1964, and had even engaged actors and a designer for the production of *Othello* with which I proposed to inaugurate it and the newly created Festival of Hammamet.

My first reaction was to fly to New York to see if I could do anything to induce the Ford Foundation to change their minds, or at least to make an exception for me. My friend Don Kingsley, then head of the Foundation's regional office situated in Beirut, was in New York, and was as distressed as I was, but there was nothing he could do: a new president of the Foundation believed that it was more important to provide technical help to raise the living standards of the underdeveloped world than to build theatres, that plumbers were more important than actors. I prepared to go back to Tunis empty-handed to face the inevitable consequences of the fiasco which threatened – consequences which I could not even foresee, especially if President Bourguiba were to refuse to come to my rescue. But I had a last card in my hand.

Before leaving Tunis on my way to New York, I had obtained from the Portuguese Ambassador to Tunisia a letter to the President of the Gulbenkian Foundation in Lisbon introducing me as a close collaborator of Bourguiba and a personal friend. I decided to pass through Lisbon on my way back to Tunis and try my luck with the Gulbenkians.

On arriving in Lisbon I went immediately to the Foundation which was then still at the hotel where the late Mr Gulbenkian had lived for many years, and was received by the Foundation's director, Mr Essayan, who had married Gulbenkian's sister, and Mr Robert Gulbenkian, the nephew. They listened to my story attentively, and, I felt, sympathetically: I think their Armenian origin, and the fact that Mr Essayan came from the same Levantine, Ottoman world as my wife's parents, whom he had known in Baghdad, helped them to understand me and to regard with some sympathy this improbable Anglo-Lebanese adviser to the Tunisian President who had come to them out of the blue. They invited me to dine that evening with the Foundation's President, Senhor Perdigão.

Senhor Perdigão was a Portuguese lawyer who had become President of the Foundation when Mr Gulbenkian Senior had

Fadlo and Soumaya Hourani with their children, c. 1918: (clockwise from top right) Albert, Wadia, Leila, George, Salwa. The author sits in his mother's lap.

The matriarchy. The author's grandmother, Um Fadlo (centre), with her son and daughters.

Zelfa and Furugh in Tunisia.

'A success'! The author with President Bourguiba.

Musa Alami with his boys at Jericho.

The theatre at Hammamet.

decided to base it in Portugal rather than in England, and he needed a Portuguese citizen to head it. Perdigão himself had no knowledge of the world from which the Gulbenkians came, nor any real interest in the problems of culture in the Arab countries, but his glamorous wife, whose interests in music and ballet he was encouraging through the generous funds at his disposal, was present at the dinner, and approved the ideas I presented for the creation of a festival of the performing arts at Hammamet, and of the symphony orchestra I was setting up. At the end of the evening Mr Essayan told me to come and see him the following day, and I took this as a polite way of breaking the news that they could not help me. Next morning when I went to see him in his office, he asked me quite casually how much I needed. I gave him the estimate on which we had agreed with our contractor, which was for 42,000 Tunisian dinars. He produced his cheque-book and signed a cheque for that amount, wished me good luck, and sent me on my way! In the theatre at Hammamet hangs a marble plaque commemorating this generous gift of the Gulbenkian Foundation, and in my heart there will always be immense gratitude for the personal kindness of Mr Essayan and Robert Gulbenkian, and the understanding of Senhor and Senhora Perdigão.

I was now saved from what was potentially a humiliating situation, and I returned to Tunis to find my friends and colleagues at the airport waiting to hear what they were certain would be bad news. As I came down from the plane I waved the cheque towards them, feeling what Mr Chamberlain must have felt when he returned from Munich, but with less disastrous consequences for humanity.

This was the beginning of a race against time. We had only six months in which to complete the theatre and inaugurate it. If it was not completed before the summer of 1964, it could not be used before 1965, and we would have lost a whole year and spent much more money than was available. But if we were to use it in 1964, a whole festival had to be planned. To plan an international festival of the performing arts in a theatre which did not yet exist, to engage artists, and issue invitations to visitors from abroad, all on a practically non-existent budget, was perhaps the most temerarious thing I have done in my life, but, as it turned out, also one of the most successful.

I doubt if any theatre has been built and finished in six months, or at so small a cost: including the lighting equipment, the architect's fees, and the contractor's bill, the total cost came to approximately 60,000 Tunisian dinars, 16,000 of which came from President Bourguiba's personal account. Only the extraordinary enthusiasm and devotion of my collaborators made this possible: among these the first was Armand Meppiel, a young Frenchman who came to help us for almost no reward, and who organized the work with an amazing efficiency, sparing himself no effort and no sacrifice. The Tunisian workmen, too, slaved to finish the theatre in time: sometimes they worked both day and night, and to spur them on we would slaughter sheep and roast them on the seashore where they would sing and dance under the stars. Our efforts, however, very nearly came to nothing after the visit by the Chief Engineer of the Tunisian Government to the site. Paul Chemetov, our architect, had been delighted to discover that the theatre was to be built on sand: this, he told us, was the best and the cheapest foundation, and all that was necessary was to enclose the sand in a framework so that it could not move. To the Chief Engineer, who had studied at one of France's most prestigious schools, this was pure folly: he returned to Tunis to inform President Bourguiba that I had embarked on a mad and dangerous adventure, and that the theatre was destined to fall into the sea. Bourguiba was naturally disturbed, for he had an unlimited confidence in his young Tunisian collaborators. He called me to tell me that I should stop the work, and it was only with difficulty that I persuaded him to receive the architects and hear their point of view. Chemetov, whose burly Russian physique enveloped a subtle and persuasive mind and manner, convinced Bourguiba that there was no danger in the work, and that we were not utterly mad. The theatre was finally completed one day before it was to be inaugurated, although the lighting system was only installed on the afternoon two or three hours before the first performance of an Arabic *Othello* was to begin.

President Bourguiba and Madame Bourguiba, most of his ministers, high officials, and a large group of distinguished foreign visitors from the world of the arts and society, including Princess Paola of Belgium, Peter Ustinov and Peter Daubeny, attended the inauguration which was followed by a ball, with the walled town of Hammamet in the background illuminated for the first time for this great occasion. I could not resist leaning across Bourguiba to say to the Chief Engineer, who was sitting nearby, 'The theatre hasn't fallen into the sea,' to which he replied, 'But it will one day.' Each time I visit Tunisia now I go to Hammamet to see if his prophecy has come true, but I see no signs that the theatre has moved one inch from its solid foundations of sand.

So the open-air theatre of Hammamet was built. It is my belief that it is among the most successful theatres built in recent times, offering directors and actors exceptional facilities in a unique setting: its background of sea, with the town of Hammamet in the distance, and the special quality of the Gulf of Hammamet's light and air, its simplicity of style combined with highly sophisticated technical equipment and scenic possibilities, make it a superb instrument of work appreciated by all of the many distinguished directors, actors, musicians and other performers who visited or worked in it during the three seasons in which I directed its activities.

My choice of *Othello* to inaugurate the theatre was based on two considerations. In the first place, it is a play whose themes of jealousy and intrigue make it easily intelligible to an Arab public, who find in it reflections of their own society and ways of thinking, and its principal character is an Arab from Mauretania, not a black African as he is usually portrayed in the West. Secondly, I wanted to use a Shakespearian play as an experiment in the Arabic language. The principal problem of the Arabic theatre lies in the wide gap between the spoken and the written versions of the language, which is wide enough to make it difficult, if not altogether impossible, for an illiterate person to follow a play, or a poem, in the literary language, or rather vocabulary: but as the colloquial speech and vocabulary vary considerably from one Arab country to another, Arabic theatre has fallen between two stools – in the classical, literary language it is unintelligible to large sections of the population, and in the colloquial version it becomes parochial and, with the exception of the Egyptian dialect, barely comprehensible outside the country from which it comes. To create a genuinely Arabic theatre it is necessary to develop a language which, while being accessible to audiences in any part of the Arabic world, does not perpetuate the stilted and remote classical style.

To test my theory that such a 'common language' could be found, and that actors from different parts of the Arab world could collaborate to create a real 'Arab theatre', not just an Egyptian or a Lebanese or a Tunisian one, I brought together an Egyptian Othello in the person of a well-known Egyptian actor, Jamil Ratib, a Tunisian Iago in the person of Ali Ben Ayad, and a Lebanese Desdemona, Theodora Racy; in addition I asked an Algerian designer working for many years with the Royal Shakespeare Company in England, Abd'elkader Farrah, to design the costumes and décor. And I commissioned a new translation of Othello from a Tunisian scholar, Dr Taher Khemiri, who had taught Arabic in Hamburg, written a standard Arabic-German dictionary, and now lived in Tunis.

The proof of the success of this first experiment in the creation of an Arabic theatre came with the extraordinary reaction of the Tunisian public. Apart from the educated Tunisians who came to the first night, the audiences for the other performances came from the town of Hammamet and from nearby towns and villages mainly in the Cap Bon area, and most were illiterate. Taher Khemiri had succeeded in combining the speech of every day with a 'correct' literary form, so that the world of Shakespeare's characters, in which the people recognized their own world, and identified with the actors and with the action, was opened up to them: Othello's tale of jealousy, intrigue, violence and remorse revealed not some imaginary or remote world, but their own, and Shakespeare, instead of remaining a writer from an alien culture, was assimilated into Arabic culture: language, instead of being a barrier, became a key which unlocked its gates.

Had this experiment been continued in Tunisia or elsewhere, it would have been possible to create a whole new dimension to Arab culture, which would have forced its way into the universal culture which is the only vital force today, without losing its Arab identity which is anchored to the Arabic language. But, as I was later to realize, it was just this possibility which frightened those in the Tunisian cultural and educational establishment who saw the revival of Arabic or Tunisian culture in terms only of 'a return to the sources', which in the case of theatre, or cinema, can only condemn it to sterility, as there are no sources for an Arabic theatre or cinema within the classical literary heritage.

The theatre of Hammamet had been built and inaugurated, but it now had to be used to its best advantage. As an open-air theatre it could only be safely used during the four months of the Tunisian summer, that is from June to September, but the Centre had to carry on its activities all year round. I did not want to imitate or to rival the Festival of Baalbek in Lebanon which for some years had been bringing some of the most prestigious artists and ensembles to a summer season. Baalbek was not a festival of creation, and the Arabic contribution was minimal except for an attempt to invent a Lebanese folklorish dance. My concept of the Hammamet Festival was that it should be the culmination of work to be done throughout the year, and I also hoped to raise the standards of the Tunisian and Arab participation in the festival by bringing well-known artists, directors, and critics to visit the Centre and to create joint artistic ventures with Tunisians.

It was in this perspective that I invited to Tunisia the one Arab musician of international reputation in the field of classical music, the Lebanese-American Anis Fuleihan, who came under contract with the American State Department to set up an orchestra. Fuleihan was a pianist and composer whose works had entered the repertoire of the New York Symphony Orchestra and had been widely performed in America for thirty years. I put him in charge of the musical section of the Centre, and together we decided that Tunis needed a classical orchestra. There were a few French and Italian musicians in Tunis, but not enough to make up the small orchestral ensemble which Fuleihan had in mind. The small budget provided by the Ministry of Culture was not sufficient to engage musicians from western Europe or

America, so we approached the eastern European embassies in Tunis for help. We were invited to Sofia and Prague and found that the Bulgarian and Czechoslovak governments were prepared to release musicians from their own orchestras to come to Tunisia. The musicians were naturally delighted, even though the salaries we offered were low. So there came into existence the 'Orchestre Classique de Tunis' which performed throughout the winter in Tunis, Sfax and Sousse, and in the summer took part in the programme of the three festivals for which I was responsible between 1964 and 1966. In addition to the orchestra the Centre organized concerts by visiting pianists, violinists and singers. Among the performers who came to Hammamet and Tunis were the pianists Samson François, Abbey Simon, Yuri Bukoff, Marie-Françoise Bouquet and Henri Ghoraieb, the Bach Orchestra from Leipzig's Gewandhaus Orchestra, and the Budapest Quartet who performed Beethoven and Haydn in the Centre's marble swimming-pool, emptied for the occasion.

A number of dance groups came to perform in the theatre, most famous of which was the Ballet du Vingtième Siècle under the direction of Maurice Béjart, which performed ballets based on Wagner's Venusberg music, Ravel's *Bolero*, and the *Birds* of Hadjidakis, and a special show in which Tunisian dancers, jugglers, acrobats and drummers joined with Béjart's own artists. In the patio of my house in Sidi Bou Said they also performed to music played by the Tunisian Rachidiyya ensemble who specialized in the classical Arabic music which has come down from Andalusia. Paul Taylor's Dance Group came from New York, and from Spain a troupe of authentic flamenco singers and dancers led by the famous dancer Rosa Duran: in one memorable programme they combined both Tunisian and Spanish traditional music and demonstrated their common origin.

In the summer of 1965 I asked Claude Planson, director of the Théâtre des Nations in Paris for many years, to organize an international summer school for young actors and actresses. He brought as lecturers and teachers a number of the most famous figures in contemporary theatre, such as Joan Littlewood, Peter Brook, Jan Kott and Gianfranco di Bosio, and our students came from Tunisia, Lebanon, France, Spain, and South America. Joan Littlewood and her friend and manager Gerry Raffles put on a show written and improvised by the students, and the experiment was so successful that we repeated it in the following year.

The Centre at Hammamet was open all through the year and received guests and members of the conferences we organized in the main house and in the pavilions which Sebastian had built in the gardens. The resident director of the Centre was Sherif Khaznadar, currently director of the newly created Théâtre du Monde in Paris after a highly successful career as director of the Centre Cultural de Rennes, ably assisted by his wife Françoise.

In the field of the plastic arts the Centre made another experiment which was to have a considerable impact on the artistic life of Tunisia. Profiting from the presence in Tunis of a young Belgian art teacher, Michel Pion, who possessed a remarkable talent for teaching the very young, we decided to open a children's workshop in Sidi Bou Said open to any child attracted to it by the opportunity to paint or draw or work with his hands. Pion's special talent was to help children to develop their creative powers without constraining them into any mould: he did not impose his ideas, but led them to discover for themselves, with help from him, what was valid and invalid. The result was a sudden flowering of talent very much in advance of anything that had been done in Tunisia before, or was done after Pion left Tunisia some years later. The standard of the work done in the children's workshop was high enough to enable us to organize an exhibition of drawings, painting, sculpture, pottery and masks in Paris in 1965, and later on in the USA where the Smithsonian Institution organized a travelling exhibition which went all around America.

All these activities – the symphony orchestra, the concerts, the children's workshop, the conferences, the theatre school, and the summer festival of the performing arts – were carried out by a very small group of colleagues and friends from our office in Tunis, and with the valuable assistance and advice of Thomas Erdos, who from his impresario's office in Paris provided the Centre with a direct link with the artistic and intellectual sources of European culture, and who helped us to achieve an international reputation among artists and critics and to establish the summer festival as one of the recognized festivals of the European and Mediterranean scene.[6]

It is not easy, at twenty years' distance, to measure the success of the Hammamet Centre in achieving the goals we had set for ourselves, but there is no doubt that it did create a cultural fermentation which left its mark on many who, in one way or another, participated in its activities. As an institution the Centre did not survive as I had originally conceived it, but it is a proof of the impact that it made that it has survived at all: at various times it has been threatened with dismemberment in order to build yet more hotels on its grounds, and its theatre has been abused and degraded by performances of shows that I would not have permitted. But the idea of an international centre has taken root, the theatre is still physically intact, the house and garden preserved for its original purpose of receiving visiting writers and artists and housing conferences : the symphony orchestra, disbanded after my departure, has been reconstituted, the children's workshop in Sidi Bou Said is still there, though unused except as a picture gallery – and perhaps one day it will all come to life again awakened by a prince's magic kiss!

The very success of the Centre, and the wide publicity it received not only in Tunisia but in the international press, the articles and the reports of visitors, critics, artists and friends who by 1966 were beginning to flock to Hammamet and Tunis, was the cause of its collapse and my departure from Tunis. Ironically, it was the Minister of Culture who played the leading role in this sad story.

My relations with the Minister of Culture, M. Chedli Klibi, had been strained during the official visit which President Bourguiba made to Ottawa and Washington in 1961, on which I and my wife accompanied him. The draft of the President's speech before the Canadian Parliament had been prepared by the Minister, but when I translated it from Arabic into English I realized that it was quite unsuitable both in style and content, and wrote another completely different draft which Bourguiba accepted and delivered with great success. Following this I wrote part of the speech he delivered to the joint meeting of Congress in Washington on 4 May 1961 after which he received a standing ovation. Such incidents do not make for harmony between a minister and a mere adviser.

Chedli Klibi, whose Ministry of Culture had been created in imitation of the French department over which André Malraux presided with brilliance, was no Malraux. His conception of his role was nearer to that of a minister in a totalitarian government responsible for the 'guidance' and 'enlightenment' of the Tunisian people: he believed, perhaps seriously, that, just as a minister of post and telephones was responsible for telephones, *he* was responsible for culture. It was no accident that his plans for the cultural enlightenment of the Tunisian people received enthusiastic support from the embassies of socialist governments. The existence of the Hammamet Centre under my direction was a source of irritation and perhaps of jealousy. As the Centre was an autonomous agency, receiving a small contribution from the Ministry of Culture's budget, but also funded by contributions from foundations and individuals which I was responsible for raising, he had no control over its programmes, and my position with the President protected me at first from his aim of bringing the Centre under the wing of his inefficient Ministry.

In addition to his functions as Minister of Culture, M. Klibi was also mayor of Carthage, a suburb of Tunis among whose ruins which still testify to the triumph of Rome over Carthage stands a classical amphitheatre. In this theatre he conceived the idea of creating a rival festival to that of Hammamet, and called in my architects from Paris to ask them to undertake the work of conversion, which out of loyalty to me they refused. A Tunisian, whose one qualification for the position was the fact that he was President of the Horse-Racing Club of Tunis, was made director of the Festival of Carthage, and aging actors from the Comédie Française were imported to put on plays from the classical French repertoire. In spite of the fact that Carthage was nearer to Tunis than Hammamet, and that its festival enjoyed much greater facilities for publicity than we did, the Tunisians sensed that what was happening at

Hammamet was far more exciting than the French tragedies which they had been seeing for many years in the more spectacular Roman theatre of Dougga in northern Tunisia: the discriminating public flocked to Hammamet. I tried to persuade the director of Carthage, who was my friend, that we should cooperate rather than compete with each other, and I offered him as a gesture of goodwill a performance by Maurice Béjart's Ballet du Vingtième Siècle, but the precedent was not followed up: Carthage was pitted against Hammamet, and the prevailing mood in the Ministry was confrontation rather than cooperation.

The culmination of the Minister's campaign to subordinate Hammamet to Carthage, and to impose his own version of Tunisian cultural revival, came in the summer of 1966. The first performance by Zambra, a Spanish flamenco troupe of singers and dancers, which I had organized in the Andalusian gardens and décor of the d'Erlanger palace in Sidi Bou Said, coincided with the opening of the Festival of Carthage by the Comédie Française: 'le tout Tunis', the diplomatic corps, and the people of Sidi Bou Said came to Zambra, hardly anyone went to see the Comédie Française.

A further source of irritation to the Minister was the performance at Hammamet of a show conceived and constructed by Joan Littlewood and her group of Tunisian, Lebanese, French, Spanish and South American students at the summer theatre school now in its second year: *Pepito* was a series of sketches portraying the comedies and tragedies in the life of a Tunisian worker in France. Unfortunately no permanent record of the text or the largely improvised performances exists, but it was a brilliant first step in the direction of a multinational theatre towards which Joan Littlewood was working. Joan had reached a point in her artistic life where she felt she could do no more on the English scene: her ideas about the theatre and the actor, revolutionary when first put into practice, were now becoming accepted in England, the USA, and France. Her own involvement in the theatre in London, where she and Gerry Raffles had created Theatre Workshop, was coming to an end, and she found herself less and less sympathetic to the political, intellectual and artistic climate which prevailed in Great Britain in the sixties. The Hammamet Centre, and Tunisia in general, with which she fell in love, opened up for her the exciting possibility of discovering a new cultural scene, of introducing and trying out her ideas and methods on a new and unspoilt society. She found in the Centre in Hammamet an atmosphere of friendship, informality, and unsophistication which she had been looking for and had not found elsewhere, and had I remained in Tunisia she might have stayed and worked there for many years, with incalculable benefits to not only the Tunisian but also the Arab cultural scene at large.

But *Pepito* was too much for Chedli Klibi to swallow. He had not understood what it was all about, he thought the title *Pepito* suspiciously non-Tunisian, and he informed President Bourguiba, whom I had invited to the first night and who had agreed to come, that this was not something he should attend: it was a foreign show of dubious character. This was communicated to me by the President who called me to tell me that he was not going to Hammamet, because I had not invited his Minister of Culture. This, of course, was not true, because the Minister was invited to all functions at Hammamet, but never came to any after the inaugural *Othello* in 1964. Bourguiba went on to tell me that he had heard that my wife and I held parties and receptions in our house of a 'Bohemian' character (at which parties his ministers and entourage were frequent guests!), that I was encouraging foreign and non-Tunisian activities, and was not mixing enough with the Tunisian people!

This unpleasant conversation with Bourguiba, the first of its kind I had ever had, convinced me that Klibi was determined to put an end to my activities at the Centre, and to bring it under the control of his Ministry. I was not mistaken, for not long after the festival of 1966 was over, and I had taken my annual holiday in Lebanon, he persuaded Bourguiba to appoint in my place as director of the Centre a tired official from the department of education, and to 'compensate' me by appointing me president of the Centre's committee! Not content with this stab in the back, the Minister adopted the classical Tunisian method of discrediting someone by sending inspectors to look for irregularities in the Centre's accounts, which they did not find. What they did find, however, were the Centre's debts, which had mounted up: the Minister of Finance had not fulfilled his promise to cover the extra costs of the theatre and house at Hammamet which we had enlarged and improved, the deficit from the festivals had not been covered by the tiny subsidy from the Ministry of Culture which never exceeded 35,000 Tunisian dinars a year, and no account had been taken of the fact that I had bought a property for the Tunisian state for 64,000 dinars which was now (in 1966) worth at least five times what it had cost.[7] These debts were reported to the President, who was particularly worked up at the Centre's debt to a butcher of Grombalia![8]

I realized that my days in Tunisia were over, and decided to visit Saudi Arabia to see if my friends there, who included King Faisal and his brother-in-law, might help me to make a graceful exit from Tunisia, but on my return to Tunis I learnt that President Bourguiba had decided to cancel my appointment as his adviser: I returned my diplomatic passport to Bourguiba Junior with a short letter of farewell, and left the next day, not to return for five years to the country which I had so much loved, and, I think, so well served.

This was not to end my relations with Habib Bourguiba, though it did end my official career in Tunisia. What I did not realize at the time was that Bourguiba was in the throes of a severe illness which affected his relations not only with me but also with others even closer to him, and made him readily believe rumours and suspicions reported to him by persons who for one reason or another resented my closeness to the seat of power.

After fifteen years I can now see more clearly than I did at the time that what lay behind the hostility of Chedli Klibi to my direction of the Hammamet Centre was not just personal, but was rather a basic difference between our conceptions of cultural revival. Nothing better illustrates this difference than the question of the place of 'folklore' in that revival. I was not opposed to giving its proper place to a genuine, authentic folklore, but I was firmly opposed to the idea of introducing a faked or a foreign folklore. My reasons were not only cultural, but also political: the totalitarian regimes of Europe, both fascist and socialist, have used 'folklore' as a way of channelling and limiting the creative spirit along lines which fit into their interests in dominating and controlling all aspects of their populations' lives. 'Folklore' is 'safe': it does not demand thought or provoke controversy: it satisfies their populations' national feelings and pride without raising dangerous memories of historical rivalries and enmities – all peoples dancing in their national costumes are free and equal; and to the outside world these healthy smiling girls and boys demonstrate the attachment of the people to their autocratic masters.

I did not believe that the new Tunisia needed to create this image, and I did not like such tendencies as I saw for the one-party system to develop along autocratic lines, and their reflection in the creation of a folklore less Tunisian than eastern European. The Minister of Culture imported instructors and advisers from Bulgaria and other socialist countries to train young Tunisians in dances derived from the traditions of the Balkans and Russia, and to dress them in invented costumes. The Tunisian public was made to believe that they were watching something 'traditional' and 'national': the Tunisian national Troupe Folklorique obtained considerable success in the festivals which became fashionable all around the Mediterranean in the sixties and seventies, and similar troupes were organized in all the different regions of Tunisia to dance and skip in Russian boots.

I regarded this facile way of 'reviving' a national culture which had never existed as dishonest and unfair to the Tunisian people: it was a way of preventing them from participating in the universal culture which is the only living one today, and in which they must participate if they are to become fully a part of the modern world. Where national traditions exist, they must be studied and built upon, not fossilized or falsified. In Tunisia, for example, there exists a small tradition in the villages and among the people of dance and music, but their movements and rhythms are extremely limited. I believed that this tradition would not be harmed or killed by showing the

Tunisians that there are other more evolved and complex ways of dancing, and I hoped that they would be given the opportunity to learn new techniques and disciplines which would make possible the evolution and enrichment of their traditional culture. I did not see that there was any contradiction or irreconcilable gap between Béjart and the Bedouin dancers of the villages: Béjart could give them a dimension which they would not get from within their own limited traditions, or from sources imported from outside which were political rather than truly cultural.

I refused to allow the theatre at Hammamet to be used by the national or local folklore troupes or to include examples of this bastard art-form in the festivals of the performing arts which I organized between 1964 and 1966. When Chedli Klibi succeeded in laying his hands on the Centre and the Hammamet Festival one of the first things my 'successor' did was to organize performances by various folklore groups from Tunisia and other countries. This was a way of trying to demonstrate to the Tunisian people that the days of the 'cultural cosmopolitanism' of which I was accused several times in the press of trying to introduce were over, and that the International Cultural Centre, so closely associated in the past with my name and personality, had now been 'nationalized'. In contrasting me with the new director of his choice, Chedli Klibi announced that 'le style est l'homme', implying that the Tunisian public would recognize and appreciate the difference between my direction and that of my successor: this they did indeed, and every time I revisit Tunisia, and in particular Hammamet, where I still have many friends among the simple people of that lovely town, I hear nostalgic recollections of the extraordinary days we spent together at the theatre and in the gardens and pavilions of the Centre, and expressions of real regret at my departure.

I lost the battle to open up Tunisia to the outside world and to stimulate a new and original flowering of Arab culture in the country which I believed at the time could be its most fertile ground. 'Cultural chauvinism' gained the day, but the real losers were the Tunisians themselves. Many of the young people to whom the Centre represented an exciting experiment, which had brought them into contact with some of the most important figures of the contemporary artistic world, were now forced to leave Tunisia if they wished to enlarge their horizons and develop their talents. Some of these young Tunisians flourished and became prominent abroad, but the country was deprived of much of its greatest talent. And in the long run, unless they can reintegrate themselves into their national cultural environment in Tunisia, these gifted young people will find themselves increasingly cut off from the sources of their own culture yet unable to integrate themselves completely into that of their new societies. This is the drama not only of the Tunisians, but of all the artists and intellectuals from the Arab countries now living abroad in whose countries of origin the conditions of political and intellectual freedom in which alone the creative spirit can flourish do not exist.

My departure from Tunisia early in 1967 was not, however, the end of my relations with Habib Bourguiba. For five years I did not return to that country. In those years he passed through many phases of illness, Tunisia went through many crises, but when he finally emerged from his physical sickness he had recovered much of his former strength and lost none of his lucidity. I was restored to his favour and received many signs of his old affection for me, and he does not fail in private and in public to make amends for what I think he recognized had been a fault in the way he had treated me: on television and radio he still frequently recalls the days he spent in Washington in 1946 and Cecil Hourani, the 'friend in need'. And on my side I have lost all the bitterness I felt, though which I never publicly expressed, at what had happened between us, and I ascribe it to the cloud of sickness which for a time overshadowed that bright spirit but which has now lifted.

VII
Rival Nationalisms

My life and work in Tunisia had given me many occasions to reflect on different concepts of nationalism in the two wings of the Arab world, the Mashriq and the Maghrib, as well as on the translation of these concepts into political life and action. I was also forced by events in which I was involved to take up a position and to clarify my thoughts and eventually my identity. Where did I stand myself in relation to the great upheavals which were taking place around me: the emergence of new regimes and states in North Africa, the formation of the United Arab Republic in 1958 and its dissolution in 1961, revolution in Iraq in 1958 and the installation of totalitarian regimes in Iraq and Syria both claiming to adhere to the same version of Arab nationalism, crisis in Lebanon in 1958, and the Arab-Israeli conflicts in 1956, 1967 and 1973?

The final outcome of my involvement and my reflections was to make me aware of my Lebanese identity, to strengthen my attachment to the land, the society, and the state of Lebanon, and to define my relationship to other poles of attraction in my quest for identity and roots. Of these there were two which in particular seemed to offer alternative answers to the Lebanon to which I finally returned: one was Syrian, the other Arab nationalism.

I had first heard of Syrian nationalism from a young cousin from Beirut who had come to live with us in Manchester while I was still at school. He told us of a wonderful man who had recently returned to Lebanon from South America, where his parents had emigrated, and who had brought with him a new vision of the history of the Mashriq, in which Syria played the central role. He taught that Syria was the mother of all Near Eastern civilizations, that this Syrian nation had a 'real' existence more extensive than the frontiers of the Syrian state created after the First World War, and he eventually came round to the view that the Syrian state of the future would embrace all the 'historic' lands of the Syrian nation between Iraq in the east and Cyprus in the west. In order to bring into being the new state to replace the fragmentation of the Syrian homeland which the Great Powers had created for their own purposes, Antoun Saadé, as he was called, founded the Syrian Popular Party, of which my cousin, as well as many of the young men from a similar Protestant and Orthodox background in Beirut, was an enthusiastic member.

When I first went to Beirut in 1939 I thought of myself as a 'Syrian'. This was the term which most of the emigrants from present-day Lebanon and Syria used to describe themselves before the First World War, although by nationality they were citizens of the Ottoman Empire, and in South America were called 'Turcos'. But the term 'Syrian' had a geographical and historical rather than a political or ethnic connotation: within the Ottoman Empire there was no political or even administrative entity called Syria, which was only a name and a memory covering an undefined geographical area corresponding roughly to the Arabs' ancient distinction between 'bilad ash-Sham' on the left of the Arabian peninsula and 'bilad al-Yemen' on the right – 'the country of Damascus' and 'the country of Yemen'. Lebanon, on the other hand, did have a distinct administrative and political entity within the Ottoman Empire which found its final definition in 1861 and its present-day form as a state in 1920. Thus, contrary to the belief propagated, for various motives, by some journalists and 'Middle East experts' today, Syria has no historical or legitimate claims on Lebanon.

In calling myself 'Syrian' I was completely unaware of the political and ideological implications of that term, but I was soon corrected by a friend who, while Lebanese himself, was an Arab nationalist and strongly opposed to the theories of Antoun Saadé. The American University of Beirut, where I received my first education in Near Eastern politics, was then the scene of an intense rivalry between Syrian and Arab nationalism. That there was at the same period a new and growing movement of Lebanese nationalism in Beirut and other parts of the country I was hardly aware, for it was usual at the American University, and among the community which had grown up around it, to refer to the Christian quarter of Beirut as 'the other side': a pejorative term which reflected the American Protestant missionary dislike for Catholics, in which general category they placed the Maronites and Greek Catholics of Mount Lebanon and Ashrafiyya, a quarter of Beirut.

Coming freshly as I did from Oxford where I shared in the allergy of many of my contemporaries to the totalitarian regimes in Germany and Italy and to the 'loyalists' in the Spanish Civil War, I suspected that the theories of Antoun Saadé about the Syrian nation, and the form he was giving his party, were another version of the fascism then rampant in Europe: certainly there was the same devotion to the *Zaim*, or Leader, as Saadé was called by his followers, and the same feeling of superiority to other peoples, in this case the Arabs who had the misfortune not to have been born Syrian. I was curious to meet him and discover the secret of the influence he exercised over many of my new friends in Beirut. Of that one meeting I remember being impressed by the contrast between his mild and modest manner and the intransigence of his views: I was treated to a long and rambling discourse in which he expounded the views he had already published in his book *The Growth of Nations*, and which were to lead him eventually to his death by execution following an attempt to overthrow the Lebanese state in 1949.

His ideas and the party he had founded did not die with him, but continued to attract support in Lebanon, whose liberal regime they sought to overthrow, although in the mother-country, Syria itself, they were suppressed. Apart from the myth which grew up around the martyred leader, the attraction of his ideas lay in the vision of a secular, non-confessional society and state in contrast to the compartmentalization of contemporary Lebanon, and in the alternative it suggested to the Lebanese state of the Kataeb[1] and the Arab state of the Arab nationalists – a vision attractive to those in the Protestant, Orthodox and Druze communities who wished to be neither

Lebanese nor Arab. But in more recent times the Syrian Popular Party was caught between the conflicting forces of Lebanese, Palestinian and Arab nationalism, split into a number of factions, and ceased to offer any realistic alternative to the Lebanese state.

It was Arab, not Syrian, nationalism which in my first period of teaching in Beirut and for many years after attracted my enthusiastic support. My childhood and youth in Manchester and Oxford, my early interest in the Palestinian Arab cause, and my first visits to Marjayoun had predisposed me to this Arab fervour. In the violent disputes which I sometimes listened to in our house between the supporters of Faisal's Arab kingdom and its pro-French opponents, my father's sentiments were with the former. Marjayoun had not been part of the autonomous Mount Lebanon created by the Great Powers in 1861; and he was not in touch with or aware of the aspirations of the Maronites and Catholics for an independent Lebanese state which found increasing expression in Beirut and Paris in the early years of the century, although when it came into existence he opted for its citizenship. And when I first arrived in Marjayoun I found still vivid memories of events twenty years before in which the town had played a historic role which, to my belief, has never yet been recorded in the annals of the short-lived Arab kingdom.

As the Arab forces led by the sons of Sherif Hussein advanced in 1918 with the British and French forces into Palestine and the lands east of Jordan, the Emir Faisal sent messengers ahead to his supporters in Syria and Lebanon asking them to proclaim the Arab Government as soon as the Turkish armies retreated, and before the arrival of the British and French of whose intentions he had already formed justified suspicions. There were Turkish forces stationed in Marjayoun, and its Austrian commander had been living in my grandmother's house: these forces left Marjayoun before the withdrawal of the Turkish armies from Damascus and Beirut, and so it came about that the Arab Government was first proclaimed, and the Arab flag first raised, at the Turkish *sérail* which still stands outside our garden wall. In that event the main role had been played by a citizen of the town who had been a Deputy in the Ottoman Assembly of 1909, and had there mixed in Arab nationalist circles, and I was a frequent visitor to the house of Mourad Ghulmiyyeh to listen to his story of the most important moment of his life.

Of those days when hopes of a new Arab kingdom under the banner of the Hashemites were still high I would also hear from the Emir Faour, whose father, their cousin, was in close and secret contact with the advancing Arab forces, and was among the first to welcome them in Syria. To the end of his life – tragically cut short in 1977 – he continued to believe that it was the destiny of the Hashemites to create the Arab state, and when we met, in Marjayoun, Beirut, Amman or Saudi Arabia, he never ceased to spell out his dream of a new capital, somewhere in the desert between Palmyra and Iraq, where he claimed there existed ancient water systems, from the days of the Abbasids and maybe earlier still, which could easily be repaired to bring life back to the desert, and to restore their former fame to the Arab tribes whose names and ancestry and history he knew by heart.

When I moved from Beirut to Cairo, I believed that the Second World War offered the chance for the British Government to rectify the errors they had made at the end of the First, and to revive the idea of an Arab state. From wartime Cairo the idea seemed plausible: British forces were in control of all the Near East, the economic and financial activity of the whole area was controlled from the Middle East Supply Centre, and it was possible to move across frontiers with an ease which it is difficult to imagine today. The problem of Palestine could, I thought, be solved within a wider framework such as that afforded by the Arab League, and the League itself would be the embryonic nucleus from whose institutions the Arab state would emerge. When, by a further stretch of my vivid imagination, the countries of the Maghrib would throw off French rule, the two wings of the Arab world would join together and form the Arab union from the Atlantic to the Gulf of which the poets of Arab nationalism sang.

The twenty years which followed my eager first participation in Arab affairs slowly but surely revealed to me the fragile and largely illusory nature of my beliefs. Had I been right, the emergence of the Arab states into independence should have brought them nearer to the unity to which I thought they genuinely aspired, but what I observed was the opposite: independence brought positions to be defended, interests to be protected, and the growth of new classes of politicians and bureaucrats who had not known the unity which Ottoman rule had imposed and whose horizons were limited by the frontiers of their little states. Ancient rivalries and historical jealousies were resurrected, new sources of conflict appeared, and in one of these conflicts I was myself caught up.

To the peoples and nationalist parties of the Maghrib, Egypt was traditionally the heart of the Arab world: it was the largest Arab country, it had had the longest experience of independence, and the literature, music, theatre and films which came out of Cairo represented to them the finest flowering of modern Arab culture. To Cairo had come the Moroccan, Algerian, Tunisian and Libyan leaders, finding there a freedom they did not enjoy in their own countries, and a platform from which to arouse support for their causes throughout the Arab and Muslim worlds, and in the world at large. But the prestige of Egypt among the Tunisians, and the friendships which Habib Bourguiba and other members of the Neo-Destour Party had formed there among politicians, literary figures and journalists did not prevent the outbreak of serious conflicts between the two countries once Tunisia achieved its independence in 1956.

One source of conflict appeared soon after. When Bourguiba had persuaded his party and the Tunisian people to accept less than full independence when offered internal autonomy by the Government of Mendès-France, a few members of the party had not agreed. Of these Salah Ben Youssef was the most prominent. He believed in 'all or nothing', and when in 1956 internal autonomy gave way to full independence, he refused to accept that this independence was real, or that it could have come through Bourguiba's leadership. From Cairo he and a small band of followers, tolerated and encouraged by the Egyptian Government of President Nasser, carried on a violent campaign in the Egyptian and

Arab press in which Bourguiba was pilloried as a 'traitor' and 'collaborator' with France, and Tunisia's independence portrayed as fictitious. This, I remember, was the view currently prevalent in Beirut in 1955 and 1956, and indeed for many years later, of the leadership of Bourguiba and the nature of his regime.

The first public signs of a rift between the Tunisian regime and the Egyptian Government came in early 1958 with the arrest on the frontiers between Tunisia and Libya of an Egyptian sent by Salah Ben Youssef to assassinate Habib Bourguiba and Hedi Nouira, one of his closest collaborators. The confession of the Egyptian, a certain Youssef Najjar, and proofs of the complicity of the Egyptian Government, were published by the Tunisian Ministry of Foreign Affairs in a 'Black Book' of which I wrote the English version. The entry of Tunisia into the Arab League did nothing to close the gap between its regime and the Government of the newly formed United Arab Republic of Egypt and Syria which challenged the authority and leadership of Bourguiba in the name of the 'Arab nation' of which President Nasser claimed to be the spokesman. But the most violent conflict between the two regimes and the two men was that which broke out as a result of Bourguiba's 'peace initiative' for Palestine in 1964 and 1965.

To some extent it was the difference in the education and culture of the two leaders which lay behind the recurring conflicts between their regimes. Bourguiba had been educated at the Saddiqi College in Tunis, then as now one of the foremost educational institutions in the country: his culture and languages were both Arabic and French, and he found no contradiction or conflict between the two, and so nourished no antagonism except on political grounds to the France he challenged. Nasser, on the other hand, had only a limited Arabic education and an elementary knowledge of the English language and Anglo-Saxon culture, and viewed the relation between Egypt and Great Britain in simplistic terms as one between subject and master. The most striking difference between the two men was that revealed by their oratorical styles and the contents of their public speeches. Nasser was able to sway Egyptian and Arab crowds by his command of the language of the common people in which he told them what they wanted to hear, while Bourguiba addressed the Tunisian masses in an intelligible mixture of colloquial and literary Arabic in which he expounded the most sophisticated political and philosophical ideas. Nasser was led by the masses, and Bourguiba led them. In more recent times the only other Arab leader who has come near to Bourguiba's mastery of the minds of his audience was Anwar Sadat, whose speeches explaining and justifying his historic visit to Jerusalem in 1977, and the agreements he later made with Israel, resembled in many ways those of Bourguiba replying to the attacks made on him by Nasser and other Arab politicians.

I had the opportunity to compare at first hand the oratorical skills of Bourguiba and Nasser in 1964. The affair of Bizerta and the withdrawal of the last French forces from Tunisia in 1963 led to a temporary reconciliation between the two men, and Bourguiba decided to invite not only Nasser, but also Ahmed Ben Bella, the first President of the new Algerian republic, to the ceremonies celebrating the first anniversary of the French evacuation. I suspect that his motive in so doing was to expose them to the Tunisian people, who could now, with their political maturity formed in thirty years of listening to him, form their own judgements of the three leaders. Ben Bella's problem was that he could with difficulty express himself in Arabic. He had no sophistication, and thought in simplistic terms, and all I remember of his speech was his dramatic announcement that after independence the Algerian people would throw away the knives and forks imported by France along with her alien rule and return to the spoon – *al maghrafa*!

Nasser's performance was very different. The Tunisian people were curious to see and hear for themselves the man who had attacked their leader. As President of Egypt he came with the prestige enjoyed by that great country as the centre of Arab culture and civilization, and his defiance of the West and his championship of the Algerian cause had made of him a legendary figure throughout the Arab world, but the violent campaigns he and his regime had waged against Tunisia and its regime had dismayed and angered the Tunisian people. His speech was full of the slogans and clichés of Arab nationalism, and the response of his audience was clear: they applauded the man, but were cool towards his ideas. Bourguiba's own address resembled that of a headmaster coming after two students had read their end-of-term compositions from the platform, and the politeness of his language did not conceal the reality of what he thought.

But the conflict between Bourguiba and Nasser was not just a personal one: it was basically one between two different conceptions of the relations which did and which ought to exist between different members of the family of Arab peoples. Nasser, whose conversion from Egyptian to Arab nationalism owed much to the ideas of Sateh al-Husri[2] and to the persuasive talents of Nadim Dimishquiyyeh, Ambassador of Lebanon in Cairo and the friend who in earlier days had corrected my indiscriminate use of the terms 'Syrian' and 'Lebanese', was, like many converts to a new-found faith, over-zealous in his fervour. Between 1958 and 1967 he made frantic efforts to put into practice the central theme of Arab nationalism – that there is one Arab nation, and therefore there should be one Arab state. Convinced that Arab unity existed in more than a metaphysical sense, that there was already a unity of language, culture, historical memory and aspirations for the future which only needed an institutional framework to make it a political reality, he believed that as the authentic spokesman of the Arab nation he had the right to override or even overthrow regimes whose existence or activities he considered prejudicial to the realization of the nation's aims. The union of Egypt, Syria and Yemen proclaimed in 1958 was intended to be the nucleus of the future Arab state, and it was in the interest of the Arab nation that he and his mouthpiece, the journalist Hassanein Haykal,[3] attempted to justify their flagrant interventions in the affairs of Yemen, Iraq, Lebanon and Tunisia. Among the trivial reasons found by Haykal to attack Bourguiba was my presence in Tunisia in which he found a sinister significance.

The pretensions of the Government of the United Arab Republic to represent the interests of 'the Arab nation' were challenged and ridiculed by Bourguiba in a series of violent speeches to the Tunisian people. I do not remember any of his speeches – and they were many – in those first years of Tunisia's independence which equalled in brilliance of argument and passion of delivery those in which he denounced, mocked, and tore to pieces the policies and pronouncements of Nasser: it was superb theatre, and Bourguiba had in fact both the talents and the inclinations of an actor. His eldest brother had actually directed a theatre troupe, and he himself had attended in his youth and maturity the performances of Egyptian and Lebanese actors such as Negib Rihani and George Abiad who familiarized Arab audiences with the works of Shakespeare, Molière, Ahmed Chawki and Moutran. He could – and still can – declaim long passages from Victor Hugo, and he incorporated into his speeches all the gestures, inflections, surprises and dramatic pauses of a practised actor.

It was Nasser's pretensions to speak and act in the name of a theoretical Arab nation which clarified Bourguiba's position on Tunisia's relations with other Arab countries. Though he felt a sympathy and an affinity with all these countries, and in particular with the Palestinian people, it was the Tunisian people and nation alone for whom he believed he was responsible, and he had no intention, when challenged by Nasserism, of merging Tunisia's national identity, which he believed had a real historical foundation, in a wider, vaguer, and still unformed Arab identity. The attempts by Nasser and the United Arab Republic to discredit and overthrow his regime in the name of a 'higher' Arab interest turned Bourguiba for ever against 'Arabism' as a political doctrine. They convinced me also, where I saw them in operation not only in Tunisia, but also in Lebanon in 1958, that between the doctrines of Arab nationalism, the activities of the Baath Party[4] and of some Palestinian organizations, and Lebanon's existence as a sovereign state there existed a fundamental incompatibility. The events which began in Lebanon in 1975 confirmed me in this conviction.

The evidence that my association with Tunisia and President Bourguiba had prejudiced my reputation and made me suspect in the eyes of many Arab nationalists in Lebanon and some other countries who were influenced by – or took their orders from – Cairo and Damascus was provided by an incident which occurred during a visit I made to Beirut in the summer of 1958. Lebanon had been for some months in the throes of a serious crisis which opposed a coalition of forces around the leadership of Saeb Salam to the President of the Republic, Camille Chamoun.[5] Although the overt cause of the conflict was constitutional, the real issue was Lebanon's relation to the United Arab Republic, the formation of which had aroused wild hopes among those Lebanese who, for one reason or another, believed that Lebanon should join the union, and among many Palestinian intellectuals who saw in Nasser a new Saladin who would lead them back to Jerusalem.

The atmosphere of excitement aroused by the formation of the new state, the virulent broadcasts by Ahmed Said and others from 'The Voice of the Arabs' in Cairo and the weekly oracular pronouncements of Hassanein Haykal denouncing with equal venom Great Britain, the United States of American, and their Arab 'lackeys' – among whom the first was Habib Bourguiba – and, in July, the bloody revolution in Baghdad which overthrew the monarchy and dragged its leaders literally in the streets of that city – all these factors had created among the Lebanese population, and principally among the Maronite Christians, a natural reaction and fear that the existence of Lebanon was threatened: they rallied around President Chamoun besieged in his palace by what was practically an armed insurrection.

Into this frantic atmosphere I returned with my family from Tunis to spend my annual vacation in Beirut and Marjayoun. I had no political mission, but I was naturally interested and intrigued by the extraordinary situation I found, and as I had friends on both sides of the barricade, as it were, I visited first of all President Chamoun, and then Saeb Salam, whose house in Moussaitbeh had become the political and military headquarters of the anti-Chamoun forces, and whose natural preference for diplomacy over the gun, demonstrated in the hot summer of 1982, had been overridden by a strange coalition of Muslim dignitaries, mercenary journalists, and armed groups of various colours. My visit to his house was observed by someone who I had thought to be a friend – and who was years later to apologize to me for his behaviour – and a few days later I was denounced in a number of newspapers and magazines as a British agent, a collaborator with Bourguiba, and a Chamounist – all of which descriptions in the minds of my accusers amounted to the same thing.

Some years later I asked one of the journalists whose attack on me was the most virulent, and, in the atmosphere then prevailing in Beirut, the most dangerous to my personal safety, why he had written about me in those hostile terms. Selim Lawzi was a man who had gone through many phases in his life, but through natural intelligence, hard work, and a certain personal warmth and charm had built up the most successful and widely read Arabic weekly until he became the victim of his frankness and over-confidence.[6] He told me that at that time, in 1958, he was being paid by the Egyptian regime, and that the services with whom he was in contact had instructed him to attack me, probably on account of my connection with Bourguiba. He apologized to me, and though his articles had rankled in my mind for many years, I forgave him.

The effect of this incident in Beirut was to increase my attachment to the person and policies of Bourguiba, and to Tunisia, where I felt protected from the violence and intolerance which, largely because of the personality and ambitions of Nasser, were sweeping over the Mashriq. When I returned to Tunis after the summer in Lebanon it was with a feeling that I was returning home. This was due in part to the fact that my family and I were members of the Bourguiba family's intimate circle, and also that in our domestic life we enjoyed the devotion and affection of Ali and Halima Chiboub, a Tunisian couple who looked after our every need: but it was due also to the climate which Bourguiba had created in Tunisian society, and to the nature of that society itself.

In Tunisia there are no indigenous Christian communities, and there is a total and open identification between 'Arab' and 'Muslim', the two terms being interchangeable. Thus the question of whether an Arab is Muslim or Christian does not arise: as an Arab he must be Muslim. Christians and Muslims belong to two different worlds – the world of Roum and the world of Islam – and the two are distinct and self-excluding.

My personal status in Tunisia was therefore clear and unambiguous: since I was a Christian, I could not be an Arab, and this, in the conflict which opposed Bourguiba's Tunisian nation-state to Arab nationalism, was an advantage. I was a foreigner, and without denying my British background, considered myself Lebanese, and this in Tunisia was another advantage, for Lebanon enjoyed a special place in the hearts of the people second only to Egypt: it was from Lebanon that had come the textbooks and dictionaries on which generations of Tunisians had been brought up, and the songs and poetry which the common people knew and loved.

From the example of Bourguiba in Tunisia, and from his conflict with the United Arab Republic and the Arab nationalists who wished to subordinate the interest of every particular Arab country to a 'higher' Arab interest of which they claimed to be the true interpreters, I learnt to look at Lebanon's place in the Arab world in a new light. Gone were my old enthusiasms for an Arab state from the Atlantic to the Gulf: not only did I now see that it was practically unrealizable, but I also came to the conclusion that, even if it were within the realm of possibility, the incorporation of Lebanon within that state would not be in Lebanon's interest, nor finally in that of the state itself.

But my disenchantment with my own romantic views did not lead me to the other extreme. I did not abandon my belief that the existing political and economic relations between the Arab countries do not correspond to the needs of their populations or to the possibilities of a sensible development of their resources. That the countries with the smallest populations and the least favourable climates and agricultural resources should have vast wealth while larger populations and potentially more favoured lands should lack the means to develop them still seems to me both unjust and unreasonable. Even within the framework of existing sovereign states a more equitable and a more rational use of Arab resources could be made, and their relations be put on more friendly and cooperative bases than the rivalries and enmities which now prevail. If the European powers, with their long tradition of war and conquest of each other's territory, have been able to form an economic community, and to create at least in embryo the parliament of the future European union, the Arab states, who enjoy a common language and culture, and many of whom lived until recently under the same Ottoman or French administration and law, should surely be able to achieve at least as much.

I did not also fall into another extreme which claims that Lebanon is not an Arab country, and has no common interests with the Arab world, or that that world does not really exist. I had lived not only in Lebanon, but in Egypt and Tunisia for long periods of time, and travelled frequently in other Arab countries. I had intimate friends from almost every one of them, and had married an Iraqi citizen and through her obtained insights into an Arab society and culture other than those of Lebanon. In none of the countries I had known or the societies in which I had mixed did I feel an alien, and all this has given me an acute sense of belonging to a cultural world in which the Arabic language certainly plays the most important role, but in which there are other factors too – social customs, ways of behaviour, food, artistic values, and common historical memories – which create a world in which the Lebanese, Christian as well as Muslim, may feel at home.

But from this point of view to jump to the conclusion that Lebanon is just like any other Arab country, or that Lebanon's identity should or could be merged in some larger Arab identity, or that more should be demanded of Lebanon for Arab causes than others are willing to give, is a step I have not been willing to take: and the events which have taken place in that country in recent years, and my own involvement in those events, have confirmed me in my present view that the survival of Lebanon as a free, sovereign, democratic country, living in peace with all her neighbours, is a matter of importance not only to those who like myself have had the good fortune to belong to her people, but also to the whole region in which she lives, and perhaps beyond.

VIII
Marjayoun Besieged

My sudden departure from Tunisia at the beginning of 1967 had a traumatic effect on me. I was shocked by what I saw as an unjustified change of heart on the part of Habib Bourguiba towards me, and by the loss of the Centre at Hammamet into which I had put so much of myself and which had been a brilliant success. I was also left without any savings and with considerable debts which it took me years to repay, and I had not taken the precaution of looking for other employment, secure as I had felt in the affections of my Tunisian friends. Partly because I still had two sisters and my brother Albert there, partly because I felt the need for a rest from the turbulence of Arab politics, I decided to go with my family to England, and for three years rented a house in Hampstead. From there I looked for freelance work, and as my experience and expertise all lay within the field of the affairs of the Arab world, I was frequently obliged to travel there as well as to the USA where I had friends in some of the major oil companies and in the Ford Foundation. I found myself living in London, but working in Arab affairs, and gradually drawn back into them by material interests and the necessity of earning a living as well as by my renewed involvement in the life of the Arab countries. I still owned the house in Marjayoun I had inherited from my family, and which during the years spent in Tunisia had remained my principal attachment to Lebanon, and it was there rather than in London, where I was not a stranger, though neither emotionally nor socially involved in its life, that I felt was home. In one of my yearly vacations from Tunis I had discovered that my father had inscribed me in the official registry kept by the Lebanese Government in the town, so that I could 'recover' Lebanese nationality without having to apply for citizenship: I had been all along, without knowing it, Lebanese – a new version of *le bourgeois gentilhomme*!

At the beginning of 1970 I found an old and typical Lebanese red-roofed house in Moussaitbeh, a 'popular' quarter of Beirut. I did not dream at the time that before long I would be involved in events much more dramatic than those I had witnessed in Palestine or Tunisia, and far more dangerous than any I had experienced in my comfortable wartime years in Cairo. Nor did I dream that Marjayoun, which had always seemed a remote and forgotten place, would play a major role in the coming storm.

To the inhabitants of Marjayoun it has always seemed that they are at the heart of things: for this belief there is some historical justification. The town's situation at the junction of roads and natural passes leading from Palestine in the south to the Bekaa Valley in Lebanon, and then into central and northern Syria, and on one of the easiest and shortest ways from Damascus to the Mediterranean, has made it throughout history an area fought over and passed through by many armies and raiders. It had been attacked and badly damaged several times in this century: in 1920, 1925, and 1941 when it was the scene of fierce battles between the British and Free French forces and the Vichy forces which resisted their entry into Lebanon; indeed the people of Marjayoun claimed – and believed – that the Second World War had been decided in that battle for their town. And an ancient prophecy told me by my Uncle Said on many occasions and ascribed by him to the prophet Ezekiel foretold that Armageddon would be fought at 'Wadi Koukaban', a site visible from the balcony of our adjacent homes. That there was more than local fantasy to these notions of the importance of their area was borne out by Patrice Bougrain Dubourg,[1] one of my dearest French friends, who visited me there early in 1978, and prophesied that the third world war would begin in Marjayoun when Israel, provoked by the activities of the Palestinians on her northern frontier, would invade the area, and when a nuclear confrontation between the two Great Powers would follow.

My interest in Marjayoun was not simply the house and garden I had inherited and partially restored, nor the family who through death and emigration were dwindling in numbers. I was involved also in the social life of the town, believing as I did that 'patriotism begins at home', and that the future generations had a right to expect to inherit some of the advantages we have received from the past. This sense of a responsibility towards the community from which I had come had led me in 1953, while I was teaching at the American University in Beirut, to set up a training centre from which both the people of the town and the Palestinian refugees in the area could benefit. I disliked the way in which the international refugee organization set up by the United Nations to deal with the problem of the Palestinian refugees had discriminated between the refugees and the Lebanese population, many of whom had been impoverished by the events of 1948 in Palestine. UNWRA provided free educational and training programmes only for the refugees, as well as rations and medical services, thereby creating a disparity between the opportunities available to them and to the Lebanese among whom they were living, and a source of friction between the two populations which did not diminish, but rather grew with time. I believed that, irrespective of what the future held for the Palestinian refugees – whether they returned to their country or remained in Lebanon – they should be treated as equals with the Lebanese, but also that the Lebanese should enjoy the same opportunities for self-betterment as were being offered to the Palestinians.

In this project, in which I was inspired by the example of Musa Alami, I was helped by the unexpected arrival in Beirut of an American lady sent by a philanthropic organization of Lebanese and Palestinian Americans to see what could be done for the Palestinian refugees. Alma Kerr had had a lifetime of experience in working among refugees ever since the end of the First World War; she was a person of infinite resource, of many skills, and deep humanity. She immediately agreed to my proposal to set up a workshop to teach various skills such as weaving, basketmaking, ironwork, and carpentry, and to try to revive crafts in the area, such as pottery, which were in danger of disappearing. The project was successful not only in training a considerable number of young men and women, but also in helping them to earn money through their newly acquired skills: markets for their products were found in Beirut, and the American Ladies' Association adopted the project. All this effort, however, came to an end when the Lebanese Government, for security reasons, decided to move the Palestinian refugees from the frontiers to places further inside the country. But I still look back to the project with some satisfaction as my personal contribution to the refugee problem, and with gratitude to the commitment and self-sacrifice of Alma Kerr, who left the comforts of her home in Dakota to share misery and deprivation in Marjayoun.

There was another and older attachment I had to the town and the area around it. My father, whose philanthropy was legendary in his native town and district, and who, although certainly not the richest among the emigrants in worldly goods, was generally considered to have been the most generous, among his other initiatives had founded a school. There was already a strong and old tradition of education in the town, but my father had realized that if Jedeidet was to survive, it had to become a centre providing educational and medical facilities to the whole area to take the place of the trading position it had lost. To that end he succeeded in persuading the Protestant and Orthodox clergy to unite their schools and to create a national college open to all communities, coeducational from kindergarten to high-school, and non-profitmaking. This project occupied most of his thoughts and activities after the Second World War and took him to North and South America raising funds from the people of Marjayoun settled there. The dream became reality in 1948, and under the dynamic direction of his nephew Labib Ghulmiyyah the school soon became the foremost educational institution in south Lebanon.

I became a trustee of the Marjayoun National College in the fifties while I was teaching in Beirut and remained one all the time I was in Tunisia. My efforts to persuade the Ford Foundation to provide funds to build a new school on land my father had purchased for the college were successful after I had gone to Tunis, aided perhaps by the increased prestige my position there gave me with the Foundation's head office in

New York. The Foundation gave us about $100,000 on condition that we raised an equivalent amount elsewhere, and that we agreed that designs for the new school should be made for us by the Greek architectural firm of Doxiades. We accepted the challenge, of course, and on my visit to Lebanon in 1958 I went to call on the American Ambassador in Beirut, Robert McClintock, to find out if there was any possibility of help there. He told me that there were PL480 funds available from the sale of wheat to Lebanon, and that if the Lebanese Government agreed there would be no objection on his part to giving us the money we needed. At that time the Prime Minister was Saeb Salam, and the Minister of Education Kamal Joumblatt, and as both were old family and personal friends, they readily agreed. So the new school was built, with ten buildings including a boarding section. Unlike most other schools in the country which have been built at different times and haphazardly, the Marjayoun National College has an architectural unity and a simplicity of design which makes it the outstanding school complex in rural Lebanon. At the inauguration of the new buildings, presided over by Saeb Salam, who has consistently supported it, I was unable to be present, but the school has continued to be one of my major interests and attachments to the town and area of Marjayoun, and a responsibility which I feel I have inherited from my father.

Commuting as we frequently did between our new rented house in Beirut and the family home in Marjayoun, my wife and I were able to follow step by step in the early seventies Lebanon's slow but sure progression to the crisis which broke in 1975. Beirut had grown and prospered, and attracted more and more foreign businesses who found its freedom and the presence of large resources of human skills an advantage not to be found in other Arab capitals, and the Arab population of Beirut also increased rapidly: Egyptians, Syrians, Iraqis, Palestinians, Kuwaitis, Saudis, flocked to the city in search of money or pleasure or freedom or all of them together. The character of Beirut changed, became less Lebanese and more cosmopolitan, and by 1974 more than 50 per cent of Lebanon's population were foreigners. From that increasing disequilibrium between the numbers of Lebanese and non-Lebanese, and from the growing disparity in wealth, opportunities and security between Beirut and south Lebanon was generated the explosion of 1975.

In Beirut, in whose newly-rich society Lebanese and Palestinians mixed and worked together, the Palestinian cause, which I had been one of the first to support years before, and in action not just in words, became an element in the city's social life. The attractive Leila Khaled, famous as the first Arab woman hijacker, was a favourite guest at ladies' tea-parties, and pretty society girls from 'good' Lebanese families, Christian and Muslim, could be seen making the round of cafés and restaurants soliciting money for *Fath* or the Popular Front for the Liberation of Palestine. And in the new hotels and nightclubs of Beirut, which equalled in sophistication and service those of any other country in the world, lavish parties, weddings, and other festivities were daily given and reported in the social columns of *Orient Le Jour*, a leading French-language newspaper, and in the weekly illustrated Arabic magazines which proliferated in Beirut.

But except for a few friends and visiting journalists whom we were able to persuade to visit us on weekends in Marjayoun, no one, and least of all government ministers and other important personalities, ever came to see what was happening in the south. And yet it was from there that the fabric of the Lebanese state, and of Lebanese society, was being undermined, as the towns and villages became increasingly the scene on which the Palestinian-Israeli drama was being played out. Forced out of Jordan, the Palestinian guerrilla or resistance movement concentrated their efforts in south Lebanon, where their proximity to the frontiers, and the nature of the terrain, with its deep valleys, wooded mountain slopes, and inaccessible ravines, provided an ideal base. The western slopes of Mount Hermon, in particular, known as 'the Arqoub',[2] became the favoured hideout of the 'fedayin'.

To the presence of the armed Palestinians' camps and bases in the south the Lebanese Government in 1969, partly under pressure from some Arab governments, and in particular that of Egypt, still presided over by President Nasser, and partly in the belief that the south in any case would one day be annexed by Israel, had given its sanction in a document commonly known as the Cairo Agreement. The Agreement was kept secret at the time, because its clauses were obviously controversial, and incompatible with Lebanese sovereignty: it permitted the Palestinians to maintain an armed presence in the Arqoub, though limited in numbers, to circulate throughout a wide area but only to pass through, and not maintain offices or bases in towns and villages. It was the same kind of agreement as the Algerians had made with the Tunisian Government in the early years of Tunisian independence when I had been in Tunis, but with a very great difference: whereas the Tunisian Government under Habib Bourguiba's leadership had been able to control the Algerians when they attempted to ignore or override the sovereignty of the Tunisian state – and Bourguiba had not hesitated to imprison Boumedienne himself when that happened – the Lebanese Government, then presided over by the deplorable Charles Helou, later by the disastrous Suleiman Frangiyyeh,[3] made no serious efforts to control the Palestinians, although it had at that time in the Lebanese army an instrument perfectly capable of doing so. It was in a clash between a group of armed Palestinians and a patrol of the Lebanese army that a Lebanese officer, Saad Haddad, who was attempting to implement the Cairo Agreement, was seriously wounded.

The Cairo Agreement had two major consequences. Firstly, it was in clear contradiction to the Armistice Agreements signed between Lebanon and Israel in 1949, which placed on both parties the obligation to prevent their territory from being used to mount attacks on each other: the whole purpose of the Cairo Agreement was to permit the Palestinians to mount such attacks. Thus it gave Israel a valid excuse to undertake reprisals against the Palestinians on Lebanese territory, in which the lives and properties of the Lebanese civilians in the areas where the Palestinians operated became increasingly the victims.

These reprisals were often visible from the balcony of our house in Marjayoun. When we heard the whish of the Israeli planes as they flew over the town we would rush out to see them dive and release their bombs, and try to guess what targets they had hit as we saw the flash and a few seconds later heard the explosion. With the regularity of a clock the Israeli reconnaissance plane MK would circle around, popularly called *Um Kemal*.[4] More dramatic were the occasions – three or four in number – when we watched the long lines of Israeli tanks and trucks as they wound round the foothills of Mount Hermon on some retaliatory raid inside Lebanese territory. On one such occasion, on Easter Day in 1974, we were sitting on our balcony eating a traditional Easter lunch with John Cooley, an American journalist and friend from Tunisian days, and watching the planes above and the invading forces in the distance.

Accustomed as we became to these frequent aerial raids, we did not at first pay much attention to the low-flying planes which came over our heads on 3 October 1973, and it was only when we came out onto the balcony that we realized that something unusual was happening: the planes were black, and clearly not Israeli, and they were flying into Israel at a low altitude. We thought it strange, but it was only when we turned on the radio that we realized that Egypt had attacked Israel, and that these were Syrian planes making their first incursions into Israeli territory. We watched the fierce battles which followed in the sky of Lebanon and in the distance above Mount Hermon and Jaulan, and the first use by the Syrians of the 'Sam' missiles which brought down many Israeli planes, one of which fell on the town of Khiam in front of us while we watched its two pilots float slowly down on their parachutes to earth.

The second consequence of the Cairo Agreement was to give the Palestinian resistance movement a clear target within Lebanon. The Lebanese army was responsible for the implementation of the Agreement, and from the point of view of the Palestinians became the principal barrier to the freedom they sought to enjoy on Lebanese territory. To weaken the army to a point where it could no longer effectively control them became the objective of the Palestinians. The cohesion of the Lebanese army depended upon a political agreement between Christians and Muslims to give their loyalty only to

Lebanon, but the Palestinians presented their cause as an Arab cause demanding sacrifices from everyone. Many Muslim Lebanese were sensitive to this demand, and some of their leaders saw an opportunity to increase their share of political power. The Lebanese army was increasingly portrayed in the propaganda of the Palestinians and their Lebanese sympathizers as the army of the Christians, while their guerrilla forces were portrayed as the army of the Muslims. This polarization of the Lebanese population paralysed the army, and led to its fragmentation. It was in south Lebanon, and in Marjayoun, that these consequences of the Cairo Agreement were first and most clearly revealed, and it was in the south that a confrontation between Lebanese and Palestinians sparked off the conflagration in 1975.

Curiously enough the occasion for this first confrontation was provided by one of my cousins from Marjayoun. He and a partner had conceived the idea of improving the fishing industry in Lebanon by introducing more modern techniques such as the use of deep-sea trawlers and a better system of distribution to enable the fishermen, a traditionally impoverished class, to earn a larger share of the profits being made by the middlemen. A company with the name 'Protein' was formed, and ex-President Chamoun became its president. But the fishermen themselves did not like the idea: they believed it would interfere with their traditional methods which included the use of dynamite. In the city of Saida in south Lebanon where political tension was high, fanned by some leaders and parties seeking to exploit the impact of the Palestinian-Israeli conflict on the population, a demonstration against Protein led to a clash with the Lebanese army in which a prominent Arab nationalist leader, Marouf Saad, was shot and killed. The battles which followed between the Lebanese army and radical pro-Palestinian and pan-Arab organizations were the opening shots in the war which was about to begin.

While the Palestinian resistance movement had been building up its strength in Lebanon, and sapping the foundations of the Lebanese army and the authority of the Lebanese state, there were Lebanese parties and individuals who saw what was happening and prepared themselves for the confrontation which they believed to be inevitable. Among these the most important were the Kataeb Party led by Pierre Gemayal and the National Liberal Party led by former President Camille Chamoun. Although in the past the two leaders had differed on many issues, they were agreed on one: that Lebanon was in danger, that the danger came from the alliance of the Palestinian resistance movement with Lebanese parties seeking to subvert the state or to destroy it altogether, and that it was their national duty to take on themselves the responsibility for the defence of the country which the Government was unable or unwilling to do. They formed para-military organizations and prepared for battle.

When that battle began in April 1975 Beirut became the scene of violent exchanges of bombardments between its east and west sections by day and night. As the violence of the combats increased, the authority of the state diminished: while in east Beirut the two Lebanese parties assured a reasonable degree of security, chaos grew in the west where we lived. In addition to the danger of the shells which fell like rain on our quarter, murder, robbery and the occupation of our houses were the daily dangers which we and our fellow citizens faced. From this increasingly intolerable situation my wife and I took frequent refuge in Marjayoun where in 1975 a relatively peaceful situation still prevailed.

But by the beginning of 1976 life in Marjayoun was also becoming more precarious, as the many organizations which made up the Palestine Liberation Organization began to infiltrate into the town and to set up the offices and bases there and in the surrounding towns, villages, and countryside which under the Cairo Agreement they had no right to do. Daily we saw new evidence of this deterioration of security: houses would be occupied, either by the sixteen Palestinian organizations which finally established themselves in the town, or by members of the local radical parties allied to the Palestinians; individuals would be kidnapped for one reason or another; small children of ten or twelve years from nearby villages, induced by the monthly wages they were paid by 'the resistance', carried guns. Though I did not feel personally threatened, I could feel how the daily diminution of the authority of the state, as represented by the army still in its garrison, and by the small numbers of the gendarmerie, was leading to a daily diminution of security, and must eventually lead to a trial of strength between Lebanese and Palestinians.

That trial of strength came in June 1976. A dissident officer of the Lebanese army stationed at the barracks in Marjayoun, Ahmed Khatib, left the town, went down into the valley of the Hasbani river not far away, and from there, with the support and encouragement of the Syrian regime, and with help from the Palestinians in the area, formed the 'Arab Lebanese army', and laid siege to the army in its garrison. A few days later the army surrendered in circumstances still not clear, and the barracks were occupied by the 'Arab Lebanese army' and some Palestinians and their local allies from Marjayoun. Although the Lebanese officer in command of the barracks fled north, a small group of Lebanese soldiers, mainly from the neighbouring village of Qleia, left with their small arms and a few armoured cars and entrenched themselves in their village. Harassed, blockaded and bombarded, they held their ground, and appealed to the Israelis across the border for help, which they received.

At the time this happened I was in Beirut, but I returned in mid-summer to find a disturbing deterioration in the situation in Marjayoun, precipitated by two events which left a deep impression on me and the whole town. The first was the murder of a member of one of the prominent families, a chauffeur in whose taxi I had often ridden, and who had no political activities or views. Michel Dabague, a cousin of the famous Dr Debakey from Houston,[5] had a son who suffered from leukemia. As the road to Beirut was extremely unsafe, particularly for the chauffeurs of Marjayoun, he had taken him to Israel to get the blood transfusions he needed. One night armed men entered the house and shot him dead for his 'crime' in visiting Israel. The second event was far more serious. A small Christian village not far from Marjayoun, and with whom the people of the town and of Qleia had close relations, was occupied by elements of the Palestinian armed groups, and almost one hundred of its inhabitants were massacred, its houses looted and burnt, its church desecrated. The massacre at Ayshia, hardly reported by the Western press, was one in the long chain of massacres, murders, and desecration of churches which sullied the name of the Palestinian resistance movement among the Lebanese people, though not apparently among the Western media men who shut their eyes to what they did not wish to see.

It was these events which decided the Lebanese soldiers in Qleia to try to reverse the situation in Marjayoun. They attacked the barracks, and after a brief battle took it, and put to flight the Palestinians and their allies in the town, who took up new positions in the neighbouring village of Blat. Two days later I returned again to the town from Beirut. The transformation was remarkable: the reign of terror of the last few months was over, and the people of Qleia and Marjayoun were reunited. From that union were to come results important not only for the area, but for the whole of Lebanon.

The entry of the Syrian army into Lebanon in June 1976 ended, for a time at least, the trials of Beirut. The city began to breathe again, many who had left for other countries returned, and it was possible to believe that life was returning to normal. But in the south, and in the Marjayoun area in particular, the situation became worse, not better. The authority of the Lebanese state no longer ran, and a 'red line' established by mutual agreement between the Syrians and the Israelis left all the area around the town of Nabatieh under the control of the Palestinians, except for a thin sliver of land along the frontier with Israel where a few villages, mainly Christian, had banded together with Qleia and Marjayoun to defend themselves. In August 1976 the President of Lebanon, Suleiman Frangiyyeh, ordered an officer of the Lebanese army still loyal to the state to go to the area and to hold it for Lebanon until the authority of the Lebanese state should be restored. That officer was Major Saad Haddad, known to his fellow officers for his courage and patriotism, which had led him to resist not only Palestinian violations of the Cairo Agreement, but also Israeli incursions into Lebanese territory.

Then began the long siege of Marjayoun and the areas under the authority of Haddad. Of that siege the story still remains to be told. I myself witnessed at first hand only part of it, for between the end of 1976 and the spring of 1977 I did not venture into that territory, besieged as it was on all sides, and only accessible from one road controlled by various organizations belonging to the 'common forces' now established between the Palestinians and their radical Lebanese allies. When I did eventually brave the blockade and arrived, though not without an unpleasant incident, in Marjayoun, it was to a hail of bullets which forced me to take cover behind a low wall. I vividly remember the astonishment with which my sudden arrival in the town was greeted by its people, who had come to believe that they had been completely forgotten and abandoned by their relatives in Beirut. My own astonishment at the situation I found was just as great. The whole town was an armed camp: on its narrow and torn-up streets rickety tanks and armoured cars rushed up and down manned by the young people of Marjayoun. The inhabitants of Jedeidet had not been known in the area for their warlike qualities: to the people of the neighbouring towns and villages they were a subject of jokes, and it was believed that one or two men from Hasbaya could dominate the market-place. Now this was all a thing of the past: every able-bodied man carried arms, and manned the few guns which defended the town, while the less fit did duty as nightwatchmen, for infiltrators were always feared from the Palestinian lines only a few kilometres distant.

I saw for myself the perils to which the people were daily exposed. To the east, my mother's erstwhile peaceful village, Ibl as-Saqi, where I used to go, in happier times, to escape from the importunities of visitors in Jedeidet, and to breakfast and dine with relatives and friends, had been transformed, along with the larger town of Khiam, into armed fortresses from where the 'common forces' bombarded, not Israeli territory, but Marjayoun. There were no shelters in the town, and only the fact that its houses were not built close to each other, and that the aim of the gunners was erratic, saved it from very serious damage, though many houses, including our own, were hit, and several citizens killed and wounded. The danger came not only from the east, but also from the west and north, for except for the road which led into Israel, the town was completely surrounded.

It was this complete blockade of Marjayoun and Qleia in 1977 which forced the inhabitants, civilian and armed, to turn to Israel for help. At one point there was almost no food left, and the water supply had been cut off by the 'common forces' which controlled its source. The small hospital had no medical supplies, and there was no possibility of taking the seriously wounded or sick to Saida or Beirut. It was Israel which saved the situation: food was sent in, water was pumped in through a new pipeline, and the sick and wounded were taken to hospitals in Israel where they received medical care completely free of charge.

Thus of the transformation of Israel from 'enemy' into 'friend', and of the Palestinians from 'brothers' into 'enemy' in the minds of the people of Marjayoun and the whole area under the command of Major Haddad, I was the witness. That this situation might have serious consequences for the future of south Lebanon and for Lebanon as a whole, if Beirut and what remained of the Lebanese state continued to ignore the problem of the south, or to surrender it in their minds to Israel, believing what every prophet of gloom and every anti-Israeli journalist predicted would be its final fate, I was fearful, and I made a number of attempts to influence the various participants in the drama to do something about it.

The first attempt was in early 1977, when the new President of Lebanon, Elias Sarkis, still enjoyed considerable support from the Syrian forces in the country and the contingents from certain Arab armies which had joined them, and from the Lebanese population who hoped that he would use his authority to end their trials. I asked for an appointment with the President and was received graciously and simply, for he was a man without pretensions or pompousness, and proceeded to give him a detailed account of the situation in Marjayoun, and to suggest, if not a final solution, at least a palliative: unless there was at least one road connecting the area to Beirut, it would become completely dependent upon Israel. The authority of the Lebanese state was represented in the nearby town of Hasbaya by the presence of security forces or 'gendarmerie', and between Hasbaya and Beirut there was a route not completely controlled by the Palestinians. I therefore requested him to send Lebanese security forces into Marjayoun, and to keep the Hasbaya-Marjayoun road open. His answer was a frank refusal: he could not put the security forces at risk, they might be fired upon! I pointed out that this was a risk which was inherent in their functions, and that the alternative was impotence. But he was adamant, and I realized that he was invoking the same arguments which had been used by Rashid Karamé in 1976, when he had been Prime Minister, to justify his refusal to use the army – a refusal which led to its disintegration and the collapse of the Lebanese state.

I realized too that President Sarkis, though he had wanted desperately to become President, did not have the will to exercise his powers, and I foresaw all the tragic consequences which were later to follow from his renunciation of power. Though I did not ask to see him again, I did try, a little later, to arrange an appointment for the mayor of Marjayoun and for the Greek Catholic bishop who, alone of the spiritual leaders of the area, had remained among his flock, and became the servant of the whole community, Christian and Muslim alike, but here again the President's response was negative: there was nothing he could do, I was told, so there was no point in his receiving them. At a time when no representatives of the Lebanese state were present in the town, his refusal to receive the two leaders of the community – the mayor, who in the absence of any official of the Ministry of the Interior represented the highest civil authority, and the bishop, the spiritual head of the whole community of Marjayoun – symbolized for me the total abdication of the President.

Having failed to move President Sarkis, there remained two other parties to whom I felt I should appeal: the Syrian Government and its fellow member in the 'Arab Deterrent Force' which the Arab League had asked to intervene in Lebanon in the autumn of 1976 – the Government of the United Arab Emirates – and the Palestinians themselves. To the Syrian and UAE governments I sent, in June 1977, through friends close to the two Presidents of those states, an almost identical memorandum in which I pointed out in detail the dangers of the continuation of the situation in the south: as a result of the blockade of the two major roads leading to

Marjayoun and the Arqoub area, 'the only source of supplies of food, fuel, employment, hospital and medical treatment, and recently in Marjayoun even of water, is Israel. It is only natural that the Lebanese civil population who have been placed, independently of their will, in a position of almost total dependence upon Israel, should compare and contrast the assistance they are receiving from Israel with the harm they are receiving from the Palestinians, and with the total absence of the Lebanese state.' In the name of the inhabitants of the Marjayoun and Arqoub towns and villages, I requested both governments to use their influence with the Palestinian leaders to persuade them to impose greater discipline on their armed elements, and to refrain from actions which would provide Israel with a pretext to invade the south. I received an assurance from my friend who had transmitted the memorandum to President Assad that it had been read and considered, and that the agreement made at Chtaura in August 1977 between the Lebanese Government and the Palestinians under Syrian auspices took into consideration the points I had made. But the Chtaura Agreement, like all the others concluded with the Palestinian leadership, was never implemented.

My appeal to the two governments was made after a meeting I had held with one of the Palestinian leaders in Beirut in which I tried to convince him that what was happening in the south, and particularly in the town of Marjayoun, was not in their interest. This meeting took place not long after the first visit I had made to the south in early spring 1977 which I have described earlier on. Together with the mayor of Marjayoun, I went to see Abu Iyad, who in the hierarchy of *Fath* occupied the second place after its chairman Yasser Arafat. He received us in his dressing-gown in the modest bedroom he was then occupying near to the headquarters of the PLO. After describing the situation in Marjayoun the mayor asked him a question: why is it that whenever your forces in Khiam or Ibl as-Saqi are attacked by the Israelis you reply by bombarding Marjayoun? Abu Iyad's reply was startling in its frankness: 'We cannot fight Israel, but we can fight Saad Haddad.' I saw in a flash of intuition the whole logic of the PLO's behaviour in the south: by equating Major Haddad and his tiny army of local militiamen, recruited from the townspeople and villagers, with Israel, the Palestinian leadership could convince their followers, and the Arab governments and Arab public opinion from which they derived their political and material strength, that they were engaged in a serious war against Israel, whereas in reality they were only fighting Saad Haddad. The fact that they had created the conditions in which Haddad had emerged as the protector of the frontier zone had to be concealed, and for that purpose the myth was propagated that he was an instrument of the Israelis who, according to the purveyors of the myth, had always coveted south Lebanon, and intended annexing it one day. This interpretation of the role of Saad Haddad, which had its origins in the situation in Marjayoun which I have described, and in the Palestinian leadership's justification for their own devious behaviour, came to be accepted as truth by most of the journalists reporting the war in Lebanon from the bar of the Commodore Hotel in Beirut, by the American Embassy in Beirut which convinced the State Department and the White House that Haddad was an Israeli stooge, and even by the representative of the Lebanese Government to the United Nations. The serious consequences of this misrepresentation of the role and character of Saad Haddad, and of the failure to understand the circumstances in which he had acquired that role, I shall later on describe.

Our meeting with Abu Iyad led to no practical result, but I did not yet despair of finding among the leaders of the PLO some understanding and appreciation of the situation which they were creating, and of the dangers it involved for themselves. The summer of 1977 brought increasing violence in the Marjayoun area, as I experienced when my visits there became more frequent and my concern and feelings of involvement grew. An additional trial for the people of the town was the destruction of the artesian well from which they derived their water, and the sniping to which their women and children, forced to use the small springs and sources which are still to be found nearby, were daily subjected. I learnt myself what it meant to be deprived of both electricity and water in a hot summer, and to go to bed not knowing if I would survive the night, for I had no shelter in our house, and rashly refused to leave the bedroom in which I had always slept. In September 1977 I decided to make one last effort to convince the Palestinian leadership that they were heading for disaster, and carrying us with them. I prepared a memorandum, and, in company with the mayor, the bishop, and a professor friend from the American University of Beirut known to everyone for his medical and personal services to the people of the south and to the Palestinians themselves, presented it to Abu Jihad, overall military commander of the Palestinian armed forces. In the memorandum I reminded the Palestinian leaders that 'in the period when the Palestinian resistance movement was in Marjayoun they were extremely well received by the inhabitants, and met with no opposition, and there are old and well-established links between Palestine and the people of Marjayoun, many of whom worked or had property there, and some of whom have been prominent in the defence of the Palestinian cause. In spite of all this, the town and its inhabitants are suffering a blockade and bombardments which have actually increased since the Chtaura agreements were reached in August.' As a consequence of this situation Israel was supplying food, water, medical treatment, and fuel, and I stated clearly and frankly that there was 'an ever-increasing build-up of sympathy and gratitude towards the Israelis on the part of the inhabitants, and conversely an ever-mounting wave of feeling of hostility towards the Palestinians'. In order to put an end to 'this deplorable situation' I made a number of proposals: the main tap controlling the flow of water from Mount Hermon to the area which was being kept shut by the Palestinians should be opened; at least one road to Beirut should be opened to permit the sick and wounded to go there for treatment; and an immediate cease-fire should be proclaimed which would enable the population to resume a normal life, send their children to school, and earn their living. In order to consolidate the cease-fire, and to deal with any breaches in it, I suggested that contacts could take place between the Palestinians and the Lebanese forces in the village of Dibbin which lay between Jedeidet and Blat, and which had managed to preserve a precarious neutrality throughout the years of war.

My suggestion for a cease-fire, and for meetings between representatives of the opposing forces was well received by Abu Jihad, who impressed me as a serious and straightforward man, single-minded in his belief in the validity of the military option, but not devious. He gave us the assurance that he would give instructions that contacts with the local Lebanese forces in Marjayoun would be accepted at any time and in any place, and also promised that something would be done to restore the supply of water. I did not feel, however, that Abu Jihad's positive and even friendly reaction was shared by the Palestinian military commander in the south, Abu Walid, a tall and sullen figure who attended our meeting. But again, nothing came out of our meeting. A few days later there was renewed fighting, and Shraiké, a strategic strongpoint held by the 'common forces' between Khiam and Ibl as-Saqi, was captured by a handful of young men from Jedeidet, none of them professional soldiers, thus seriously hampering the military and logistic activities of the Palestinians in the area.

The failure of my initiatives, which were entirely personal and not made at the instigation of anyone, convinced me that an Israeli invasion, or at any rate incursion into the south, was inevitable. It came in the spring of 1978, and it eliminated the Palestinian presence in all the area east of Marjayoun, and thus relieved considerably, although not totally, the town's security. It was not surprising that to the beleaguered people of Marjayoun and to their neighbours the Israelis came, not as invaders or conquerors, but as liberators. That was a feeling only to be understood – and eventually shared – by the inhabitants of Beirut in the summer of 1982: but to the Government of Lebanon in 1978, still cowering under the shadow of the Syrian presence and the increasing hold of the Palestinians on the capital, it was an unacceptable and inexplicable phenomenon which it tried to wish away, and in the effort the Government became grounded in a futile policy of trying to 'liberate' south Lebanon before it controlled Beirut. To the Lebanese Government the 'liberation' of south Lebanon meant the elimination of Saad Haddad and his men, who had fulfilled the mission entrusted to them by President

Frangiyyeh, and whose only 'crime' was to have prevented the occupation of their towns and villages by the 'common forces' of the Palestinians and their Lebanese allies, and the massive reprisals and destruction by Israel which would inevitably have followed. In this attitude they were unfortunately actively encouraged by the American Embassy in Beirut, which knew little if anything of the real situation in the south, and was guided, in part at least, by its concern to maintain a discreet connection with the PLO under whose protection it believed it lived.[6]

That the Israeli invasion in the spring of 1978 did not solve the problem of south Lebanon, caught as it was in the middle of the Palestinian and Israeli conflict, was due to a number of factors. One was the pressure of Washington on the Israelis to withdraw as quickly as possible; another was the intervention of a United Nations peace-keeping force. Following discussions in the Security Council in 1978, resolution 425 set up an international force under the direct orders of the Secretary-General of the United Nations, Dr Waldheim, with the mission of assisting the Lebanese Government to extend its sovereignty over all of Lebanon, and in particular of the south. I personally welcomed the resolution, and in a memorandum which I presented to the Foreign Minister, Fuad Boutros, I pointed out that the invasion of the south by the Israelis achieved what the Lebanese state had been unable to do by itself, and had at the same time created an international situation in which Israel received more blame than credit, and Lebanon won international political support.

The United Nations peace-keeping force in Lebanon – UNIFIL – was the brainchild of three friends of mine: Ghassan Tueni, representative of Lebanon at the United Nations; Brian Urquhart, Assistant Secretary-General of the United Nations; and Richard Parker, American Ambassador to Lebanon. Though I saw some merit in the idea of introducing the international organization into the Lebanese scene, I disagreed with increasing vehemence with the way it was interpreted and implemented on the ground, and the heart of my disagreement centred on the attitude of UNIFIL to the area controlled by Major Haddad at the request of the Lebanese state.

When the time came for the Israelis to withdraw from Lebanon, they handed over to UNIFIL the areas they had occupied since their invasion, but maintained Haddad's authority and forces in the area he already controlled before they had entered Lebanon. The Lebanese and American governments and the UN secretariat saw this as sabotage of their brainchild, and in a series of debates in the Security Council, one of which I attended in 1979, Haddad was repeatedly and savagely attacked by every delegation, including that of Lebanon, with the exception of the Israelis. The attitude of the delegates who attacked Haddad and Israel coincided with that of the Palestinians, who wanted him removed, not because he was an obstacle to peace or to the restoration of Lebanese sovereignty, but because he stood in the way of their own implantation on the frontiers with Israel. And the identification of Ghassan Tueni with the point of view of the Palestinians and of the Arab members of the Security Council was a measure of the degree to which the Arabs had succeeded in dominating the climate of the United Nations, and of the failure of the Lebanese regime to separate its cause from that of the Palestinians. This failure was very largely due to the attitude of the Lebanese Prime Minister, Dr Selim Hoss, a man who, out of hostility to the Kataeb Party and a deep-rooted dislike of the Maronite community, came to identify himself more and more with the aims and policies of the so-called Lebanese 'national movement',[7] and had become obsessed with the question of Saad Haddad.

In Beirut, New York and Washington, which I visited in 1979 and 1980, I argued with my American, British, Lebanese and Palestinian friends in a position of influence that they were making a mistake by refusing to look at the situation in south Lebanon realistically or objectively: that the elimination of Haddad and his enclave which they were so insistently demanding would not solve the problem of the south and might aggravate it, since UNIFIL would not be able to prevent the infiltration of the Palestinians and their Lebanese allies into the areas it had taken over, and the dangers of annexation by Israel would be increased; and that therefore the presence of Haddad and his forces, and the existence of the 'Free

Lebanon'[8] which he had proclaimed in the summer of 1978, were the best – and indeed the only – guarantee that Lebanese sovereignty in the area would be safeguarded. My arguments were not successful. Under the pressure of the Palestinians, the Syrians, and some Arab governments whose representatives met with the Lebanese Prime Minister at Beiteddin in October 1978, Haddad was severed from the Lebanese army and the pay of himself and his soldiers stopped, with the predictable result that they became completely dependent on Israel's support, and a strange situation was created in which the Israelis found themselves defending the interests of Lebanon against the wishes of the Lebanese Government!

As I had foreseen, the presence of UNIFIL in south Lebanon did not solve any problems although it created new ones. It did not establish a safe line of communication with Beirut, and was not even allowed by the Lebanese Government to establish its headquarters in the southern city of Saida, so that while logistically it depended for supplies on Israel, it became increasingly dependent for its functioning on the degree of good relations it could maintain with the PLO, who had managed to preserve their headquarters in Saida and Tyre. Instead of helping the Lebanese state to extend its sovereignty over south Lebanon it became the instrument whereby the PLO maintained its control over large areas of the south, and was able to reintroduce the long-range artillery and other armaments they had lost to the Israelis in the spring of 1978. From the dominating site of Beaufort Castle and other positions they held not far from Marjayoun they were able to recommence their harassment of the town and of the towns and settlements of northern Galilee. Thus the ground was prepared for the Israeli invasion of June 1982 by the misguided faith of the Lebanese Government in the United Nations and its unthinking alignment with the policies of the Palestinians. But the Lebanese Government did not blame the impotence of UNIFIL on itself or the Palestinians, but only on the Israelis and Haddad because he refused to allow the international force to take over the area which he and his men had saved for Lebanon and where UNIFIL's presence was not necessary. Thus in addition to being the target of the Palestinians Haddad became the target of his own government, of the Arab governments, of the Western powers led by the American and British governments, and of the Communist bloc. All these governments, who paid lip-service to Lebanese sovereignty and territorial integrity, succeeded only in encouraging the Lebanese Government to waste its time and efforts on the problem of south Lebanon which it identified with the problem of Major Haddad, to the exclusion of its real problem, which was the usurpation of Lebanese sovereignty in the south by the Palestinians, and the transformation of the 'Arab Deterrent Force', created by the Arab League to restore the Lebanese state, into a Syrian army of occupation.

In the aftermath of the Israeli invasion I was able to see for myself the situation in the areas taken over by UNIFIL and in Major Haddad's enclave of Free Lebanon, as I resumed my frequent visits to Marjayoun. The elimination of the Palestinian bases in the Arqoub area to the east relieved the town from the bombardments to which it had been previously subjected: I could now sleep safely but not comfortably in our battered house whose stone façade will always display the marks of the shells and shrapnel it received. I decided we must reopen the National College, closed since 1976 and badly damaged, but the doors and glass windows and roofs we repaired at considerable expense were soon shattered when the bombardment of the town began again from the Palestinian guns in Beaufort Castle. Situated next to the army barracks at the top of the town, our school was an easy target, and we were obliged to move our classes down to the abandoned government *sérail*, in whose underground prison we held our kindergarten classes. From 1978 until 1982 our teachers and principal, Maurice Dabague, shivered with their students through four winters in the unheated classrooms, without any of the normal facilities of a school, but no journalists or representatives of the Government in Beirut came to see us or to write about our plight. Only the Israelis came to ask what we needed, and in the absence of any Lebanese doctors except one aged general practitioner it was Israeli doctors and surgeons who provided medical services in the town's small hospital.

Difficult as life still was, the town of Marjayoun had been saved from major physical damage, but in the nearby village of my mother's family, Ibl as-Saqi, the situation was very different. I went to visit it shortly after the Palestinians and their Lebanese allies had fled, and the signs of their passage and of the Israeli bombardments were too painfully evident. Gone were the pretty red-tiled roofs of its charming houses, of my grandfather's house there remained only the walls, but the greatest shock awaited me in the three churches in the village – Protestant, Orthodox and Catholic. Their roofs were shattered, and on their floors and walls could be seen the legacy the 'common forces' had left behind: excrement, broken pieces of marble and ecclesiastical furnishings, crude political slogans and symbols on the walls, some in Arabic, others in Turkish, German and French – proof, if any were now needed, that among the Palestinians and their Lebanese allies there had been adventurers, mercenaries, and terrorists from many countries. What spirit of evil, what hatred of Lebanon, what anti-Christian fanaticism there must have smouldered in those 'progressist' hearts I could not fathom or understand. Now the Norwegian contingent of UNIFIL were setting up their headquarters in the village, repairing the least damaged houses to live in, and basking in their shorts beneath the summer sun. Little by little, as the villagers began to trickle back and to repair what could be saved of their houses, the character of the village changed; it was now more profitable, and less hard work, to supply the needs of the Norwegians than to cultivate the land: bars, restaurants, wayside stands selling beer and whisky sprang up along the village's main roads where formerly there strolled old men and young boys talking of things long past and still to come.

In the neighbouring town of Khiam the situation was far worse, for there not one human being remained after the Israeli invasion. When it had been occupied by the 'common forces' of Palestinians and their allies only a few old people had remained, but now they were gone, and no living creature – not even a cat or a dog – was to be seen, and in the town's two churches the same desecration as in Ibl told of the passage of the uninvited 'guests'.

Here, in the contrast between the condition of Marjayoun, damaged but still standing and still inhabited by its people, was to be seen – if anyone from Beirut or the world outside had come to see – the justification of Saad Haddad and the men of Free Lebanon who had banded together to save their villages and homes, for had they not done so, and allowed the Palestinians and their allies to remain, they would have suffered the same fate as Ibl and Khiam. Forced to choose between protection by the Israelis and occupation by the Palestinians, could they be blamed because they had chosen the former? Would the destruction of Marjayoun and the other towns and villages of Free Lebanon have helped the Palestinians to regain their land, or brought them one inch nearer the statehood they legitimately demanded? These were questions I put to those who in Washington and New York, and in the bar of the Commodore Hotel in Beirut, had transferred to Saad Haddad the rancour they harboured against Israel. It was only in 1982, when Tyre and Saida and Beirut tasted for themselves the fires that had consumed Ibl and Khiam, and a hundred other towns and villages in south Lebanon, that what I had been saying since 1976 came to be believed. But had the Lebanese Government, the American Embassy in Beirut, the State Department, and the secretariat of the United Nations followed the logic of my ideas, Lebanon, and the Palestinians themselves, might have been spared the bitter summer of 1982.

Although the Israeli invasion in 1978 relieved the situation in Marjayoun, it did not make life easier in Beirut, or diminish the hazards of my journeys between the two: on the contrary, the roads became now more dangerous. To reach Marjayoun I had to make long detours, and the journey took five or six hours instead of the one and a half hours in normal times, and what one might meet on the road was never known. A variety of checkpoints were now installed, each one a law unto itself: some were Syrian, some Palestinian, some Iraqi, some the 'Arab Lebanese army' of Ahmed Khatib, but none were manned by representatives of the Lebanese state. On more than one occasion I was stopped and questioned, and though I went on the business of the school, Marjayoun, because of its association with Saad Haddad, had become an object of suspicion. To my family and friends I put on a brave show of indifference to the dangers which they rightly feared, but I admit that I never approached those checkpoints without a sinking feeling that this might be my 'final solution', for there were many precedents of innocent travellers kidnapped or killed. Once outside Beirut the writ of the Lebanese state no longer ran, and it was only when I saw the tattered flag of Lebanon flying at the border between the area controlled by UNIFIL and Free Lebanon that I felt safe.

Nor was the situation inside Beirut much better. There the roads which linked the two sides of the city had been dangerous for years, as snipers took their daily toll of lives. On more than one occasion I risked my life to visit friends in east Beirut, partly in response to some inner urge which tempts me towards dangers and risks, partly because I refused to accept that in the country I considered mine I could be denied the right to go where I pleased and to meet whom I wished. Though many of my friends were in west Beirut where I lived, there were others in east Beirut whom I wished to visit. Over there was 'the other side' of which in earlier days I had known so little, but which I had come to understand and appreciate for its resistance to the forces which sought to overwhelm it. Having lived through all the stages of Marjayoun's struggle to remain free, I could now better understand the efforts of the Lebanese Front to save Lebanon from destruction, and I came too to know and admire Bechir Gemayal, leader of the Lebanese Forces who represented to me, and to the Lebanese people at large, Lebanon's will to survive and to be free.

In the years between 1978 and 1982 I did indeed become increasingly convinced that the consolidation of the areas controlled by the Lebanese Forces under Bechir Gemayal and by the forces of Free Lebanon under Major Haddad represented the only hope of saving the country from a partition between Syria and Israel, and the subjugation of Beirut to a combination of Palestinian and radical Lebanese parties: the Lebanese state, with its President confined to his residence in Baabda, a suburb of the city, would have become for ever what it had been since 1976, a phantom. The outside world, including most of the governments of western Europe and the USA, was prepared to accept the virtual dissolution of Lebanon and its disappearance from the map of the world, although this would have meant an important extension of Soviet influence, acting through Syria, at the expense of Western interests. In the spring of 1981 serious fighting broke out between the Lebanese Forces and the Syrian army in and around the town of Zahle. At the request of Bechir Gemayal I went to Washington to find out whether there had been any real change in American attitudes towards Lebanon since the Reagan administration had taken over from President Carter's team, and to try to convince Washington that the liquidation of Lebanon was not in Western interests. I found a greater willingness to listen than I had met with from members of the previous administration, but there was still in the spring of 1981 no clear-cut American policy, still a timid acceptance of the status quo and a preference to react rather than to act. There seemed little that could be done except to hold on to the small areas of Lebanon which still remained free and hope for some miracle which might transform the situation.

I was aware that any such transformation could only come about at a high cost to the lives and property of both the Lebanese and the Palestinians in Lebanon. Too many mistakes had been made, too many opportunities lost, to make it possible for a peaceful solution to be found. That I was right in my judgement was proved by the Israeli invasion of Lebanon in June 1982. At the beginning of June I was in London, and from afar watched in anguish as the towns and villages of south Lebanon which I knew so well felt the full impact of the Israelis' assault. As their army approached Beirut I could not any longer bear to be away from my home and friends and relatives, and in early July returned by sea from Cyprus, and so saw for myself Beirut under siege and bombardment. Our house in Moussaitbeh I found had become a refuge for the families of our faithful cook and housekeeper Kerima, our friend for over thirty years, who throughout the siege maintained an iron discipline and order in the house among the thirty-five men, women and children of all ages who lived there. I myself slept in the comparative safety of east Beirut, visiting my own quarter when a lull in the bombardment permitted, and when I summoned up enough courage to cross on foot the mountains of sand and the many checkpoints which separated the two sections of the divided city along its one way of passage.

When the fighting ended, and the PLO left Beirut in August, it did seem that the miracle for which I and most other Lebanese had been waiting had happened. The youthful Bechir Gemayal, who symbolized Lebanon's will to resist and to survive, was elected President by the Deputies of Lebanon's Parliament, who represented the continuity of the country's democratic life. For twenty-three days the Lebanese people lived in a state of euphoria. The Christians rejoiced because their leader had become President, and the Muslims, many of whom had feared him, were won over by his enthusiasm and dynamism and by the vision he offered of a new Lebanon.

That dream of a new Lebanon, that hope for a new leadership, was shattered on 14 September when Bechir Gemayal and more than twenty of his colleagues were blown up in the Ashrafiyya quarter of Beirut. But the euphoria of those few days in which he had been President elect, in which he had electrified the country in a series of speeches and broadcasts, ensured the election by an unanimous vote of the Deputies of his brother Amin to take his place.

The new President benefited from the enthusiasm which his brother had generated and from the grief caused by his death: the Lebanese state began to emerge from the long night which had enveloped it. We could sleep once again in our houses without the sound of gunfire. Armed bands no longer roamed the streets by day or night. Public services began to function, the streets were cleaned of the accumulated garbage of seven years, and the centre of Beirut, largely destroyed, slowly began to come to life again through the public spirit and generosity of a remarkable Lebanese citizen, Rafiq Hariri. The winter of 1982 and the spring of 1983 seemed to herald the final return of peace to Lebanon. For the first time in many years I could envisage living a normal life and enjoying the simple pleasures which Lebanon so generously affords: visits to friends, weekends in the mountains, walks and reveries in their spectacular scenery.

It was in such an atmosphere of optimism and relaxation that I began to write this book, but as I come to finish it black clouds once again cover our sky. The story of how, in the space of a few months, the golden opportunity offered to Lebanon was lost must await another book. Was it a dream, or a mirage, or was that a real shore on the horizon, towards which we hopefully sailed? I do not know, and though my optimism and belief in the ultimate resurgence of Lebanon remain, it is clear that my odyssey has not yet ended.

Epilogue

The road from Manchester to Marjayoun has been a long one: it has taken me through many countries and many episodes. I have been involved in many causes and many problems, and a large part of my life has been turbulent and troubled.[1] But on this road, while many illusions have been shed, I have also made many discoveries about myself, about the societies in which I have lived, and where I belong. My experiences in Lebanon in the last decade helped me to discover that at heart I am a Lebanese patriot, attached to a land, a landscape, a way of life, and a state which, though weakened by the events I have described, still promises to safeguard the traditional values of Lebanese society and life.

It is a source of sadness and regret to me that my discovery of the strength of my attachment to Lebanon has come about largely because of the conflict which has opposed Lebanese and Palestinians, whose cause I had for so long believed in and actively supported. I had always had doubts about the wisdom of the Arab League's decision in 1964 to create a Palestinian resistance movement which time has revealed to be the source not only of many of Lebanon's problems, but also of those of the Palestinians themselves. A resistance movement created by a political movement which has leaders and discipline can be used when necessary, and put aside when necessary. I had seen how Habib Bourguiba had created the 'fellagha' or guerrilla movement and unleashed a war on the French in Tunisia, but I had also seen how at the right moment he had ordered his men not only to lay down arms, but to hand them over to those they were fighting: how he had been able to impose his decision on those within his party and among the fighters who regarded it as treason; and how once independence had been won, very largely because he had demonstrated that he was a leader, and not being led, he repressed without hesitation those who still hankered after the gun with which they believed *they*, not he, had won that independence. But with the Palestinians the situation was the reverse: the resistance movement was created before there was a political movement to control it, so that the leaders of the guerrillas *became* the movement, and set themselves up as the sole legitimate representatives of the Palestinian people, thus preventing the emergence of a real political movement with responsible leaders. The Palestinian resistance movement was born not from the people who remained on Palestinian soil, but from those who had left it, and the midwife which brought it into this world was the Arab League, whose conflicts, rivalries, and impotence were mirrored in its own behaviour.

Of that behaviour both Lebanon and the Palestinian people were the victims. I have related my small efforts to convince the leaders of the Palestine Liberation Organization that they were making a mistake in alienating the sympathies of the Lebanese people among whom they were living, but they were too confident in their ability to manipulate the political scene in Beirut to listen, and they came to believe that they could take over Lebanon and afford to ignore the Lebanese. With time they became more callous, and did not care that the towns and villages of Lebanon were being destroyed: a phrase which I often heard from the lips of our Palestinian friends was that 'the world is ruined, let it be ruined more', and some of them believed that the more Israel expanded the nearer it would come to the collapse which they hoped would return them to their land as dramatically as they had left.

Thus my anger at the behaviour of the PLO was a double one. I was angry at the destruction they were causing in Lebanon, and the disruption of our lives which, had I believed it would lead anywhere, I might have accepted; and I was angry at the way their involvement in Lebanon's internal affairs was diverting them from their real objective of achieving statehood for their people. It was not difficult for me to predict the final outcome of their behaviour; the Israeli invasion in the summer of 1982, more destruction in the cities and towns of

Lebanon, the dislocation of the Palestinian leadership, and the abandonment of the Palestinians in the camps in Lebanon and on the soil of Palestine to what fate might hold in store for them. Like a ship without a navigator and a crew fighting among themselves, the Palestinian cause has been left to the mercy of the winds and the waves.

It was not difficult for me to see also that if Lebanon was to be saved its cause had to be separated from that of the Palestinians. Although I believe that the solution of the problem of the Palestinians will be of benefit to Lebanon, I do not see what Lebanon can now do to help them, except to demonstrate the advantages of negotiation over confrontation, and of peace over war. In that perspective I was not shocked by the agreements signed between the governments of Lebanon and Israel in May 1983, believing as do the majority of Lebanese that they were necessary. By ending the state of war between the two countries they make inevitable a state of peace, and although the full implications of peace may take some time to manifest themselves, I can only rejoice at the prospect, and hope that this will be one more step towards ending the conflict which has for thirty-five years diverted all the peoples of the Middle East from the pursuit of their genuine interests.

While I consider myself a Lebanese patriot, I do not feel superior to the Palestinians, Syrians, or other Arab peoples, nor, in spite of the damage they have done to Lebanon, do I hate them. Although I accept that we belong to the family of Arabic-speaking peoples, I do not believe we constitute one nation, or that our interests are necessarily identical with theirs. Some versions of Arab nationalism have made a conscious effort to distinguish it from Islam, but these efforts have not succeeded in persuading the Arab masses that their Arab identity is more important than their Islamic one, for while feelings of Arab solidarity show themselves from time to time when some particular political crisis stirs their indignation or enthusiasm, they live with their faith in their everyday existence and are conscious of it in every corner of their lives. The feeling of belonging to a people, a community (in Arabic the *umma*), is stronger than that of belonging to a nation, and it is to the *umma* of Islam that the loyalty of the Arab masses is given.

This identity between Arab and Muslim is incorporated into the constitutions of the Arab countries, but not of Lebanon. The Lebanese state came into existence in response to the wish of the Christian communities to have a country where they would not be a protected or tolerated minority, not live on sufferance but by right. In Lebanon all communities are minorities, and therefore none can be dominated by a majority: all are free to regulate their private lives and practices according to the laws and principles of their beliefs. Lebanon therefore can only live in freedom, and the condition of its existence is the agreement of all its communities to live together, and to owe loyalty only to the Lebanese state and its constitution. There have been times in recent years when this coexistence has been gravely threatened, and when it seemed possible that Lebanon as a state might disappear. Other loyalties have tempted some of its citizens – some to Arab, some to Islamic, some to Marxist causes – but the trials and tribulations through which the Lebanese people have gone have created a renewed commitment to the Lebanon we so nearly lost. That today some 'leaders' and groups have tried to profit from the international conflicts and rivalries which still dominate the region to re-assert their influence and to advance their private interests at the expense of the Lebanese people, does not change my belief that in the long run a national consensus will prevail.

So in spite of everything it is still on a note of optimism that I end this part of my story, and also of thankfulness that the two countries and societies to which I have had the good fortune to belong, England and Lebanon, have survived all attempts to overthrow the freedom which is the supreme value they share. I have lived through, and in a small way participated in, the struggles of both countries to remain free, and have come to reconcile in my mind what once seemed to be a conflict of identity and loyalty. What Englishmen and Lebanese have in common – their attachment to freedom, their spirit of initiative and self-reliance, their love of their country – seems to me more important than differences of culture, language or history. I feel no incompatibility between the heritage of East and West, but like all my fellow Lebanese I shall always cherish, wherever I may still wander, a special attachment to the land of my origin: a small but significant country, and, as its people call it, 'a mountain no wind can shake'.

يا جبل ما يهزّك ريح

Notes

Chapter I: A Manchester Childhood

1   A phrase I learnt from my orientalist friend Paul Kraus (see Chapter II).
2   El-Jedeidet, or simply Jedeidet, which means in Arabic 'the new (town)', is situated above a valley – Marjayoun – 'the valley of the springs', so called because of its many springs and rivulets: as el-Jedeidet is the administrative centre of the area, and was until recent times the largest town, it came to be identified with Marjayoun as a district. I have used Marjayoun as the name of both town and area throughout the book.
3   Mutannabi and Ma'ari are two famous classical Arab poets whose verses are still studied and quoted wherever the Arabic language is taught.
4   *Kibbé*, a mixture of meat and cracked wheat, eaten raw or cooked, could be called the national dish of Lebanon and Syria: *mujaddara*, a village dish from Lebanon, combines lentils and rice, or lentils and cracked wheat, to make a rich pottage.
5   Another uncle, Salam Racy, has collected and published the stories of his and other Lebanese villages in a popular series of books on the *Literature of the People* (Naufal Books, Beirut, 1970s).
6   Sherif Hussein Ibn Ali, head of the Hashemite family, governed the Hejaz under the Ottoman Empire, but declared the Arab Revolt in 1916, the first attempt in modern times to create an Arab state in the Near East. His son Faisal became King of Iraq in 1920, and another son, Abdullah, was Emir of Transjordan in 1921, then King of Jordan in 1946.
7   'Sherifian' is the adjective of 'Sherif', which indicates descent from the Prophet Mohammed, but in this case it refers to the Emir Zaid's status as a member of the Hashemite ruling family, who are descendants of the Prophet.
8   Saeb Salam, leading Muslim notable from Beirut, Minister and Prime Minister in many governments of independent Lebanon, of which he was one of the architects.
9   The Mufti of Jerusalem, Haj Amin al Husseini, was the leading opponent of British rule and Zionism in Palestine in the 1920s and 1930s: he went to Germany in 1941 and spent the rest of the war there, returned to Cairo, and eventually retired to Lebanon, where he died.
10   Gouin, who was Jewish, was imprisoned during the German occu-

pation of France, but survived to return to his beloved Royaumont.
11 Jean Wahl was also Jewish, was sent to Drancy during the German occupation, but returned after the war to resume his post at the Sorbonne and to find happiness in marriage.
12 Published by Geoffrey Bles, London, 1950.

Chapter II: Return to the Sources

1 In the mountains of Lebanon a venerable age is reached when a child can call to her grandmother 'grandmother, call your grandmother': several members of my father's family could boast of this status.
2 Wadi Teym, the Arqoub, and the district of Marjayoun are the foothills, the slopes and the valley on the western side of Mount Hermon. Together they form a geographical and human unity whose people – Christian, Muslim and Druze – have lived together for centuries.
3 Roman 'Africa' was the coastal land of today's North Africa between Algeria and Libya, including Tunisia.
4 The Arabic letter *qaf*, which corresponds to a guttural 'k' in the English alphabet, is commonly omitted in Lebanese colloquial speech, hence the peculiarity of its use in Jedeidet and Ibl. The Druze community, an offshoot of Islam, has had its headquarters since the twelfth century in the Wadi Teym area, and preserves in its speech, dress and social customs many vestiges of a distant past.
5 The first Protestant church – Presbyterian – was that of Hasbaya, founded in the early 1840s.
6 The invasion began on 1 August 1941.
7 *Ornament of Honour* (Cambridge University Press, 1937).

Chapter III: Discovery of America

1 The daughter of Ihsan Jabri and niece of Saadullah Jabri, both leaders in the Syrian nationalist cause: her father became the first and the only President of the Arab Union established in 1958 between Egypt, Syria and Yemen, and her uncle was independent Syria's first Prime Minister.
2 Faris Nimr Pasha, Lebanese writer and journalist, settled in Cairo after the British occupation of Egypt in the late nineteenth century, and through his Arabic newspaper *al Moqattam* achieved considerable influence.
3 George Antonius was a Lebanese who lived and worked for most of his life in Egypt and Palestine, and was influential in both British and Palestinian Arab circles. His book *The Arab Awakening*, published in London in 1938, is the most readable account of the origins and ideas of the Arab Revolt and its aftermath.
4 David Ben Gurion, first Prime Minister of the state of Israel, and one of its 'founding fathers'.

5 Moshe Shertok, a leading member of the Jewish Agency, first Foreign Minister of Israel, and Prime Minister: after 1948 he became Moshe Sharrett.
6 High officials in the State Department responsible for Near East affairs.
7 Sir Harold Beeley, scholar and writer on Arab affairs, entered the British Foreign Service after the Second World War, eventually becoming Ambassador in Cairo.
8 The valley of Huleh, consisting of a lake, marshland and also rich agricultural land, was taken from Lebanon and incorporated into northern Palestine through an agreement between the British and French mandatory authorities in 1923. Much of its land was owned by families from Marjayoun who in 1948 lost their properties but received neither compensation nor the status of refugees.
9 A dunam is the equivalent of one thousand square metres, thus there are four dunams to an acre.
10 See my article in the *Middle East Journal*, Washington, October 1951.

Chapter IV: Wars of the Middle East

1 *Middle East Journal*, October 1949.
2 Hussein Afnan, who died in 1941 and whom I never had the privilege of meeting, was Secretary to the Council of Ministers in Iraq in the early twenties, and later chargé d'affaires at the Court of St James's, London. Bedia Afnan was the daughter of Bedi Nuri, Ottoman Governor of Basra in Iraq, assassinated there by order of Taleb al Naqib; and the niece of Sateh al-Husri, government minister and high official in Ottoman Turkey, Syria, Iraq and the Arab League, writer, educator and 'father of secular Arab nationalism'. She represented Iraq for many years at the UN on the Fourth Committee, and was a member of the UN Committee on Human Rights in her individual capacity.
3 Maghrib and Mashriq are the terms which the Arabs use to describe the two wings of the Arab world: the Maghrib, 'where the sun goes down', is the West, i.e. North Africa from Morocco to Libya: and the Mashriq, 'where the sun rises', is the East, i.e. the Arabian peninsula. Egypt, in the middle, is just Egypt.
4 In recent times relations between the Tunisian Government and the PLO have become close, but as I was not involved with either Tunisia or the Palestinians in this period I have not given my views on the motives or the likely outcome of this *rapprochement*.
5 Wasfi Tal was assassinated in Cairo in 1971 by 'Black September', an offshoot of the PLO.
6 The 'Golan Heights' is the international press's term for the Jaulan, the district of Syria mentioned in Chapter II as the home of the Emir Faour and the Fadl tribe.
7 Leo d'Erlanger was the banker son of Baron Rudolf d'Erlanger, author of an authoritative study of classical Arabic music. In the Andalusian palace

built by Rudolf in Sidi Bou Said Leo and his wife Edwina entertained thousands of guests from the worlds of the arts, business and society.
8   Julius Fleischmann, whose family fortune came from a famous brand of yeast, vodka and other products, was a generous patron of the arts and culture in the USA and Europe.
9   For example, *A Middle East Reader*, edited by Irene Gendzier (Pegasus Press, New York, 1970) and *The Israel-Arab Reader*, Walter Lacquer (Bantam Books, New York, 1969).
10   'Mr Hourani's article raises the curtain on a new era in the contemporary discussion on the Israeli-Arab conflict' (Joel Carmichael, *Midstream*, New York, January 1968). 'To anyone familiar with the dangers and restraints which the Arab-Israel crisis has imposed on men in print, particularly in the Arab world, Hourani's article is a demonstration of great courage' (Irene Gendzier, *Midstream*, April 1968).
11   George Hakim was Professor of Economics at the American University of Beirut: he became Lebanon's Ambassador to the USA, and Foreign Minister of Lebanon.
12   Kemal Nasser, a Palestinian poet and political activist, was assassinated in Beirut by an Israeli commando group in 1973.

Chapter V: An Arab Leader: the Tunisian Experience

1   General Louis Spears was sent by Winston Churchill to represent the British Government with the Governments of Lebanon and Syria after the invasion of those two countries by British and Free French forces in 1941. From 'Spears' mission' in Beirut he played a decisive role in transforming the theoretical independence of Lebanon and Syria under France into a real one.
2   The friend, Si Slaheddin, is now the owner of an elegant and prosperous restaurant in Sidi Bou Said, 'Le Pirate'.
3   A plaque in the hotel, which has since changed hands, commemorates the visits of Habib Bourguiba.
4   Mohammed Masmoudi became a Minister in several Tunisian governments after independence, and as Foreign Minister was father of the aborted union between Tunisia and Libya signed and immediately buried in 1974.
5   Salah Ben Youssef had been a close colleague of Bourguiba, and at one time Secretary-General of the Neo-Destour Party. He quarrelled with Bourguiba on the issue of internal autonomy and turned into a bitter enemy of the newly independent regime.
6   A fascinating though fictional picture of the social, intellectual and political conditions of the Tunisian Jewish community between 1840 and 1956 is given in *Les Belles de Tunis* by Nina Moatti (Le Seuil, Paris, 1982).
7   Abulqassem Chabbi was Tunisia's most famous poet of the twentieth century: his essay on the poetic imagination is one of the most important contributions to modern Arabic literary criticism.
8   Sekou Touré and Léopold Senghor were the first Presidents of inde-

pendent Guinea and Senegal: the former was an intractable opponent of France, the latter a Francophile.
9 Ahmed Ben Salah was dismissed from the Tunisian Government in November 1969, tried and sentenced in March 1970 to ten years' hard labour. He eventually escaped from prison and went to Europe. Bahi Ladgham was removed from the office of Prime Minister in 1969.

Chapter VI: Hammamet: a Cultural Adventure

1 Denis de Rougemont, best known as author of *Passion and Society* (Faber, London, 1940), has been active for many years in European literary and cultural affairs. He warmly supported the idea of cultural centres of the kind I envisaged, and wrote a lyrical description of the Centre at Hammamet for the Tunisian review *Carthage*, January 1965.
2 A volume reproducing some of the paintings done by Klee and Macke during their visit to Tunisia in 1914 has been published by H. N. Abrams (New York, 1959).
3 George Hoyninghen Huene was a German photographer famous in the 1930s: a spectacular exhibition of his work was shown at the Photographers' Gallery in London in 1981.
4 I have not been able to establish the authenticity of this statement, but Wright certainly visited Hammamet and stayed with George Sebastian.
5 Jean Duvignaud incorporated the research into one of the most penetrating studies of a 'Third World society' written in recent times, published under the title *Chebika* by Gallimard (Paris, 1968), and translated into English with an introduction by myself by Allen Lane in 1969. A film of great visual beauty, *Ramparts d'Argile*, was made from the book by Bertucelli.
6 During the years when I was its artistic director the Festival of Hammamet was listed in the international press with the most prestigious European festivals, and I was invited to meetings of their directors.
7 The Tunisian dinar is at the present time the equivalent roughly of a pound sterling. It can safely be estimated that the property of the Centre in Hammamet is now worth three million Tunisian dinars, so that the Centre, apart from its cultural achievements, was a highly successful financial venture.
8 Bourguiba was not told that by my own efforts and through my contacts and friendships I had raised over $200,000 for the Tunisian Treasury, and that I had taken no salary for myself.

Chapter VII: Rival Nationalisms

1 A party founded by Pierre Gemayal before the Second World War which believed in Lebanese nationalism and which resisted the merging of

Lebanon's identity with Arab, Syrian or Palestinian causes.
2 See Chapter IV, note 3.
3 Hassanein Haykal was editor of *al-Ahram*, an Egyptian daily paper with the widest circulation in the Arab world. His weekly editorials were generally believed to reflect the policy and ideas of President Nasser. He was removed from his position by President Sadat and has since devoted himself to writing books.
4 The Arab Baath Socialist Party is a pan-Arab nationalist movement presently in power in both Syria and Iraq, although the two governments which it controls are hostile to each other.
5 Camille Chamoun was independent Lebanon's second President (1952-8). He founded the National Liberal Party and as a prominent member of the Lebanese Front played a leading role in resisting foreign intervention in Lebanon in recent years.
6 In 1980 Selim Lawzi was seized near a roadblock manned by Syrian troops near Beirut airport, and was found dead a few days later.

Chapter VIII: Marjayoun Besieged

1 Patrice Bougrain Dubourg joined de Gaulle in London in 1940, becoming an early *Compagnon de la Résistance* and carrying out many missions in occupied France: he was the youngest Deputy in France's first post-war Assembly, and has remained active in many branches of French society.
2 See Chapter II, note 2.
3 Charles Helou was President from 1964 to 1970, Suleiman Frangiyyeh from 1970 to 1976.
4 *Um Kemal* means 'the mother of Kemal': by this the people of the south were mocking their traditional 'leader', Kemal Assad, who, unlike MK, never came to visit his people at all.
5 Dr Debakey, the famous heart specialist, comes from Marjayoun, which he left as a child when his father emigrated.
6 I was told by more than one American ambassador in Beirut that the Embassy was 'protected' by the Palestinians. This 'protection' did not, however, prevent the assassination of Ambassador Meloy in August 1976.
7 The 'national movement' was an alliance between certain radical Lebanese and non-Lebanese parties and militia; it was closely linked to the PLO, which supplied it with arms and money.
8 'Free Lebanon' was the name given by Haddad to the area he controlled to mark its freedom from a Palestinian or Syrian presence.

Epilogue

1 My readers will perhaps have been impressed by the number of friends

and acquaintances listed in these pages as assassinated. I could add other names, such as those of Hashim Jawad, a Foreign Minister of Iraq and regional director of the UN Development Programme in the Middle East, and Mohammed Naaman, Foreign Minister of North Yemen, both assassinated in Beirut in the 1970s: and there are many others.

Index

Abdullah, Emir of Transjordan, 17, 41
Abdulwahhab, Hassan Husni, 127, 128
Abdulwahhab, Khaled, 128
Abiad, George, 155
Abla, Raif, 38
Abla, Zakia, 38
Abulhuda, Luli, 18
Abusamra, Alfred, 58
Acheson, Dean, 100, 101–2
Acre, 47
Afnan, Bedia, 57, 81
Afnan, Hussein, 5, 81
Akaba, Gulf of, 90
Alami, Musa, background, 50–1; friendship with C. H., 51, 74, 103; plans for post-war Palestine, 52; and the Arab League, 53–7, 65; Azzam Pasha and the Mufti intrigues against, 60, 65; and the Arab Office, 65, 84–5; and creation of Israel, 66, 68–9; and Israeli War of Independence, 71–2; Arab Development Society project, 72–3, 74, 85, 162; article on the Palestinian situation, 79; relations with Wasfi Tal, 85; Bourguiba visits, 87; plans for 1967–occupied territories, 94–5
Alami, Saadia, 50, 85
Aleppo, 40–1
Alexandria, 28, 55
Alexandria Protocol, 55
Algerian revolution, 113–14, 117, 166
Ali, Rashid, 51
Allio, René, 128–9
Altounyan, Dora, 40
Altounyan, Ernest, 40–1
American Ladies' Association, 163
American University of Beirut, 37–8, 77, 81–2, 84, 108, 123, 147–8
Amman, 73
Anglo-American Committee of Inquiry, 67–8
Anti-Defamation League, 60
Antonius, George, 51
Arab Club, Oxford, 18
Arab Deterrent Force, 182
Arab Development Society, 73
Arab Higher Committee, 67–9, 91
Arab League, formation, 52, 53–6, 150; officers of, 57–8; and creation of Israel, 61, 64–70; creates Palestinian resistance movement, 84, 189
Arab Lebanese army, 170
Arab nationalism, 146–59, 191–2
Arab News Agency, 75
Arab Office, Jerusalem, 58, 67, 79
Arab Office, London, 71, 75, 79, 103
Arab Offices, personnel, 57–8; in Washington, 49, 58–70, 79, 99–103
Arqoub, 31, 165–6, 182
Askeri, Rafidh al, 102
Assad, President, Chtaura Agreement, 175
Atiyah, Edward, 57
Auranitis, 2
Austin, J. L., 19
Ayer, A. J., 19
Ayshia, 170–1

Azzam, Abdurrahman, 56, 60, 65, 71

Baabda, 185
Baalbek Festival, 135
Baath Party, 155
Bach Orchestra, 136
Badawi Abdurrahman, 43–4
Baghdad, 71, 73
Bakunin, 16
Balfour Declaration, 54
Ballet du Vingtième Siècle, 136, 140
Beaufort Castle, 181, 182
Beeley, Harold, 66, 114
Beirut, 73; C.H.'s first visit to, 28; Bourguiba in, 88; growth, 164–5; Palestinians in, 165; and PLO occupation of the south, 165–87; violence erupts in, 169; 1976 return to normality, 171; dangers in, 185; Israeli invasion, 186–7
Béjart, Maurice, 136, 140, 144
Bellagha, Lamine, 104
Ben Ayad, Ali, 128, 134
Ben Bella, Ahmed, 153
Ben Gurion, David, 58
Ben Milad, Mahjoub, 127
Ben Salah, Ahmed, 115, 121–2
Ben Yahmed, Bechir, 108
Ben Youssef, Salah, 151, 152
Berdyaev, Nicolas, 25
Berlin, Isaiah, 20
Bevin, Ernest, 66
Bizerta, 111, 113, 115–19, 153
Blat, 171
Bliss, Daniel, 3
B'nai B'rith, 60
Boumedienne, Houari, 166
Bouquet, Marie-Françoise, 136
Bourguiba, Habib, background, 98; ideas on Palestine, 79–80, 83–9; and de-Zionization of Jews, 79–80; 1965 Near East tour, 84–9; Jericho speech, 87; first meeting with C. H., 97; friendship with C. H., 98–9; seeks support in America, 99–103; meeting with Acheson, 101–2; and his son's name, 103; plots to restore Moncef Bey, 104–5; exile on La Galite, 105, 106; Tunisia granted independence, 106–7, 112, 151; C. H. joins his staff, 110, 112–13; and evacuation of French forces from Tunisia, 114–15; and French base at Bizerta, 115–19; and de Gaulle, 116–17; and nationalization of foreign assets, 119–22; and the International Cultural Centre, 126, 132–3, 141; and C. H.'s departure from Tunisia, 141–2; illness, 142, 145; restores C. H. to favour, 145; Nasser and, 151, 152–5; assassination attempt, 152; and the United Arab Republic, 154–5; and 'Arabism', 155; C. H.'s relations with, 157, 160; and Algerian revolution, 166; resistance movement, 189
Bourguiba, Habib Jr, 103, 118–19, 142
Bourguiba, Mathilde, 103
Bourguiba, Sitt Wassila, 114, 126, 132
Boutros, Fuad, 179
Bowra, Maurice, 23–4
Brazil, 3, 5, 11
British army, C. H. joins, 38, 41–9
Brook, Peter, 136
Brooke, Rupert, 26
Budapest Quartet, 136
Bukoff, Yuri, 136
Bunting, John, 15
Burns, Robert, 3
Butler, Samuel, 15

Cairo, C. H. joins British army in, 38, 41–6, 48–9
Cairo Agreement, 166–8, 169, 171
Cane, Mr, 14
Carthage, 139–40
Cénacle du Liban, 88
Chabbi, Abulqassem, 113, 127
Chabbi, Lamine, 127

INDEX

Chamoun, Camille, 70, 156, 168, 169
Champigneulle, M., 22, 124
Chemetov, Paul, 128–9, 132
Chiboub, Ali, 157
Chiboub, Halima, 157
Chtaura Agreement, 175, 177
Churchill, Sir Winston, 46, 54, 66
Clayton, Gilbert, 41
Clayton, Iltyd, 41–3, 48, 52, 54, 55, 98
Comédie Française, 139, 140
Communist Party, 13, 15–16
Congress for Cultural Freedom, 62–3
Cooley, John, 167
Crossman, Richard, 66, 67
Crum, Bartley, 67

Dabague, Maurice, 182
Dabague, Michel, 170
Dajani, Auni, 18
Dajani, Burhan, 57
Dajani, Musa, 85
Damascus, 32–3, 73
Daubeny, Peter, 133
Dayan, Moshe, 96
Debakey, Dr, 170
Declaration of Human Rights, 70, 77
de Gaulle, Charles, 116–17
d'Erlanger, Leo, 89
Deroche, Jean, 129
Desjardins, Mme, 25, 124
Desjardins, Paul, 24, 25, 124
de-Zionization of the Jews, 79–80
Dibbin, 177
di Bosio, Gianfranco, 136
Didsbury Preparatory School, 9
Dimishquiyyeh, Nadim, 154
Dougga, 140
Doxiades, 164
Dubourg, Patrice Bougrain, 161
Duran, Rosa, 136
Duvignaud, Jean, 127–8

Eban, Abba (Aubrey), 45, 58, 90
Eddy, William, 59, 100

Eden, Sir Anthony, 54
Egypt, and the Arab League, 54, 55–6; Six Days War, 89–91; as centre of Arab world, 151; and Tunisia, 151–2; union with Syria, 154
Eisenhower, Dwight D., Suez crisis, 90
Elgar, Sir Edward, 14
Ellis Island, 59
Encounter, 92, 94
Erdos, Thomas, 137–8
Essayan, Mr, 130–1
Ezra'a, 32

Fahmi, Ali, 100
Faisal, King of Saudi Arabia, 70, 142
Faisal I, King of Iraq, 5, 17, 41, 53, 149
Faour, Emir, 36, 150
Faquih, Assad al-, 102
Farha family, 36
Farrah, Abd'elkader, 134
FBI, 60, 62
Fleischmann, Julius, 89–90
Focillon, Henri, 24–5
Ford Foundation, 160; and grant for International Cultural Centre, 124, 127, 128, 129–30; funds for Marjayoun National College, 160, 163–4
Forte, Mme, 25
France, 78
France, and Tunisian independence, 99–107, 111, 113; evacuation of forces from Tunisia, 114–15
France, Anatole, 15
Francis, Francis, 38, 39
Franco, General, 18
François, Samson, 136
Frangiyyeh, Suleiman, 166, 171, 179
Free Lebanon, 184, 185
Freedman, Ben, 61
Fuleihan, Anis, 135
The Future of Palestine, 69

Gandhi, Mahatma, 16
Gaza, international trusteeship proposed for, 94–6
Gemayel, Amin, 187
Gemayel, Bechir, 185, 187
Gemayel, Pierre, 169
German, Edward, 14
Gezira Club, Cairo, 43
Ghassan, 2
Ghazzeddin, Chafiq, 18
Ghoraieb, Henri, 136
Ghulmiyyah, Labib, 163
Ghulmiyyeh, Mourad, 150
Gibb, Professor, 27
Gibran, Khalil, 4
Gide, André, 25
Girgis, Marjory, 41
Goldmann, Nahum, 62
Gorse, Georges, 117
Gouin, Félix, 22
Grafe, Inno, 44
Grafe family, 24
Greene, Henry, 23
Groethuysen, Bernard, 24, 25
Gulbenkian, Robert, 130, 131
Gulbenkian Foundation, 130

Habash, George, 82
Haddad, Saad, 166; holds Marjayoun for Lebanon, 171, 173, 175–6, 178–82, 184
Hakim, George, 94
Halévy, Daniel, 23
Hallaj, 44
Hallé Orchestra, 12
Hariri, Rafiq, 187
Hammamet, 124–45, 160
Hampstead, 160
Hannah (cook), 13
Harlech, Lord, 118
Hasbaya, 31, 173
Hashem, 36
Hashemites, 150
Hauran, 2, 31–3
Haykal, Hassanein, 154, 156
Hegel, Georg, 19, 23
Heidegger, Martin, 23, 77
Helou, Charles, 166

Henderson, Loy, 63, 100
Hermon, Mount, 2, 28–9, 31, 165, 167, 177
Herzen, Alexander, 16
Hopkins, Garland, 61
Hoss, Selim, 180
Hourani, Albert (C. H.'s brother), 27, 44, 160; at the Jerusalem Arab office, 58; evidence to the Anglo-American Committee, 67–8, 69
Hourani, Cecil, family background, 1–3; Lebanese background, 2–3, 30–5; early life, 3–13; inherited nostalgia, 4; name, 9; education, 9–10, 13–22; interest in music, 12, 14; and communism, 13, 15–16; awakening interest in Arab politics, 17–18; first contacts with anti-semitism, 23; first visit to Lebanon, 28–39; joins British army in Cairo, 38, 41–6, 48–9; military training in Palestine, 46–8; demobilization, 48; at Arab Office in Washington, 49, 58–70; and creation of Israel, 64–70; and the Palestinian cause, 73, 74, 75; turns to journalism, 75–6; ghost-writes speeches, 76; joins Charles Malik's staff, 77; enters family business, 81; marriage, 81; returns to teaching, 82; advocates containment of Israel, 92–4; article on the 'Alami plan', 94–6; joins Lebanon UN delegation, 94; helps Bourguiba in Washington, 99–103; settles in Tunisia, 81, 83, 107–8; and relations between Tunisia and USA, 109–10; joins Bourguiba's staff, 110, 112–13; and Bourguiba's 1965 Near East tour, 84–9; not welcome in Cairo, 84, 88; and evacuation of French forces from Tunisia, 114–15; and French base at Bizerta, 115–19; International

Cultural Centre, 123–45; restlessness in Tunisia, 123; leaves Tunisia, 89, 141–2, 160; Bourguiba restores to favour, 145; visit to Chamoun, 156–7; relations with Bourguiba, 157, 160; standing in Tunisia, 158; Lebanese nationality, 160–1; sets up as free-lance writer and consultant, 89, 160; interests in Marjayoun, 161–2; returns to live in Lebanon, 161–4; and Palestinian involvement in Lebanon, 165–88
Hourani, Fadlo (C. H.'s father), origins, 2–3, 28–9, 30, 34–5; Presbyterianism, 3, 6; life in Manchester, 3, 4, 5, 11–12, 35; suggests C. H. might change his name, 8–9; and English life, 9; sets up a school in Didsbury, 9–10; business, 10–11, 23; temperament, 34–5; wants C. H. to join the family business, 35, 75, 81; support for Faisal, 149; and C. H.'s nationality, 160; founds school in Marjayoun, 163
Hourani, Furugh (C.H.'s wife), 81, 103, 105, 108–9, 113, 164, 169
Hourani, Isa (C. H.'s cousin), 32, 39
Hourani, Soumaya (C. H.'s mother), 4, 6, 8, 28, 31; characteristics inherited by C. H., 35; death, 81
Hourani, Zelfa (C. H.'s daughter), 108
Howard, Harry, 101
Huberman, 23
Huene, Hoyninghen, 125
Huleh, 72
Husri, Sateh-al, 154
Hussein, King, 85
Hussein, Sherif, 5, 17, 18, 53, 149
Hussein, Taha, 44, 45
Husseini, Haj Amin, Mufti of Jerusalem, 19, 50–1, 60, 65, 68
Husseini, Jamal, 17, 50, 51, 52–3, 67, 71

Husseini, Musa Abdullah, 18–19

Ibl as-Saqi, 4, 31, 34, 172, 183
International Cultural Centre, Tunisia, 89, 123–45, 160
Iraq, 5; Arab League, 54, 55
Irbid, 84
Israel, foundation, 61, 64–70, 72; war of independence, 71–2; Bourguiba's ideas on de-Zionization of Jews, 79–80; Six Days War, 89–91, 96; C. H. advocates containment policy, 92–4; plans for international trusteeship of occupied territory, 94–6; reprisals against Palestinians in Lebanon, 166–7; Yom Kippur War, 167; support for Marjayoun, 173, 175, 177, 181, 182; 1978 invasion of Lebanon, 178–80, 182; 1982 invasion of Lebanon, 181, 186, 190; peace with Lebanon, 191
Issawi, Charles, 57
Iyad, Abu, 175–6
Izzeddin, Najla, 58

Jacks, Maurice, 14
Jackson, Commander, 51
Jamali, Fadel, 70
Jankelevitch, Vladimir, 25
Jaulan, 36
Jawdet, Ali, 100
Jedeidet, 2, 31, 34, 163, 172, 178
Jedeidet-Marjayoun, 2–3
Jellouli, Hedi, 104
Jericho, 72–3
Jerusalem, 39; Arab Office, 58, 67, 79; division, 72; Jewish Agency, 68
Jews, de-Zionization, 79–80; see also Israel
Jihad, Abu, 177–8
Jones, Lewis, 109, 111
Jordan, Arab Development Society, 73; Bourguiba visits, 85–6; military capability, 86; expels Palestinian resistance

movements, 96, 165
Joumblatt, Kamal, 164

Kant, Immanuel, 19, 23
Karamé, Rashid, 174
Kataeb Party, 148, 169, 180
Kennedy, John F., 119
Kerima, 186
Kerr, Alma, 162–3
Khairi, Khulusi, 57
Khaled, Leila, 165
Khalidi, Walid, 57
Khalifa, 106
Khatib, Ahmed, 170, 184
Khattabi, Abdulkerim al, 18
Khazars, 61
Khaznadar, Françoise, 137
Khaznadar, Sherif, 137
Khemiri, Taher, 134
Khiam, 167, 172, 183
Khouri, Boutros (Peter), 5, 13
Khouri, Faris al, 61, 70
Khouri, Juliette, 99
Kierkegaard, Søren, 23
Kingsley, Don, 124, 130
Kisbany, Amin, 4–5, 15, 17, 26, 81
Klee, Paul, 125
Klibi, Chedli, 138–44
Koestler, Arthur, 61
Kott, Jan, 136
Kraus, Paul, 44–6, 90
Kropotkin, 16–17

Ladgham, Bahi, 115, 116, 121–2
La Marsa, 116
Lampson, Sir Miles, 51
Lawrence, T. E., 5, 40
Lawzi, Selim, 157
Lebanese Front, 185
Lebanon, and C. H.'s family background, 2–3, 30–5; C. H.'s first visit to, 28–39; Second World War, 35–40; independence, 52; Arab League, 55; refugees from Palestine, 72; Bourguiba visits, 87–9; becomes Palestinian resistance centre, 96; Syria's historical relationship with, 147; Arab nationalists and, 155; and United Arab Republic, 156; Tunisia and, 158; place in the Arab world, 158–9; Palestinian refugees, 162–3; disequilibrium between Beirut and the south, 164–5; Palestinian resistance movement in, 165–87, 190; Cairo Agreement, 166–8, 169, 171; blockade of Marjayoun, 171–8, 181–4; 1978 Israeli invasion, 178–80, 182; UNIFIL move into the south, 180–5; PLO re-established in the south, 181; 1982 Israeli invasion of, 181, 186, 190; return of optimism, 187–8; peace with Israel, 191
Lebanon, Mount, 149
Lenin, 13, 15, 16, 80
Lesur, Daniel, 23
Libya, union with Tunisia, 115
Lisbon, 130
Little, Tom, 75
Littlewood, Joan, 136, 137, 140–1
London Arab Office, 71, 75, 79, 103

Ma'ari, 3
Macadoo, Dale, 47
Macke, Auguste, 125
Mahmud, Nureddin, 71–2
Makarios, Shaheen, 34
Malik, Charles, 70, 77, 100, 108
Malraux, André, 24, 128, 139
Malraux, Clara, 24, 25
Manchester, C. H.'s early life in, 3–13; C. H. enters family business in, 81
Marco Polo, 28
Marcus, Liselotte, 23
Marib, 2
Marjayoun, C. H.'s first visit to, 30–1, 149; and C. H.'s ancestry, 31, 32; characteristics of people of, 33–4; and Second World War, 35–6, 38–9; visits by the Emir Faour al Faour, 36; Ben

INDEX

Gurion claims as part of Israel, 58; and Arab nationalism, 149–50; C. H. takes part in life of, 161–4; PLO moves into, 169–70; besieged, 170–84; support from Israel, 173, 175, 177, 181, 182
Marjayoun National College, 163–4, 182
Marx, Karl, 15, 16, 20
Masmoudi, Mohammed, 106, 115
Massignon, Louis, 44, 103
May, J. L., 15
McClintock, Robert, 164
Mclelland, Mr, 14
Mehiri, Taieb, 116
Mekkawi, Jamil, 104
Mendès-France, Pierre, 106, 151
Mendoza, Rabbi, 10
Meppiel, Armand, 132
Metulla, 39
Middle East Supply Centre, 51, 150
Mill Hill School, 13–17, 27
Mohammed Ali Club, Cairo, 43
Mokaddem, Saddoq, 108
Moncef Bey, 104–5
Morris, William, 16–17
Moussaitbeh, 161
Moyne, Lord, 45–6, 51
Mur, George, 18
Murphy, Robert, 115
Murray, Sir James, 14
Mutannabi, 3

Nabatieh, 171
Nahar, 92
Najjar, Youssef, 152
Nasir, Jamal, 57
Nasrullah, Salim, 32
Nasser, Jamal Abdul, impact of, 83; and Bourguiba, 87, 88–9, 151, 152–5; and military defeat of Israel, 88; Six Days War, 90–1; Cairo Agreement, 165–6
Nasser, Kemal, 96
National Liberty Party, 169
Neo-Destour Party, 101, 104, 107, 120, 151

Nimr Pasha, Faris, 43, 51
Nokrashi Pasha, 55
Nouira, Hedi, 115, 127, 152

October War (1973), 167
'Orchestre Classique de Tunis', 136
Owen, Wilfred, 26
Oxford University, 17–22, 27

Palestine, 1936 revolution, 17–19; C. H.'s military training in, 46–8; Jewish settlement in, 57; creation of Israel in, 61, 64–6, 72; British policy towards, 66–8, 80; Britain withdraws, from, 71; Israeli war of independence, 71–2; Bourguiba's ideas on, 79–80, 83–9; plans for international trusteeship of occupied territories, 94–6
Palestine Liberation Organization (PLO), proposals for a 'democratic Palestinian state', 64; formation, 84; Bourguiba and, 87; and democratic Palestinian state, 93; expulsion from Jordan, 96; moves into Marjayoun, 169; and siege of Marjayoun, 171–8, 181–4, 190; Chtaura Agreement, 175, 177; re-establishes itself in south Lebanon, 181; leaves Beirut, 187; attitude to Lebanon, 190–1
Palestinian, refugees in Lebanon, 96, 162–3; resistance movement formation, 189–90
Paola, Princess, 133
Paris, 27, 36, 37, 103, 104
Parker, Richard, 179
Parry, Hubert, 14
Peel, Lord, 68
Pepito, 140–1
Perdigão, Mme, 131
Perdigão, Senhor, 130–1
Pion, Michel, 137
Planson, Claude, 136
Poe, Edgar Allan, 23
Pontigny, 23, 24–5, 124

Popular Front for the Liberation of Palestine, 165
Protein, 168
Presbyterian Church of England, 3

Qandil, 32
Qleia, 170, 173

Rachidiyya, 136
Racy, Munah, 4, 35
Racy, Theodora, 134
Racy, Yuakim, 6
Raffles, Gerry, 137, 140
Ratib, Jamil, 134
Ray, Miss, 12
Reform Club, Manchester, 11, 12
Rihani, Negib, 155
Romilly, Esmond, 15
Roosevelt, Franklin D., 59
Roosevelt, Kermit, 61, 100
Rougemont, Denis de, 124
Rousseau, Jean-Jacques, 19
Royal Institute of International Affairs, 27
Royaumont, 22–4, 124
Ruskin, John, 40
Russell, John, 22, 24

Saad, Marouf, 168
Saadé, Antoun, 147–8
Sadat, Anwar, 93, 153
Saddiqui College, 152
Said, Ahmed, 156
Said, Nuri Pasha, 53–4
Saida, 168, 181, 184
Sainte-Beuve, 21
Sakiet Sidi Yusuf, 114, 115, 116
Salam, Saeb, 17, 87–8, 156, 164
Salam, Selim Bey, 17
Salloum, Zaal, 36
Sarkis, Elias, 173–4
Satterswaithe, Bob, 63
Saudi Arabia, Arab League and, 55
Sayegh, Fayez, 77
Schiaparelli, 125
Scott, C. P., 11
Sebastian, George, 126, 137
Second World War, 26–8, 35–49

Segal, Ruth, 28
Sfax, 136
Shertok, Moshe, 58, 62
Shevikar, Princess, 43
Shraiké, 178
Shukairi, Ahmed, 57, 89, 96
Sidi Bou Said, 127, 136, 137, 138, 140
Sidon, 6
Sieff, Daniel, 10
Siemens, 129
Simon, Abbey, 136
Sinai, 89
Six Days War (1967), 89–91, 96
Slim, Mongi, 109
Smithsonian Institution, 137
Solh, Taqieddin, 97
Souk al Khan, 31
Souq al Arba, 114
Sousse, 136
Soviet Union, and creation of Israel, 70; influence in Middle East, 186
Spanish Civil War, 18
Spears, General, 99
Stalin, Joseph, 16
Stern Gang, 45–6
Super, Charles, 14
Supervielle, Jules, 23
Syria, settlers from Yemen, 2; C. H.'s family origins in, 32–3; independence, 52; and Arab League, 55; Six Days War, 89; nationalism, 146; historical relationship with Lebanon, 147; union with Egypt, 154; Yom Kippur War, 167; 1976 entry into Lebanon, 171; and the siege of Marjayoun, 174–5; attacks on Lebanese Forces, 186
Syrian Popular Party, 147, 149
Syrian Protestant College, 3, 4
Szeryng, Henri, 23

Tal, Wasfi, 57, 84–5
Tannous, Izzet, 91
Taylor, J. P., 14
Taylor, Paul, 136

Thant, U, 95
Tolstoy, Leon, 16
Transjordan, Arab League, 55
Trotsky, Leon, 13, 16
Tueni, Ghassan, 92, 179, 180
Tunisia, C. H., settles in, 81, 83; independence, 99–107, 111, 113, 151; United States cooperation with, 109–10; post-independence success, 110–12; and Algerian revolution, 113–14, 117, 166; evacuation of French forces from, 114–15; union with Libya, 115; French base at Bizerta, 115–19; nationalization of foreign assets, 119–22; International Cultural Centre, 123–45; and Egypt, 151–2; and Lebanon, 158
Tyre, 181, 184

UNIFIL, 179–85
United Arab Republic, 146, 154–6
United Nations, 60; and creation of Israel, 68, 69–70; Palestinian refugee camps, 73; C. H. reports from, 75–7; resolution 242, 94; Tunisia and, 99; and the French base at Bizerta, 118; Palestinian refugees, 162; Lebanese crisis, 179, 180, 184
United States of America, Arab office in, 49, 58–70, 79, 99–103; and creation of Israel, 61, 63, 67, 70; Bourguiba seeks support in, 99–103; cooperation with Tunisia, 109–10; and French base at Bizerta, 118–19; Lebanon crisis, 179, 184, 186
Universal Declaration of Human Rights, 70, 77
UNSCOP, 68–9
UNWRA, 162
Urquhart, Brian, 179
Ustinov, Peter, 133

Venice, 28
Victoria, Queen, 11

Wadi Teym, 31
Wahl, Jean, 23, 24
Waldheim, Kurt, 179
Walid, Abu, 178
Washington, Arab Office, 49, 58–70, 79, 99–103; Bourguiba's second visit, 108–10
Wasit, 36
Weizmann, Chaim, 21, 61
Weldon, T. D., 19
West Bank, Jordan's sovereignty over, 86; international trusteeship proposed for, 94–6
Whitehead, Alfred North, 77
Whitehorn, A. D., 14
Whitehorn, Katharine, 14
Wilde, Oscar, 23
Williams, A. J., 14
Wilson, Harold, 66
Wittgenstein, Ludwig, 19
Woodruff, Dicky, 126
Woolf, Virginia, 23
World Zionist Federation, 62
Wright, Edwin, 101
Wright, Frank Lloyd, 126

Yemen, C. H.'s family origins in, 2, 32; Arab League, 55; union with Egypt and Syria, 154
Yom Kippur War (1973), 167
Young Communist League, 15
Youssef, Salah Ben, 108

Zahle, 186
Zaid, Emir, 17
Zambra, 140
Zasulich, Vera, 16
Zionism, 10; support in United States, 60–1; Bourguiba's de-Zionization plans, 79–80
Zorara, 32
Zurayk, Constantin, 100

An Unfinished Odyssey
Lebanon and Beyond

Book II

To the Memory of all the many companions of my life whom I do not forget. And to All who still sustain me by their friendship, tolerance, and affection.

Acknowledgments

To Russell Harris, Tony Naufal and Zelfa my sincere thanks for their invaluable assistance in advice and editing at all stages of this book.

Contents

Preface	7
Chapter 1: From Manchester to Mecca: the Hashemite Vision	11
Chapter 2: Baghdad Days	29
Chapter 3: Two Sides of the Jordan	40
Chapter 4: Albania: The Last Adventure	61
Chapter 5: Lebanese Dilemmas	72
Chapter 6: Garlic Identity and Language	93
Chapter 7: From Iran to Tunisia	100
Chapter 8: Cheese	109
Epilogue	114
Appendix I	118
Appendix II	129

Preface

When I chose the title *An Unfinished Odyssey* for my first book of memoirs published in 1984, I had hoped that my journey would end when land was sited. As I write this in early 2011 none of the problems which have engaged my thoughts and activities for most of my life have been solved: Lebanon still suffers from external pressures and internal divisions; next door, Palestinians and Israelis still suffer the legacy of an aborted partition; two international invasions have all but destroyed Iraq's unity and threaten it with fragmentation. There are however some signs on the horizon which may indicate a coming change in the air: peoples are moving, tyrants are falling, and freedom is calling. Could those still dim lights predict the longed-for land?

This second volume of memoirs recollects some episodes in these three countries, and others in Tunisia and Albania. In the chain of events which link together all the stages of a long life, there are some which preceded it but which impinged upon it at certain times and in certain places. My story began before I was born and will continue after my life: that story and not the history is all I can claim to relate in these brief souvenirs.

To illuminate the story I have chosen to reproduce a number of documents which I believe shed light not only on the past, but also on the present, and perhaps on the future too. The Arab debacle in June 1967 enthused me to write an angry pamphlet, which I titled *Torrero or Bull*, implying that some Arab leaders – and I had in mind primarily Gamal Abdel Nasser – could not decide what they wanted to be. Later widely reproduced, the pamphlet was renamed *The Moment of Truth*. It reads today as if it had been written yesterday, and its bitter criticisms and prophetic doom are still relevant to the follies and the futilities of both the peacemakers and the war-mongers, of whom there are a surplus both in the Middle East and in the West. In early 2003 I wrote another *Moment of Truth* (Appendix I). Its proposal for a new 'Road Map' is equally relevant to the present impasse and offers a way ahead.

Events in Lebanon between 1975 and the present day dragged me, as it did many others, into a series of still-ongoing crises. In terms of the official policies of the official Lebanese Government my involvement in the ambiguous situation in South Lebanon was marginal. That former unsettled situation has become central with the passage of time: the artificial frontiers drawn by the British and French governments after the First World War between the natural and historical 'Lebensraum' of lower and upper Galilee have become the flash-point of a conflict which could easily expand far beyond the confines of the neighbouring combatants, and involve the whole world. Two documents, in chapter four, between Lebanese unofficial leaders and official Washington shed light on a situation which has not changed in its essence since the documents were written in the late 1970s and early 1980s – a situation which, irrespective of the interests or wishes of the population of South Lebanon, makes of their territory a chess-board on which the game of nations is ruthlessly pursued. The players have changed, but the game goes on.

My youthful dreams, my political attachment to the 'Hashemite vision' of a united, multi-national, and multi-cultural Arab space to replace but not to destroy what Ottoman dominion had best displayed, were all shaken but not erased by the sequence of events which began with Iraq's invasion of Kuwait in 1990, continued with the multinational invasion of Iraq in 1991, and reached its horrific climax in the wholly illegal and scandalous attack on Iraq's soil and its political foundations initiated and led by an American President and a British Prime Minister in 2003.

The prelude to that first invasion gave me an occasion to make a statement in defence of a major player in the battle for reason and humanity: an unprovoked and vicious attack, made in the press, on the motives and actions of the Jordanian monarch needed a reply, and I supplied it. This led to my re-introduction into the heart of the Middle Eastern problem – the Palestinian and Arab conflict with Israel – and crystallized my views on how it might be resolved.

A long association with the Jordanian scene added a new territory and a new involvement to my story. The collapse of Chinese-style communism in 1992 opened up a new chapter in the history of Albania. To restore the monarchy ousted by the Italian invasion in 1939 was the mission of Leka, the exiled Crown Prince of the Albanians, whose acquaintance I made in Amman and of whose friendship I was the beneficiary. Two visits to that lovely land and people convinced me that his mission was not only realizable, but highly desirable: the re-emergence of a Muslim-Christian kingdom on European soil would be a powerful antidote to Islamophobia, and compensate both components of its population for the almost contemporaneous falls of Granada and Constantinople in the 15th century. The referendum on the monarchy in May 1997 gave the would-be king a majority of the popular vote, but the intervention of the OECD falsified the figures and returned to power remnants of the former regime. The Albanians in their scattered territories have still to find their way.

Not all my memories are of failures and frustrations: there have been smiling as well as dangerous chances. Friendships in many countries and on many dimensions sustained me in difficult times: ventures and adventures compensated for the uncertainties of self-employment, some successful, others opening up new horizons and whetting appetites for more. Unexpected widowhood brought me solitude but not loneliness, and family relationships provided the link in the chain between the past and the future – the ancestral whispers, the comforts of the living, and the future promises of the young and the yet-unborn.

Of my own place in the chain I became aware not long ago during the course of a dinner given by Prince Hassan and his gracious wife, Princess Sarvath, in their domed house in Amman. Seated between foreign diplomats, guests from abroad, and Jordanian academics, I was surprised and apprehensive when the Prince suddenly stood up and announced in a grave tone of voice that 'Cecil and I used to be brothers': of what serious shortcomings, what unintended faux-pas had I been guilty and deserved this demotion from brotherhood? After a disturbing pause he continued: 'in the past I was the brother of the King, and Cecil was the brother of Albert Hourani; now I am the uncle of the King, and Cecil is the grandfather of Skandar Keynes'.

This was followed by one of those boisterous and startling

bursts of laughter which endear the Prince to his friends – and they are truly very many of them in East and West. It was a touching compliment to me, and at the same time a salutary reminder of the fragility of fame (King Hussein died in 1999, Albert Hourani in 1994).

Chapter 1
From Manchester to Mecca: the Hashemite Vision

Few were the men and women who left their native lands in Lebanon, Syria or Palestine at the end of the 19th and beginning of the 20th centuries to seek their fortunes in Europe or the Americas who did not hope that they would soon return for good with money to help their families. And few were those who did return: wars, revolutions, famines in the 'old countries' discouraged, and the prospects of greater prosperity than they could expect at home diminished their original optimism of an early return. Like transplanted trees they began to put down new roots, and the old ones started to wither away, but they were not always conscious of the change. They faced their new situations bravely, but they clung to their illusions.

My parents were such. The slow process of realization that their sojourn in their new home was likely to be prolonged, perhaps indefinitely, was reflected in the names they chose for their children. My three sisters, who preceded my brothers and myself, were born before the outbreak of war in 1914 made the prospect of early return impossible; nevertheless, because my parents still assumed that their daughters would marry men from the old country, they gave them two names, the first Arabic: Salwa, Wadia, and Leila, and the second English. My brothers and I on the other hand were given English first-names: George, Albert, and Cecil, and then Arabic middle names: Fadlo, Habib and Amin. The reversal in the order of Arabic and English names must have reflected a change in my parents' perception of the future of the family. As their stay in England grew longer, and the prospect of an eventual return to their native land grew dimmer, they must have realized that whatever might be the future of their sons, the cultural environment in which they were growing up was English. Although they spoke it to each other they did not think it necessary to teach us Arabic. And they did not envisage that we might find it difficult to cope with a situation which they had not faced themselves: while our intellectual processes were English, our sensibilities were Arabic: to think and to feel are not always compatible, as I was later to discover.

The six children: George, Wadia, Cecil, Salwa, Leila and Albert in 1921.

It took me many years before I understood my parents' choice of my name. Cecil was not a common name in the Edwardian times in which our family was formed, although Cecil Rhodes was a famous but not yet controversial figure. I found the key to the choice in one of the talks which my father gave on the BBC Arabic service for which he had volunteered during the dark years of World War II. Although nearly seventy in 1940, for five years he went regularly from Manchester to Evesham sometimes in dangerous circumstances, to join the small group of Arabic-speakers recruited to counter the virulent anti-British propaganda being broadcast from a radio station in Berlin in

FROM MANCHESTER TO MECCA

which, curiously enough, a first cousin of my mother from Haifa collaborated with the notorious Iraqi Yunis al-Bahri.

In one of these talks my father wished to illustrate the role played in British life by what is now commonly known as 'civil society'. He took as an example the story of a young English boy in the 17th century who, orphaned, had been sent to Aleppo to work in the Turkey Company which traded between England and the Ottoman lands. There John Morden (1623-1708) made money and invested it in goods to be sent by sea to England. His ship however did not come home, and John Morden was reduced to poverty, working at one time as a butcher's assistant; but another reversal of fortune restored his wealth, he ended his life as Sir John Morden, 1st Bt., and in his will left money to found an institution to support 'decayed merchants'. Morden College three hundred years later still exists in Blackheath, London, and as an example of the continuity of England's tradition of philanthropy, my father mentioned – without giving a name – that a friend of his in Manchester whose 'ship had not come home' had benefited from a grant from the College. When I read this I remembered that a frequent visitor to our house in Manchester, who had a special affection for me, and would seat me on his lap, had lost all his money. On a hunch I telephoned to College and asked if any record could be found of a grant to a certain Shaker Rihan sometime in the 1930s.

A few days later I received a letter from the archivist. Yes, in 1932 Mr Shaker Rihan had been granted a yearly sum of £60 until his death in 1936. In his application for the grant he stated that his income which had varied between £60,000 and £300,000 yearly, had been lost due to 'the misconduct of partners in Beirut', and when asked for information about any illnesses or handicaps

Fadlo Hourani.

he might have, he had replied, 'none except a stroke'. When I read this I was convinced that I had been called Cecil out of friendship and sympathy for Shaker Rihan and his wife, a lady from South Africa, who had lost their son called Cecil in the early years of the war. Now too I knew why Uncle Shaker had a special affection for me, and why also I never received the £500 which he had generously left me in his will.

More recently I learnt by chance that Shaker Rihan had gone to Manchester from Marjayoun a year or two before my father in 1891, and that they may also have known each other in their childhood. One day at the local bakery in the town I was introduced to a lady married to a member of the Abu Rihan family; I asked her if she knew anything of a Shaker Rihan who had been in England many years ago; she told me that they knew that there had been a very rich man from the family in Manchester, but nothing more about him. I asked her to take me to the family home, perhaps two hundred years old, now derelict but still beautiful. As I stood at the entrance I remembered vividly the figure of that loving old man with a wide moustache and a generous paunch across which hung a gold chain between the two probably empty pockets of his waistcoat.

The author with Uncle Shaker.

My second name, Amin, was easier to explain. It was the name of a classmate of my father at the American University of Beirut, Amin Habib Kisbany from Kfarshima, a small Lebanese town which has produced many distinguished men and women. Amin Kisbany was a member of one of the two main branches of the Lebanese family. For members of the first branch the pursuit of wealth provides the principal motivation of their lives; an end in itself, when achieved it sometimes permits the pursuit of other subsidiary interests. Kisbany was a member of the second branch for whom achievement in fields other than the accumulation of wealth takes precedence: literary, academic, artistic success, or power, influence, or simply service in a cause, even if not recognized, motivates them. Amin Kisbany, with whom my father maintained a lifelong friendship, provided me not only with a name, but also the attraction of an adventurous, restless, idealistic, imprudent and improvident man; and it was a period in his life spent in Baghdad which formed a link in the chain of events which was to lead to my marriage.

Unsuccessful in converting Jews in Morocco to Christianity, or selling Singer sewing machines in that country, Kisbany attempted at various periods in his life to earn, through commerce, enough money to pursue his real interests: history, theology, languages, of which he had mastered Hebrew and Aramaic in addition to Arabic and English. Before 1914 he had set up a small business trading between Manchester and New York where his brother was settled; and when war broke out in June 1914 he and my father found themselves, like other members of the small Near Eastern community of merchants in Manchester, as subjects of the Ottoman Empire, liable to detention or imprisonment once Turkey declared war on Great Britain, France, and the Russian Empire.

Through an influential friend in the Presbyterian Church of which my father was an active member all his life, he approached the Home Office to put the case that he and his fellow Ottoman subjects, as peaceful law-abiding citizens, should not be considered enemy-aliens, and in his own case he wished to acquire British nationality. A reply came from the Home Office: Mr Hourani had no reason for anxiety about his status, although his request for British citizenship could not be considered at the present time (in fact, it was not until 1926, thirty-five years after he had come to England, that he was granted citizenship). In a typically British pragmatic way our family, along with others in a similar situation, were permitted to continue their lives and activities undisturbed apart from some minor administrative regulations which they were asked to follow. Some families such as the Gabriels and the Idilbys lost sons on the battlefields of France, but in general the Christian, Jewish, and Muslim families from Beirut, Damascus, Aleppo, Baghdad, and Alexandria, now well integrated into the commercial and social life of Manchester, escaped the less fortunate fate of many German and Austrian citizens who were interned or imprisoned. I remember as a child hearing of only one case of a lady from our small community being fined for hoarding sacks of sugar and rice – an activity normal in her own country in times of war or want, but not looked upon favourably in war-time England.

Their special and rather privileged situation created among the Levantine families, Christian, Jewish and Muslim, in Manchester a sense of close community. My father and Amin Kisbany were prominent in founding in 1915 what came to be known as the Manchester Syrian Association, and my father became its secretary. The Association's original purpose was to look after the interests of the community and to assist any members who might be in need of help, but it later acquired a political character. This was largely due to the influence of Sir Mark Sykes, who had been appointed by the British Government to be in contact with communities from the various territories of the Ottoman Empire whose views on the future of their homelands would be of interest. Both Sir Mark Sykes and his French counterpart, M. Georges Picot, visited the Manchester Syrian Association in 1917, and on that occasion my father delivered an address on behalf of the group which was highly complementary to both, and handed over to Sir Mark a cheque for £300 to be sent to General Allenby for medical supplies in his campaign in Palestine, and another for ten thousand French francs to M. Picot as a donation to the French Red Cross. He concluded his address with a vibrant *'Vive La France'*.

The Manchester Association was indeed highly successful in collecting money not only from its members, but also from the entire Manchester business community. I have documents which list the names and the contributions from all the benefactors, and they give a vivid picture of the wide spectrum of British involvement in commerce and industry in the lands of the Ottoman Empire in the years before World

War I. In 1916 the sum of nearly £5,000 had been raised, and by 1917 it had reached £7,500.

At an early stage in the Association's existence the question had been raised by certain members whether members of the Jewish community should be admitted; the move was defeated by the Committee, and Jewish merchants from Baghdad, Aleppo, Damascus, Alexandria and Beirut contributed generously to all the fund-raising and social activities of the Association. The Manchester organization was thus a true reflection of the multi-confessional and pluralistic society of the Arab provinces of the Ottoman Empire. It was this 'reflection' which Sir Mark Sykes hoped he might channel into a political expression of the views of the Arab community on the future of their homelands. Much criticized, and often denounced, for what has usually been interpreted as a plan to annex the territories of the Ottoman Empire and to partition them between the British, French and Russian Empires, the Sykes-Picot Agreements, which he had secretly drafted with his French counterpart in 1916, while they did for the first time specifically envisage the establishment of 'an Arab state or confederation of Arab states', left the question of boundaries and administrative arrangements to be decided at a later stage between Great Britain and France. It was within this ambiguous framework that Sykes conducted his consultations with the Manchester Association and with Count Maurice Zugheib, a Lebanese resident in London who represented a point of view restricted to the future of the autonomous province of Mount Lebanon.

Sir Mark Sykes visited the Manchester Association again in June 1918. On that occasion my father challenged him on the implications of the secret agreements of 1916 which the new rulers of Russia had published after the 1917 revolution: how did he reconcile the impression he had given that His Majesty's Government supported the project of an Arab State or confederation of states with the revealed terms of the secret agreements which assigned large areas of the Near East to Great Britain and France? Sir Mark, clearly embarrassed, replied weakly that he had done his best to promote the Arab State, but that French pressure to assert their claims to what is now Syria and Lebanon had been too strong. This was the first chink in my father's hitherto solid belief in the integrity of the British word, later to be further widened by events in Palestine.

At a subsequent public meeting with members of the Association, Sykes spoke about the progress of the war in the Near East. Then, in private, he invited my father and two other members to a meeting at the War Office in London. While I have found no record of what transpired at that meeting, it appears to have been supportive of the movement initiated by the Sharif Hussein bin Ali, ruler of the Hejaz, known as 'the Arab Revolt' – against Turkish sovereignty in the Arab provinces of the Empire. A letter dated July 1918 from my father to Sir Mark Sykes informed him that the sum of £1,500 had been collected to be sent to Sharif Hussein, and that there would be some volunteers from the community to join his forces. In the same letter he mentioned that the Syrian Jewish community had contributed £500, and the Baghdad Jewish community £1,000, to the Association's support fund for the Allied war effort in the Near East. In a further letter dated 19 July my father informed Sykes that at a 'General Meeting today after a conference with Syrian officers (presumably from the Sharif's Arab army) five thousand pounds was raised for propaganda, recruiting, and other objects of the Association.'

In one of his BBC Arabic broadcasts my father quoted the reply of Sharif Hussein to these gestures of financial support from the Manchester community in a letter communicated to my father by Mark Sykes: 'My dear children: I thank you from my deepest heart for your generous sentiments and your valuable donation. When I learnt that the needs of your people in Syria are greater than in my country, I sent the sum to those on whom I rely to distribute to the needy in your country, but I accepted five per cent in respect for your wishes.'

This message, according to my father, had a profound effect on the members of the Manchester community, many of whom from that time onward felt supportive of the Arab revolt. These feelings found expression on the occasion of the visit of Sharif Hussein's son, Emir Feisal, to London in December 1918. The Manchester Association decided to send a delegation to London to invite the Emir to visit

FROM MANCHESTER TO MECCA

Manchester, and my father, along with Amin Kisbany, who was now the assistant secretary of the Association, and two other members, were chosen to fulfil this mission. My father gives a vivid description of the Emir – his handsome face, slender figure, captivating smile, and the fervour with which he asked his visitors to demand the complete independence of all the Arab territories. At one point he removed his Arab head-dress and struck it on the table to emphasize his determination to restore the former greatness of the Arab nation.

The visit to the Emir and his address was a turning-point in Amin Kisbany's life, as though he had been waiting for such an occasion: from Manchester he wrote to the Emir offering his services in any capacity he might choose. My father, a cautious man, attempted to dissuade him from leaving his commercial career, to no avail. The Emir invited Kisbany to join his entourage, and took him to Damascus and from there sent him to the United States of America to organize members of the Near East community, largely concentrated in New York and Brooklyn, in support of the Arab movement.

At the Peace Conference to be held in Versailles in 1919 the victorious Allied Powers were to invite the Emir Feisal to present the views of 'the Arabs'. In anticipation of that occasion, and inspired by the Emir's words, my father and three other members of the Manchester Association (Messers Kahla, Chiha, and Doki) sent a letter to the British Foreign Secretary, Arthur Balfour, in support of the Emir's vision for the future of the Arab peninsula, and suggesting that Syria – its frontiers defined as 'the

Sketch of King Feisal I prepared for the equestrian statue by the Italian sculptor Pietro Canonica and erected in Baghdad.

Taurus mountains to the north, the Euphrates river in the east, the confines of Arabia on the south-east, Sinai and the Hejaz to the south, and Sinai and the Mediterranean to the west' – should be under one single administration and be independent. A further suggestion was that this independence should be 'under the guidance of Great Britain, France, and the United States of America'. The letter went on to propose 'a scheme of federation between Syria, Mesopotamia and Arabia by which each of these countries would have an administration best suited for its population while all are united to a Central Authority somewhat on the model of the United States.'

An official of the Foreign Office commented in a note written on the document 'I think [this document] ought to go to Paris. The Manchester Syrian Association is, I believe, a body of some importance, and this, I think, is the first British source in favour of an undivided Syria – to include Palestine. The novel feature is the advocacy of a triple guardianship of Great Britain, France, and the USA in place of the French clamour for an exclusively French guardianship.' The office of Lord Curzon, who was in charge of the British participation in the Versailles Conference, replied evasively to the letter from Manchester: 'the question will receive the fullest consideration of His Majesty's Government in conjunction with their Allies at the forthcoming Peace Conference', but the real reaction of Curzon is revealed in an initialled handwritten comment on the document: 'nonsense'.

President Woodrow Wilson visited Manchester in 1919 and met with the Manchester Syrian Association. On that occasion my father addressed the President and concluded: 'if at this time we are permitted to express our innermost thoughts it would be to request that Your Excellency's great influence may be exercised for the benefit of our beloved country so that she may come to enjoy the blessings of liberty and become worthy of her glorious past'.

In New York, Kisbany had been active in rallying support among the Arabic-speaking communities for the cause of Sharif Hussein, and two organizations also sent memoranda to London along similar lines. He was then requested by someone in the Emir Faisal's entourage to proceed to France to join his delegation to the Versailles Conference. The delegation consisted of Nuri Said, an Iraqi officer who had played an important role in the military operations of the Arab revolt; Auni Abdulhadi, a member of a prominent Palestinian family from Nablus; Rustom Haidar, a member of a notable Lebanese family from Baalbek; and other Iraqi, Palestinians, Syrian and Arab personalities. While the Emir knew French from his education in Istanbul, and Abdulhadi and Haidar from their studies in France, Kisbany was the only one who knew English well. It was these four advisors who drafted the Emir's address to the Conference on 6 January 1919 in which he attempted to convince the assembled delegations of the legitimacy of the claims made by his father, Sherif Hussein, to the independence of Arabia - claims based on the Arabs' role in the war against Turkey, and on the commitments which he believed had been made to him by the British.

Amin Kisbany's ID card at Versailles Peace Conference, 1919.

King Feisal II on the lap of Hussein Afnan.

There exists a fascinating record of the preparation of Feisal's speech. Rustom Haidar had kept an almost daily record of his activities ever since he left his teaching post in Damascus to join the invading Arab army in Transjordan, and these diaries were published long after his untimely death by assassination in Baghdad in 1940. On the day before his speech the Emir Feisal gathered his advisors in his rooms at the Hotel Crillon in Paris. From such experience as I have had in my own life of drafting speeches for important and sometimes crucial occasions I can well imagine the atmosphere in the meetings which lasted several hours: the hopes, the doubts, the fears and suspicions which simultaneously occupied the thoughts of Feisal who by now realized that battles in the field are easier to confront than battles in the corridors of power. At an all-night session, after Emir Feisal had retired, the small group drafted the document in Arabic and French, and Kisbany translated it into English.

Emir Feisal's efforts at the Versailles Conference and in private meetings with the delegates – and most importantly with Clemenceau – were not successful in convincing them of the validity of his vision of a united Arabia.

King Feisal I (seated) with Gertrude Bell and Hussein Afnan standing behind, 1923.

Feisal's short-lived Syrian kingdom was overthrown by France, and after a period of exile in Europe he was compensated for this loss with the territory of Iraq, where he was proclaimed king in 1922. Among the small and loyal group of friends who followed him to Baghdad was Amin Kisbany, whom he appointed second secretary in his Diwan, or Royal

Court. There he was to serve for eight years. There too he was to form a friendship, and to share a house, with my future father-in-law, Hussein Afnan. Between Manchester and Baghdad a link in a chain was formed which brought me together with my wife Furugh thirty years later.

Amin Rihani, a brilliant Lebanese journalist, poet, and historian of contemporary events visited Baghdad in 1923 in the course of researching his book on 'The Kings of Arabia', a major source for the modern history of the Arab countries. In a still-unpublished work he devoted several chapters to describing his personal and social life in Baghdad, where he stayed in the house shared by his two friends, Amin Kisbany and Hussein Afnan. Social and political life in the capital revolved around King Feisal and the royal court. Feisal did not assume or enjoy the trappings of a monarchy alien to the traditions of the Arabs, and on one occasion declared 'they call me King, but my only purpose is to serve my people'. He was bored with the protocol of the palace and official dinners, and felt most at ease with the companions of his years of warfare in the desert and the days of exile, and in the company of the tribal and ethnic components of the country, although a few such as Gertrude Bell among his new British mandatory officials were admitted to his inner circle.

Amin Kisbany and Hussein Afnan were of that inner circle, as was Rustom Haidar, who became their intimate friend. Haidar was perhaps the most trusted advisor of King Feisal, and was several times appointed Minister of Finance in Iraqi governments. The closeness of these 'outsiders' to the centre of power inevitably gave rise to jealousies and sometimes intrigues against them by politicians anxious to take their places or to demonstrate their own 'patriotism'. Rustom Haidar was assassinated in his office by a disgruntled official, although the real motives for the crime, and its possible instigators, were never revealed. By then Amin Kisbany had left Baghdad and returned to his native village in Lebanon, and Hussein Afnan, who had served as chargé d'affaires of the Iraqi government in London and Ankara had been demoted to a banal function in the Department of Railways, and did not long survive the death of his closest friend.

In the late summer of 1939, shortly after I arrived for the

first time in Lebanon, I went almost immediately to visit Amin Kisbany in his home in Kfarshima. I found him lying on an iron bedstead in an almost empty room, coughing ceaselessly. He did not live long after my visit, and my father, in his first Arabic broadcast, announced with sadness the death of his oldest friend. Kisbany had asked me to visit Amin Rihani who had also returned to his native village Freike. This I did. Rihani, who was also unwell, told me stories of those days in Baghdad when that happy band of 'outsiders' had worked for a cause and for a man in whom they believed without thought of material gain, and without the prospect of recognition of their services. After Rustom Haidar's assassination, it was discovered by his brother that he had nothing to his name but fifty dinars in the bank and a small house. This 'happy band' have been role models for myself in the different stages of my varied career, and from them I learnt to have no illusions about the prizes which may be won, and the price which must be paid, by the 'outsider' who indulges his thirst for adventure. As R. L. Stevenson wrote in *The Dynamiter* life as 'a bazaar of dangerous and smiling chances' is my own experience.

My father was certainly attracted by the personality of the Amir Faisal and by the story of the Arab Revolt. The people of Marjayoun were very conscious of their Arab origins: I remember hearing some of them describe themselves as 'hadhrami' – from the Hadramout in Yemen from where history or myth said they came, and in an essay he wrote as a youth in the American primary school in Beirut (miraculously preserved in the archives of the American missionaries) my father describes his grandfather as a 'Bedouin'. Some of his contemporaries in the town, such as Mourad Ghulmiyyeh, who had been a member of the last Ottoman Parliament in Istanbul, and known the Amir there, had openly supported the movement of revolt against the Turks, and was to be penalized later by the French authorities who expelled the Amir from his Syrian kingdom. On my first visits to the town I sat with him often and listened to his story: not all his fellow townsmen shared his views, and some who were French-educated or Catholic like the Barakat family, supported the French presence, and had their houses pillaged or burnt by the Arab tribesmen from Transjordan and Syria who attempted an unsuccessful revolt against the French in 1920. How much politics and religion were entwined in peoples' minds at that time I was able to understand from an Arabic catchword which the Greek Orthodox Mourad Effendi often used: *'Mekki wa la Bkerke'* (Mecca rather than Bkerke), indicating his preference for Mecca over the Maronite Patriarch's seat in Bkerke – a sentiment which is still shared by some in Lebanon today.

The events which led to the detachment of the Arab provinces from the Ottoman Empire after 1918 have often been mistakenly described by both historians and popular mythology as an ethnic or racial Turkish-Arab conflict. After four hundred years of co-habitation the separation did not come easily, and for many of the partners not happily. What has come to be called 'Arab nationalism' had its roots in what is often called by western historians 'the decline of the Ottoman Empire', also termed 'the Sick Man of Europe'. As a description of the political and military influence of the Empire within Europe it was true, but it did not take into account the intellectual and cultural climate which in the Empire's capital Istanbul, Salonika and other Ottoman cities in the last half of the 19th century was teeming with new ideas. Some of these reflected currents of thought and culture in France, Italy, England, Germany, Russia and the Austro-Hungarian Empire, filtered either through the provinces which the Empire still retained in Europe, or through the foreign educational institutions which began to open in that period; but there were other currents of thought reflecting the prevailing religious, social and cultural climates in the Muslim components of the Empire, and further afield in the wider Muslim world of India and the Far East. These diverse currents of thought co-existed peacefully and not in confrontation, because the authority and the prestige of the *Dawlet* (the State) was still accepted, with varying degrees of willingness, among the many ethnic and sectarian components of the Empire as an almost immutable fact of life.

The idea of 'Pan Islam', of a political framework which would embrace all parts of the *Umma*, which found followers in the Muslim communities of India as well as among Turkish, Arab, Iranian and Afghan thinkers found a secular challenge in liberal, nationalist, and revolutionary ideas coming from Europe. Voltaire, Rousseau, Fichte, Mazzini, Flaubert. Zola, Turgenev and Tolstoy were read eagerly by the young students of the French, German, Russian and Italian schools in Istanbul: the music of Chopin, Rossini and Verdi was played in the salons and Opera houses of Istanbul, Tunis, Cairo and Beirut, while in the coffee-houses and *yalis* along the Bosphorous, serious intellectuals from all parts of the Empire discussed and dissected the latest periodicals and books published in Istanbul, Sarajevo, Salonika, Cairo, Beirut, Damascus, Lucknow and Bombay.

So long as the structure of the Empire remained intact, it was possible for the individual citizen to reconcile in himself two parallel though not convergent currents of thought. Ottoman Man or Woman, Muslim, Christian or Jewish, could be politically loyal to the *Dawlet*, but at the same time, according to choice or conviction, be modern, conservative, liberal, revolutionary, *croyant* or *libre penseur*. The two great reforms of the Tanzimat in the mid-19th century established the *qanun*, or fundamental law, which gave equal political rights to members of all communities in the Empire, but did not please some sectors of Muslim societies which clung to the idea of the *sharia* as the legitimate basis of civic rights. The dispute between *qanun* and *sharia* was less lively in Istanbul than in Cairo and Damascus where the traditions of Muslim theology were still strong, and where fear of westernization favoured retreat into the past, while in Beirut, looked at by many Ottoman officials and intellectuals as an escape to freedom and pleasure from the boredom of official life in Istanbul, French, British and American ideas of liberty, equality and democracy dominated the cultural and social scene.

In 1908 the Ottoman structure was shaken by a successful movement to restore the constitution granted by the Sultan in 1876, but revoked by Sultan Abdulhamid. The revolution was greeted with enthusiasm among the populations of the Ottoman provinces in the Balkans, some of whom, like Romania and Bulgaria, saw it as encouragement to their own hopes for self-government, while others, as in Albania, saw it as a confirmation of their status as equal citizens within the Empire, a sentiment shared by many of Muslim liberals in

Turkey and by non-Muslim communities in the Arab provinces. The Ottoman Parliaments, with representatives from all quarters of the Empire, provided the opportunity to discuss and debate the great issues of the nature of the State and the relations between its peoples. This question became crucial when power was seized by a group of officers calling themselves the Committee of Union and Progress, but some of whom aspired to transform the Empire from a multi-ethnic into a Turkish state.

The idea of such a transformation was greatly promoted by the reaction of the European Great Powers to this political and intellectual ferment in the Empire. Instead of encouraging the forces of liberalism, pluralism and constitutionalism they interpreted them as a sign of weakness. The Balkan wars in Europe and the Italian invasion of Libya in 1911 dealt a deadly blow to the forces of progress, and strengthened the attraction of Turkish nationalism as the answer to European aggression. This left the Arabs out in the cold and posed a new and agonizing problem of identity: if the Empire was to be transformed into a Turkish state, what would be their status in the new configuration? As Ottomans the Arabs had enjoyed a privileged situation in the administration as well as in all other walks of life: as subjects of a Turkish state, would they be any different from the Armenians, the Greeks, and the other ethnic communities? And if the *Dawlet*, under whose comfortable shade they had grown up were to disappear, what would be the fate of the Arab provinces of the lost Empire?

In the disturbed and disturbing atmosphere of Istanbul between 1908 and 1914 some of the Arab deputies in the Ottoman Assemblies and Councils, as well as Arab officers in the imperial army and Arab members of the civil service began to make decisions about where they wished to stand. There were some who felt at ease with the idea of a Turkish state, and as Muslims believed that they might easily integrate into Turkish society whose language and way of life they already shared: others, with close ties to their cities and families in the Arab provinces began to create in their imagination the vision of a new Arab entity which would replace Turkish rule, but conserve the Ottoman values of pluralism and multiculturalism.

At the centre of these political and cultural debates was the Hashemite family whose head, Sherif Hussein bin Ali, had recently been re-instated in their traditional role as governors of Mecca. His sons received a double education of Turkish and French in Istanbul, and Arabic in the Hejaz where their father sent them to acquire the Arab culture of the cities and the desert. It was the Amir Abdullah, the Sherif's second son, who made the first tentative move along the road of separation from the Turks; in 1916 he entered into correspondence with Lord Kitchener in Cairo to sound out what might be the reaction of the British Government to an Arab movement of independence from Turkish rule. This was to lead to a detailed correspondence between his father and British authorities on the basis of which he declared 'the Great Arab Revolt'.

This was the first political expression of Arab nationalism. It was not born out of an ideology but out of circumstances on the international scene: it was a risky gamble on the odds of an Allied victory over the Central Powers, but it was also an attempt to fill the vacuum which the defeat of Turkey would create in the Arab lands with a new political structure. That structure, as proposed at Versailles, and supported by Lebanese and Syrian communities like those in Manchester and New York, was to link the former Ottoman provinces in a federation taking into account the specific characters of the regions and people of the Arabian Peninsula. It was hoped, not to eradicate the multi-ethnic and multicultural formula of the Ottoman Empire, but to continue it under the rule of an *Arab Dawlet*. From its very beginning the concept of Arab nationalism was thus inextricably linked to the project of Arab unity.

The Hashemite plan did not succeed, but the vision did not die. The fortuitous circumstances of my life have associated me in various ways and at different stages with this vision, which I believe to be a still viable, and even necessary project if the Arab states which now control the truncated territories of the Peninsula are to survive the perils to which their fragmented policies expose them.

Chapter 2
Baghdad Days

In my childhood Baghdad was the city of my dreams. The stories of *The Thousand and One Nights* were one of the first books I read: the visit of Sherif Zaid, young brother of King Faisal, to lunch in our house in Manchester, and the frequent visits of Amin Kisbany and some of his friends made me conscious of Iraq before any other Arab land. Later on the *Letters of Gertrude Bell*, two volumes of which stood on the bookshelf above the fireplace of our dining-room, introduced me to many of the Iraqi and British figures at the centre of Baghdad's social life, among whom was Hussein Afnan. He is mentioned several times in Miss Bell's letters, for she had chosen him to edit an English newspaper in Baghdad, and he later became the secretary to the Council of Ministers, in which capacity it was he who read the public proclamation of Feisal as King of Iraq on 23 August 1923.

Of the social life of Baghdad in those few years before the Second World War disrupted its stability, and before the *coup d'état* of 1956 destroyed it, I was able to catch a glimpse during my first visit to the City of Peace. In the summer of 1948, shortly after the debacle in Palestine which began in May and has continued ever since, I accompanied Musa

Emir Zaid, youngest brother of King Faisal I in Baghdad in 1923.

Alami, head of the Arab Offices in the West of which I was a member, on a mission to seek support for the already failing Arab military effort. We lodged at the Zia Hotel, at that time the Ritz of Baghdad, and during my stay I was able to meet some of the many friends of the family of Hussein and Bedia Afnan, and of their daughter Furugh: the Khayyats, Rassams, Khandans, Daftaris, Chelebis, Haidaris, Omaris, Jawdats, Pachachis, Babans, as well as many of the statesmen and politicians with whom Musa Alami had become intimate during his own sojourn in the city in the early 40s.

On one occasion I was invited to attend a large gathering of both the private friends and the public figures: the occasion was the visit to Baghdad of Habib Bourguiba and Tayeb Slim, one of the younger Tunisian companions of his 'jihad'. At that time Bourguiba was still an almost unknown figure on the Arab political scene, where concern with the Palestinian question took precedence over the nationalist movements in North Africa.

Habib Bourguiba and Tayeb Slim at Hotel Zia, Baghdad 1949.

I had convinced Musa that the Palestinian and Tunisian causes were part of the same struggle, and it was he who was instrumental in introducing Bourguiba into the Baghdad political and social world. Among the luminaries of that scene was Mahmud Subhi Daftari, a benign, urbane and hospitable gentleman whose greatest pleasure in life was to entertain his many friends in the garden and orchards of his farm outside Baghdad. In honour of Habib Bourguiba he had invited *le tout Baghdad* to his private paradise; there among the orange and lemon trees, the date palms and the roses, large tables were spread with dishes from the Arabic, Turkish, Iranian and Indian cuisines. Like the guests, the food was a true reflection of the multicultural society of Iraq, and I was as fascinated by the one as by the other. No-one foresaw then that ten years later the exile would be the President of Tunisia, and some of his fellow-guests at the party would be exiles in that country, where Furugh and I were able to repay in our house in Sidi Bou Said some of the generous hospitality I had so enjoyed in Baghdad.

Mahmud Subhi Daftari and Bedia Afnan in his Baghdad paradise.

My visit to Baghdad had another purpose, to discover the world from which Bedia and Furugh had come. I had met them first in London on their way to the United States of America, where the mother was to join the Arab Office and the daughter to go to Wellesley College. Like myself, Bedia Afnan was totally new to the American scene; our salaries were too small to allow us to play much of a social role individually in Washington, and so we set up house together in a small house in Georgetown at 32nd Street and Q with an Assyrian cook whom we found living in Detroit.

In the turbulent years between 1946 and 1948 when the small band of scholars, amateur publicists, and intellectuals who joined the Arab Office attempted to present a reasonable and acceptable view of Arab opinion on the Palestinian problem to the American public and to the Washington establishment, the Iraqi, Saudi, Egyptian, Lebanese and Syrian Embassies helped us beyond measure to enter into the social life of the city, and to make political contacts which, on our own, would have been difficult to achieve. Our modest house in Georgetown was often the meeting-place of State Department officials, journalists, and socialites where Bedia Afnan's conversational talents, her daughter's vivacity, and our Assyrian cook's culinary skills, provided the certainty of many an evening's entertainment. The presence of Furugh during her vacations soon broke down the distinction between my public duties and my private life, and between Reason and Enthusiasm.

Cecil and Furugh, Washington DC, 1947.

I was perhaps psychologically and emotionally predisposed to fall in love with a girl from Baghdad. Furugh Afnan was not an ordinary girl: her genetic heritage, her cultural roots – part Iranian, part Turkish – her education in a British missionary school in Beirut, a startling physical beauty of features, and a vivacity which made her, as many of friends were to describe her after her death, 'life itself' – all these made her for me the incarnation of oriental femininity which to a romantic Presbyterian and sexually repressed young man made her irresistible.

It was only after a period of passionate attachment, then of marriage, that I was able to unravel partially the many strands in Furugh's character and to understand, though never perfectly, what made her so fascinating to me, but so difficult for her to live with herself. To the outside world she was brilliant, vivacious, amusing, generous, but there was a reverse side: from great gaiety to deep depression was a not infrequent sequence. She often doubted herself, felt that she was unachieved, and uprooted from one world, found it difficult to find another. In her a variety of inherited and acquired cultural genes jostled together to create an identity which was unique and 'different', while she really wanted to be 'the same'.

On her father's side Furugh was closely related to two of the most famous but controversial figures of Iran in the 19th century. The Afnans were the family of the maternal uncles of Sayyid Ali Mohammad, known as the Bab, or Gateway, and Mirza Hussein Ali Nuri, known as Bahaullah, was her great-grandfather whose daughter, Furughiyya Khanum, after whom she was named, married Sayyid Ali Afnan, Furugh's grand-father. On her mother's side Furugh was the great-niece of Sateh al-Husri, an Ottoman educator and scholar who after the break-up of the Empire decided he was an Arab and not a Turk, and became the father of secular Arab nationalism whose ideas and vision were to have a profound influence on the course of 20th century Arab history.

Furughiyya Khanum eldest daughter of Bahaullah.

Her parents had been able to live happily with their very different, and even opposing cultural and intellectual backgrounds. The Bab and Bahaullah proclaimed the vision of a regenerated Islam and Muslim society; Sateh al-Husri envisaged a regenerated secular Arab society and a politically united Arab State. What kept them together was their involvement in what they hoped would be a new

Sateh al-Husri uncle of Bedia Afnan.

flowering of the Arab and Iranian civilization which had made Baghdad a great capital in the past. They both shared in the Hashemite dream encapsulated in the person of King Feisal; after his death they were both disappointed, but not disillusioned.

Childhood in Baghdad in the thirties was a small paradise. As members of its privileged, though not moneyed, circle of which the royal palace was the centre, the children enjoyed the pleasures which Iraq and Baghdad offered: the beauty of the river scene, with its skyline of date-palms and the *belems* crossing it; night parties on the river-bank with *masgouf* roasting on the spit; excursions to the gardens of Hajji Naji and Subhi Daftari; summer vacations in the Kurdish mountains to the north; picnics in their green valleys when a caravan of horses and mules would carry tents and carpets ahead to pitch them under the shade of giant mulberry trees; a happy life at home with Najm, a young Bedouin servant, Anna, the Assyrian cook, Rex, a giant Kurdish sheepdog, and Olga the cow.

Hussein Afnan in 1939.

The early and unexpected death of Hussein Afnan in Beirut in 1940, and war in Europe were the beginning of the end of that Baghdad paradise. Furugh had the natural strong attachment of a daughter and only child to her father. I never met him, and she was always reluctant to talk to me about him. Behind her reluctance, and behind her father's smiling face I guessed there was concealed some secret and sad story. From her mother and her uncles and cousins, and from my researches into the still

Furugh with Rex in Baghdad.

only partially-revealed history of the revolutionary events in Iran in the 19th century sparked by her forefathers, Sayyid Ali Mohammad, the Bab, and Bahaullah, I later on came to understand the tragedy in the life of Hussein Afnan and of his whole family, and the sad story of a great movement which has strayed far away from its original mission.

By a curious coincidence, before I knew anything of the Bahai story, and its origins in Iran, two houses in Palestine – one in Haifa and the other in Acre – formed a connection between my family and the Afnans. When I first landed in late 1939 on the soil of the lands from where my parents had come I had stayed in Haifa in the house of maternal cousins of my mother. The Doumit family lived on the lower slopes of Mount Carmel, but not long before I arrived they had owned a house higher up and very close to the shrine built by AbdulBaha, the son of Bahaullah, to hold the mortal remains of Mirza Ali Mohammad, known as the Bab, martyred in Tabriz in 1850. On the door of that shrine Shoghi Effendi, the grandson of AbdulBaha nominated by him as the Custodian or Guardian of the legacy of the Bahai Cause, placed a powerful light which disturbed the Doumits and other residents of that area.

Mirza Ali Mohammad, Sayyid al-Bab.

Failing to reach any agreement either amicably or through legal action, the Doumits placed a large illuminated cross on the roof of their house. The conflict between the light and the cross ended by the sale of the house in 1935 to Hussein Afnan's cousin, Shoghi Effendi, who immediately demolished it and used the stones, doors and window frames, to construct an annex to the Pilgrims House next to the shrine. So it came about that the pilgrims who came from Iran and the East to visit the shrine of the Bab and lodged in the reconstructed house of my mother's cousins, would continue their pilgrimage to worship at the shrine of Bahaullah who is buried in the house of my father-in-law Hussein Afnan's family!

To understand the story one must go back to the early years of the 19th century in Iran where the expectation of the arrival of a messianic figure was current among the Shia Muslim communities spread through the Middle East, Central Asia, and India. Mirza Ali Mohammad, born to a merchant family in Shiraz in 1819, after some years of study, travel and pilgrimage, advanced from a first cautious interpretation of Quranic texts and law, to an open declaration of revelation, in which he claimed to be the *Qaim*, the Riser, whose coming would announce the advent of the Day of Judgement. In this new phase of human history the *Mahdi*, the Guide to the True Path, the Right Way, would initiate a new dispensation. This would not cancel or abolish the Muslim faith, but would replace the accepted 'sharia' by a new set of rules which would govern the conduct of human affairs. Mirza Ali Mohammad took for himself the name and the role of the Bab as the gateway, the door into this new path to the Truth.

The Bab gained some of his first followers among members of his own family, the Afnans. The charm of his personality, the eloquence of his words, and the unworldliness of his private life quickly spread the news among towns and villages in Iran far away from the centre of political authority. The Muslim clergy at first accepted to discuss and debate with him within the accepted framework of Shia scholasticism in which the door of interpretation is open, and he even found a friendly audience within the inner circles of power at the court of the ruling Qajars. But the rapid growth of the Bab's following aroused the fears of both clergy and government that their authority was being challenged; the movement was repressed with extreme cruelty, though many members of the educated and comfortable classes of Iranian society were prepared to become martyrs for the new cause. Tried by a court of the clergy, and refusing to renounce his claim that he was indeed the *Qaim*, Mirza Ali Mohammad was executed by a firing-squad in Tabriz on 19 July 1850.

Among the early followers of the Bab was Mirza Hussein Ali Nuri, a member of a family of notables, who following the execution, found it prudent to leave for Bagdad. On his return to Teheran, an attempted assassination of Shah

Nasireddin led to a ferocious persecution of the new sect: Mirza Hussein was thrown into prison but was released through the intervention of the Russian Ambassador. While in prison he wrote a letter to the Shah announcing that in a dream he had received a message from God that he was to fulfil a new mission. Exiled to Iraq he declared eight years later that he was 'the Manifestation of God' who he claimed had been foretold by the Bab. According to this new discourse the role of Mirza Ali Mohammad was that of a precursor, a John the Baptist. Henceforward a new dispensation, that of Bahaullah – the Glory of God – was to replace that of the Bab. This was equivalent to proclaiming that the revelation of the Prophet Mohammad was not final, and that revelation itself was progressive. The contemporary Darwinian theory of physiological evolution found its equivalent in this new theory of theological evolution.

AbdulBaha – Abbas Effendi – known as The Master.

The repression and persecutions which the Babis had suffered in Iran threatened to put an end to the movement; to save it from extinction Bahaullah was able to divert the immense devotion which the Bab had aroused by his messianic claim into less radical and more pacific channels. He now claimed that he was the Messenger through whom God had spoken to reveal a new formulation of the eternal truths which had been revealed to previous Messengers. It was not a new religion, but a wrapping-up of all preceding revelations which established the principles on which human behaviour should be based. These principles are laid down in the writings of Bahaullah and still constitute the ethical core of the Bahai movement.

In the years of exile in Palestine which followed Bahaullah's departure from Iraq, he and his son AbdulBaha were successful in incorporating the now legendary prestige of the Bab into this new 'dispensation'. The mission of Bahaullah now broadened its dimension to include all the major religions of the world; the esoteric innovations of the Bab were changed into a milder message which reconciled all religions in a broad and not too explicit vision of a New World Order and of Universal Peace, so that it was possible within this new 'revelation' to be a Bahai, a follower of Bahaullah, without ceasing to be a Muslim, Jew, Christian, Buddhist, Confucian or Hindu.

As a pacific, moral, and simple message which reconciled all religions and rejected none, and enjoined love of one's fellow-humans, honesty, justice and charity, the new revelation attracted followers from both the old and new worlds. Streams of visitors especially from the United States of America and Europe converged on Haifa and Acre where the family of Bahaullah lived along with the followers and disciples who had accompanied them to their new home in Palestine. It was into this family that Hussein was born to the daughter of Bahaullah, Furughiyya Khanum, and her husband Sayyid Ali Afnan, a maternal cousin of the Bab himself. With his Afnan cousins and the cousins from the family of AbdulBaha, Hussein grew up in what to the followers of the Cause was a Holy Family.

In a succession of wills written before he died in 1921 the Master entrusted his eldest grandson with the task of ensuring the continuity of the movement which by now had acquired thousands of followers in the Old and New Worlds, by setting up a body of trustees to administer its affairs. Shoghi Effendi interpreted the instructions of his grandfather differently: claiming that it was premature to form this 'Universal House of Justice', he assumed for himself absolute authority not only over all followers but also over his own family, as well as the authority of interpreting all the writings and sayings of his illustrious grandparents with infallibility. Anxious not to repeat the schisms and disputes which had plagued the movement ever since the Bab had died, the family acquiesced in Shoghi Effendi's increasingly autocratic actions and decisions: his closest cousins attempted to help him in a role which was clearly too large for him to play alone, but all incurred his mistrust and eventual displeasure. Hussein Afnan, who had gone to Bagdad and become secretary to the council of ministers in the Iraqi regime, worked hard to recuperate for the movement properties lived in by Bahaullah and purchased by the Master, but incurred the displeasure of the 'Guardian' for working in politics. After his marriage to a Canadian lady, daughter of an early follower, Shoghi's relations with his own family deteriorated to a point when he 'excommunicated' them all, either for disobeying his wishes, or accusing them of being enemies of the cause. By the end of his life, when he was living in London, his wife was to write later that the entire family of Bahaullah had betrayed the cause, and that he alone – with his wife – were the only true Bahais!

For Hussein Afnan, as for all the other members of the family, this was a tragedy: not only had they been ejected from the cause in which they had all been reared and in which they believed, but that cause had been deflected from its original definition and purpose. Whereas Bahaullah and AbdulBaha had lived, spoken, and written in the vocabulary and idiom of Islam, and been accepted in Palestine as part of Muslim society, Shoghi Effendi used his autocratic power and control over the financial affairs of the movement to take it out of Islam and to attempt to turn it into a new religion. Using the Bahai community in the United States as a cover for his own decisions and his control over the revenues contributed by the faithful, he set up an administrative organization which restricted the cause to its card-carrying members. Not only was Bahaism separated from Islam, but Islam became an enemy, and one of his closest cousins was excommunicated for marrying a Muslim girl! From its status as a questionable heresy, Bahaism was transformed into apostasy, and its followers in Iran and other Muslim lands are still paying the price of that fatal error.

Although I never met Hussein Afnan, I knew from my mother-in-law, and from my wife, of the deep unhappiness which the disintegration of the Bahai cause at the hands of the 'Guardian' had caused him, and I learnt from other members of that family of the same distress. One of them, Suhail Afnan, in whose green and piercing eyes I saw reflected the image of his great ancestors, told me in tragic tones, 'Cecil, you know our story... we *were* a great family'. I realized then that the loss of a Cause may be greater than the loss of a Country.

Chapter 3
Two sides of the Jordan

If Iraq was the land of my childhood dreams, it became in later life a land of nightmares: the revolution of 1958 which bloodily eliminated all save one member of the ruling Hashemite family, as well as many of the personalities who had in one way or another made of Iraq a modern and forward-looking society; the sequence of *coups d'état* which followed the revolution and led to ever-increasing degrees of ruthlessness and despotism; the devastation and hardships inflicted on the Iraqi people as a result of Iraq's invasion of Kuwait, and the international interventions in 1991 and 2003 which have dislocated Iraq's unity and threaten to fragment it permanently.

In the tragic story of modern Iraq an episode of the first Gulf War was to provide the occasion for a new chapter in my own life. In the weeks which preceded the invasion of Kuwait in 1990 a crisis between the Iraqi government and its oil-producing neighbours fore-shadowed that event. The intimate relations between these countries and the United States of America internationalized the crisis, in which Washington became a player although its role was

Assem Salam and Furugh in Highgate Cemetry, London.

ambiguous. During this period I received an invitation from Yale University to give a lecture on the topic of the crisis, which usefully concentrated my mind. The lecture which stirred considerable debate and controversy was a highly critical analysis of American policies in the Middle East.

In August of that year I was in London and heard early in the morning of the 2nd the news that Iraq had invaded Kuwait. I immediately telephoned Assem Salam, my friend of many years, who was also in London on a visit from Beirut, to inform him; his reaction which proved accurate was 'this is an earthquake'. Why was this? It was not because this was one Arab state invading another of which there had been other examples in the 20th century: Saudi Arabia had invaded and annexed the Yemeni provinces of Najran and Asir in the 30s, and Egypt had committed aggression against Yemen in the 60s. What was new and potentially explosive was not only Iraq's challenge to the authority of both the United Nations and the Arab League, and to the oil interests of the industrial world, but also to the whole structure of the post-1918 map drawn up by Great Britain and France on the former territories of the Ottoman empire.

While the occasion for the invasion was Iraq's claim that Kuwait was undermining Iraq's oil interests by production over agreed limits, the real causes were two. It was an universally-held belief among the Iraqi population that Kuwait historically and legally belonged to Iraq, and its eventual re-integration had been the policy of all the regimes which had preceded that of Saddam Hussein. It was also an attempt to translate into reality the ideology of a certain version of Arab nationalism based on the writings of my wife Furugh's great uncle Sateh al-Husri, namely, that there is one Arab people or nation, and that therefore there should be – and eventually will be – one Arab State. It was a theory which could be used to justify the fusion of any two or more existing states on the ground that they were only parts or provinces of the greater Arab entity. The role of the 'Arab Bismarck' who would unite the Arab provinces which Gamal Abdel Nasser had unsuccessfully tried to assume was now taken up by Saddam Hussein. His invasion of Iraq was doomed to failure because he united too many opponents and touched the interests of the industrial world in the supply of cheap oil.

But while most Arab governments naturally opposed his adventure, their peoples saw it in a different light: it was seen as a welcome challenge to the legitimacy of the post-1918 frontiers, and a defiance of 'the West' on whose heads many of the grievances of the Arab peoples against their regimes were placed.

In my own home the feelings ran high. Furugh had been brought up in Iraq, regarded herself as an Iraqi, and shared the emotions of her friends and the ideals if not all the arguments of her great-uncle. Like all her friends and contemporaries she regarded Kuwait as part of Iraq, and the prospect of a war to reverse the invasion was as odious to her as it seemed unnecessary to me. Although I could not deny that Saddam Hussein's action was imprudent, I was impressed by the efforts of the Jordanian monarch to prevent the internationalization of the crisis and to resolve it within an Arab context. A declaration by the Iraqi president linking the problem of Kuwait to both the Palestinian-Israeli and the Lebanese-Syrian problems incited me to write a letter to *The Times* advocating a wider approach to the crisis, but it was another letter which provided an occasion for me to work off some of my frustration, and which was to open a new chapter in my life.

On September the 26th I was astonished to read in *The Times* the text of a letter written and published in the Washington Post and New York Times by Prince Bandar bin Sultan, ambassador of the Kingdom of Saudi Arabia in Washington and an intimate counsellor and friend of President Bush. The letter, addressed to the person of King Hussein of Jordan, was an unprovoked and ferocious attack on the King who was pursuing his efforts to form an Arab consensus within which Saddam Hussein it was hoped could be convinced to retire peacefully from Kuwait. While King Hussein roundly condemned the invasion he was advocating a negotiated and peaceful settlement, fearing rightly as events were to show that war would create a situation worse than the one it was supposed to remedy. The Ambassador's letter accused the King of complicity in the invasion and questioned his motives for the search of an Arab solution. Perhaps the letter was intended to please his friends in Washington who saw in the invasion of Kuwait an opportunity to pursue other and wider aims than a mere reversal of the invasion, or perhaps he was motivated by a wish to play a greater role in his own country. In either case, coming from an Arab diplomat of exceptional influence at the time, it was not only harmful to the efforts of King Hussein, but insulting to his person.

Letter from Prince Bandar bin Sultan Al Saud to King Hussein.

Your Majesty, you gave a moving speech to the American people this past week which appears to have been done over the head of your long-time friend, President Bush. In it you say you were moved to do it because of a letter from Mr Brown of North Carolina, USA. Would it not be more honourable and truly moving if you were moved enough by Kuwaiti women and children with tears in their eyes because they lost their country as a result of an aggression of your friend, Saddam Hussein? Would it not be more honourable and honest to speak to the Iraqi people over the head of your friend Saddam Hussein and tell them what he has dishonourably done in invading and annexing a brother Arab and Muslim country? And the horrifying acts of rape and destruction unprecedented in Arab history... that is fact. And facts are stubborn things.

You say, Your Majesty, that the Holy Places in Saudi Arabia have been desecrated by friendly forces and those forces must leave immediately. But those forces are actually hundreds of miles away, with tens of thousands of Muslim and Arab forces (your forces are not among them) between those forces and the holy places. And all those forces are dedicated to help defend Saudi Arabia and are respectful of its custodianship of the holy places, and will not leave until your friend Saddam Hussein leaves Kuwait, which we hope will be peacefully and immediately. Tell us, Your Majesty, what have you done to safeguard the Al-Aqsa Mosque and the Church of the Holy

Sepulchre that you lost to the Israelis in 1967, almost a quarter of a century ago. Is that the kind of protection you want us to give the Holy Places in Saudi Arabia? Your Majesty, the Holy Places in Saudi Arabia are protected only by your brother Muslims, and no non-Muslim is anywhere around, as millions of Muslims can daily attest and you know that to be a fact.

And, Your Majesty, you claimed to defend the Palestinian people's right to self-determination and a state of their own. I support you. But you were responsible for the Palestinian homeland on the West Bank from 1948 to 1967. Why, in all that period, you did not give them their rights and statehood? And how would the occupation of Kuwait give our brother Palestinians their homeland? Facts are stubborn things.

You talk of 'haves' and 'have-nots'. Saudi Arabia record as one of the 'haves' is clear in helping the 'have-nots' and we are proud of it. Just turn to the records of your finance minister, and see how much has been given to you and your country for many years by Saudi Arabia, willingly and happily, as brothers. Are not facts stubborn?

When you needed Saudi troops to help you, they came and spent ten years in your country at your asking. And we did not question why or why not, nor raise 'ifs' and 'buts', as you do now. Facts are stubborn things. You are a very intelligent man. And you have a fine memory. You say the Kuwaiti-Iraq border is disputed and based on a historical record created by colonial British. Your Majesty, you should be the last one to say that. Not only are your borders but your whole country was created by the same colonial British. Facts are stubborn things indeed, Your Majesty. And do you remember when the British troops were invited by you into your country in 1958? We did not object or question your motives. Facts are stubborn things.

Your brother, King Fahd, is proud to have as

friends President Mubarak, President Assad, King Hassan, the Presidents of Pakistan, Bangladesh and Senegal, the leaders of the Mujahideen, Presidents Gorbachev, Bush, Mitterrand, Prime Minister Thatcher and so many more heads of state who have joined in the world-wide consensus of the United Nations, arrayed against the naked aggression and annexation of our brother state Kuwait. And we are proud of our friends. I hope you are proud of your new friends – Saddam Hussein, Abu Abbas, Abu Nidal, Habash, Hawatmeh and the rest of that unholy crowd. Facts are stubborn things.

You tell us the situation is like 1914, when the world was going to a war which it did not want but could not stop, which led to World War I. That is not true. Your Majesty, we are today like the 1930s, when a madman decided to annex his neighbour and the world did nothing, which led to World War II. These are facts. Facts are stubborn things.

Your Majesty, please remember what caused this crisis in our region – it was the invasion of the Arab and Muslim state of Kuwait by Saddam Hussein. Only after that and because of that Muslim, Arab, and friendly forces were invited. They will all leave when this aggression is turned back or when we ask them to leave. These are facts Your Majesty... and facts are stubborn things.

Finally, Your Majesty, I long had a great respect and affection for you. And I continue to have deep respect and affection for your people. But I no longer can feel that you are the same man I knew. I hope that I am wrong. And if I am wrong, please accept my sincere apologies, Your Majesty. But facts are stubborn things.

The letter aroused my intense indignation: it had to be answered, but by whom? Clearly the King could not reply himself, but as the days passed and no answer from Amman was forthcoming, I decided that I must write it although not solicited. I drafted a reply which while without descending to the level of the Ambassador's insults, would match its insolence. I realized that I could not publish this under my name, even if the two newspapers which had published the letter of Prince Bandar accepted to print it, so I sent it to the Royal Palace in Amman, suggesting that someone of equal stature to the Prince put his name to it. The suggestion was accepted, and my letter, under the signature of Hazem Nusseibeh, a former student of mine at the American University of Beirut who had been a Jordanian Ambassador and Foreign Minister, was published on October the 6th in both Washington and London.

Reply to Prince Bandar bin Sultan al-Saud's open letter to King Hussein.

Your Excellency: His Majesty King Hussein is precluded by a natural preference for the language of diplomacy and reason over the language of passion and personal denigration from replying himself to the open letter you addressed to him through the Sunday Times last week. He is also restrained by his wish to respect the agreement made between his grandfather, King Abdullah, and your distinguished grandfather, King Abdul Aziz Al Saud, to bury the circumstances in which the dynasty of Al Saud replaced the Hashemite family as sovereigns of the Hejaz and custodians of the Holy Places.

Your letter, inspired by King Hussein's broadcast through the CNN channel to the American public, was perhaps a personal initiative of your own rather than a decision by your government to open an ill-advised and unwarranted campaign against King Hussein. Nevertheless it calls for a reply because of the wide publicity it has received on both sides of the Atlantic, and because while it claims to present 'facts', some of those facts are only half true, or not true, and there are other facts that have no mention at all.

King Hussein did not say that the Holy Places

had been desecrated by what you call friendly forces, and out of discretion – a quality which you would be wise to learn from him – he did not mention the occasion when your government called in French forces to evict, not foreigners, but your own citizens, from the precincts of the Holy Kaaba. What he did say was that the presence of non-Arab and non-Muslim forces in Saudi Arabia united secular nationalism and religious conservatism against it, which might, in the event of war, 'result in incalculable grave consequences involving Arabs and Muslims the world over'. He therefore advocated that these forces should be withdrawn 'within the shortest possible period of time'. It is difficult to understand why you, as the representative of your government, should object to that unless you want those foreign forces to prolong their presence beyond the present crisis

You make the extraordinary statement that King Hussein was responsible for 'the Palestinian homeland on the West Bank' from 1948-67, and you ask why he did not give Palestinians their rights and statehood. King Hussein acceded to the throne in 1953; and there was no 'Palestinian homeland on the West Bank'. The territories of Palestine which remained in Arab hands after 1948 and 1949 joined the Kingdom of Transjordan at the request of the Palestinians themselves, who did not wish to consecrate partition by accepting a Palestinian state on only part of their land. Their homeland is Palestine, not the West Bank.

You sarcastically remark that 'your whole country was created by... the colonial British', as if any country in the Arab Peninsula achieved its present frontiers other than through arrangements made by Great Britain and France during and after the first World War. King Hussein's great-grandfather, Sherif Hussein, favoured a united Arab state in the whole of the Peninsula.

Jordan has not opposed the right of any sovereign country to invite troops to aid its defence. The reference you make to 1958, when Jordan called for foreign assistance, came in the context of the Cold War.

Like some Western statesmen you seek to draw a parallel between this crisis and Germany's invasion of neighbouring countries in 1938 and 1939, forgetting that the rise of National Socialism took place against the background of frustration and resentment caused by the Versailles settlement. Iraq's invasion and annexation of Kuwait cannot be correctly described as the sole cause of the crisis; it has its roots in other annexations, other problems created by the international community but left unresolved.

In calling not only for the withdrawal of Iraq from Kuwait, but also for a serious international effort to solve the equally serious problems in the region, King Hussein has consistently put forward a point of view to which the governments of France, the Soviet Union, Great Britain, and even the United States of America are gradually coming around. It is difficult to understand in whose interest it is to discredit and denigrate King Hussein's efforts just when they seem to be bearing fruit.

Could it be that the real cause of your outburst against the king is his statement that 'as regards all countries and peoples in the region, every encouragement must be given to their governments to ensure their orderly and rapid transformation into democracies recognized as such by any yardstick in this world, where citizens enjoy equal rights, and where human rights are recognized, enjoyed and respected.'

You state that you have lost 'the great respect and affection' you had for King Hussein, though you retain them for the Jordanian people. I do not think King Hussein will be unduly upset by whatever change of mind you may have had about his personality. He is quite happy with the solid support he enjoys not only of the Jordanian people, but also of a broad and perhaps major spectrum of the Arab peoples, of whose aspirations he is the authentic spokesman.

(The author is a former Jordanian foreign minister)

As a result of the publication of the reply to Prince Bandar's letter, my wife and I were invited to spend a week or ten days in Jordan. At the time of our visit King Hussein was abroad, and to my astonishment and great pleasure it was the director of the office of the Crown Prince who was at the airport in Amman to receive us. Michel Hamarneh had been one of my many students at the American University of Beirut, and was to prove a faithful colleague and friend in the years which followed. This was the beginning of a long association with Crown Prince Hassan, King Hussein's younger brother.

In the months which preceded the Gulf War in February 1991 the position taken by Jordan, and in particular the intense efforts of King Hussein and his brother to seek a peaceful resolution of the crisis had been widely either ignored, misunderstood, or misrepresented in Washington, London, and in many other capitals, by governments and the international media. The King had been portrayed as an accomplice of the Iraqi regime, and Jordan was being penalized for its choice of principle over expediency. From London where I had watched the war in a state of indignation I took another initiative: Jordan had to defend its stand and provide a convincing record of what had actually been said and done by its authorities. The same idea was already circulating in Amman, and my offer to put together a document for that purpose was accepted by the Palace.

I was invited to Amman and given access to speeches, letters, memoranda, and interviews given by King Hussein and the Crown Prince, and to other official documents. As I conceived it, the White Paper would be a summary of the principle initiatives taken by Jordan to try to prevent the war, and present truthfully the reasons for their failure even at the cost of embarrassing or angering other parties to the conflict.

The argument was to be supported by supporting texts chosen from among the many items I was shown. In this truthful but potentially controversial document there were some among the Palace's advisors who would have preferred to omit the dangerous details, or even to publish nothing, but the King agreed with the unchanged document, and it was published. As expected, the White Paper irritated Washington, and angered the Egyptian Government which published a rival 'Black Book', and also the Kuwaitis who published their own 'White Paper'. I have been happy to learn that the Jordanian White Paper has been widely used in some American colleges and at Oxford University as a sourcebook for the history of the first Gulf crisis.

A few weeks after the publication of the White Paper my wife Furugh died suddenly in London. Emir Hassan and Princess Sarvath came to my house to present their condolences. He then suggested that I might like to come to Amman to work with him as an advisor. I believe he did this because he realized that I would be in need of a path to lead me out of grief, and to involve me in a new and challenging adventure. I shall be eternally grateful for this gesture of friendship from a family who from childhood I had admired, and with whom in old age I have been privileged to work.

The opening of this new chapter in my life coincided with a new stage in the Palestinian-Israeli conflict. The months preliminary to the outbreak of the Gulf war, and the conflict itself, had revealed clearly the linkage in the minds of the Arab population in the region between America's policy towards Saddam Hussein and its traditional policies in the Israeli-Palestinian conflict. What were perceived as 'double standards' became the main cause of Arab resentment: Iraq's defiance of the international community was seen as either equivalent to or less flagrant than Israel's persistent refusal to accept United Nations' resolutions on a wide variety of subjects, and American support for this refusal. Before the war in the Gulf had ended President Bush and his advisors began an attempt to soften Arab resentments, closely connected as they were to America's oil interests in the Arabian Peninsula, by offering an olive-branch to the Palestinians in the form of a new initiative towards a 'peace process'. While still denying any linkage between the two problems, the connection could not be concealed. Optimists saw hope in President Bush's 'New World Order', and cynics saw it as just one more attempt to pursue old policies under another name.

The first American step towards this 'new world order' was the convening of a conference in Madrid on 30 October 1991, in collaboration with the new Russian regime, to which Egypt and the Arab governments, although still theoretically at war with Israel, were invited. Not being a state, the Palestinians were at first not invited nor consulted on its agenda. This agenda was laid down in a series of letters addressed by Bush's Secretary of State James Baker to the invitees: the Israeli-Palestinian conflict was to be addressed within the framework of Security Council Resolutions 242 and 338, although these resolutions only related to the parties to the 6-Day War of June 1967, namely Israel, Egypt, Jordan and Syria, and they were not relevant to the conflict between Israelis and Palestinians which had begun with the partition recommended by the General Assembly in 1947. King Hussein at first refused the invitation to Madrid because the Palestinians were not invited, but as a compromise with Israel's refusal to sit with the PLO, a joint Jordanian-Palestinian delegation was invited to Madrid. It was at this point that I arrived in Amman in my new function as an advisor to the office of the Crown Prince who had been appointed by the King to organize the participation of the joint delegation to the Madrid Conference.

In the initial stages of the preparations for this participation, divergences of views already began to appear. The Jordanian team included a former prime minister, academics, economists, past and present advisors to the royal court, a Jordanian international lawyer and two foreign international lawyers; among these were some Jordanians of Palestinian origin whose loyalties were to Jordan. The Palestinian delegation was composed partly of members who had remained on Palestinian territory before and after Israeli occupation, and partly of members of the Palestinian Diaspora This was a less homogenous group, for the 'insiders' and the 'outsiders' had different perspectives: the insiders tempered their views of what was legally or morally just with a perception of what was possible, while the outsiders leaned towards confrontation rather than compromise, an easier choice for those who lived far away from the daily tragedies of conflict on the ground.

In my role as an observer and advisor I soon sensed that there was a major question which needed to be addressed, and not put aside for fear of discord: what role could and should Jordan play in any settlement of the Palestinian-Israeli conflict? Did it have a legitimate role at all, or had that role been cancelled by two decisions taken by King Hussein: the first in 1968 after the Rabat Conference in which he had accepted the Arab League's recognition of the Palestine Liberation Organization led by Yasser Arafat as the sole legitimate representative of the Palestinian people, and the second in 1988 when he had seemed to relinquish all claims to sovereign rights in the Palestinian territories?

The first decision, while it did not amount to a legal renunciation of Jordanian de facto sovereignty exercised over territory which remained in Arab hands at the end of 1948, complicated matters. Between Jordan and Israel, as two sovereign states, agreement about territory, possible though difficult, would have international acceptance and legitimacy; but between a sovereign Israel and an as-yet unformed Palestinian authority any agreement that might be reached, could only be a diktat from the strong to the weak. This was then, in 1991, and still is today, the basic problem which eludes solution within the framework of an embryonic Palestinian state and a fully-grown and powerful Israeli state.

As I perceived it the agreement on a joint Jordanian-Palestinian negotiating team opened the possibility of bridging the gap between Jordanian rights and Palestinian hopes. If it had been able to speak with one voice it could have both re-asserted Jordan's claim to recuperate most if not all of the territory lost to Israel in the 6-Day war, and inserted within any agreement with Israel the terms on which all three parties would establish the Palestinian state. Peace based on a triangular structure would be solid: on two pillars it could only be incomplete and unsafe. Unfortunately this was not to be: once in Washington where the negotiations were to take place the Palestinian members started to break away from their Jordanian partners, and thus to cut the ground from under their own feet. To some Palestinian members of the joint delegation the umbrella which Jordan had provided in order to enable the Palestinians to go to Washington was irksome: it reminded them of what they would prefer to forget, namely that Jordan had accepted to hold a trusteeship over Palestinian territory at the request of Palestinian leaders in 1949; and it reflected a widespread prejudice among many Palestinians in the Diaspora against Jordan and its Hashemite regime.

This led to the separation of the two teams in Washington, and no attempt was made from Amman to assert Jordanian rights. Inevitably the negotiations reached an impasse: there was no longer the *interlocuteur valable* in the shape of Jordan with whom the Israelis could negotiate, but only a team of Palestinian negotiators whose authority to speak on behalf of the Palestinian population in the territories was being progressively sabotaged by the exiled leaders of the PLO in Cairo who feared that their role as 'the sole legitimate representatives of the Palestinian people' was being eroded.

Seeing the negative consequences of the *impasse*, at a meeting in the house of the Crown Prince, I suggested to King Hussein a way out of the deadlock: Yasser Arafat's moral and material authority as the head of the PLO had been seriously weakened both internationally and among the Palestinians by his support for the Iraqi regime's invasion of Kuwait; in spite of his personal inclinations King Hussein had continued to support Arafat's Palestinian leadership, but need no longer do so. In order to rescue the negotiations in Washington, I suggested that he meet with the Israeli Prime Minister, Yitzhak Rabin, and set the negotiations on a new track which would break the deadlock. Rabin, I argued, had as much interest in a successful 'peace process' as the King, and this could be the occasion to regain the chance which had been lost after 1967, both to end the Jordanian-Israeli conflict and to create the framework for an end to the Palestinian-Israeli conflict. The King was amenable to my suggestion and sent me to Washington to prospect the terrain.

I arrived in Washington on 25 March and next day went to the office of two of the King's American advisers: Richard Weitz, a former Ambassador to Jordan, and Jack O'Connell, a former CIA station head in Jordan. My second contact was Professor Itamar Rabinovitch, the Israeli Ambassador in Washington, known to be a close and influential adviser to Prime Minister Rabin, and then negotiating with Syria. I explained that my views were my own and in no way committed the King or Crown Prince. They had consented to my meeting with him as a way of perhaps opening up a channel of communication which, without being a substitute for other channels, might be fruitful. There was now a dangerous situation in Gaza, the West Bank and Israel: an escalation of violence which the Israelis were unable to control, and no apparent Palestinian authority. The growth of extremism on both sides posed a problem which needs to be addressed. While King Hussein was absolutely committed to peace, this was not necessarily the same as a commitment to the process started at Madrid, which anyway had come to a dead-end. No solution, for example, which left Jordan carrying the main burden of the Palestinian refugee problem could work. The Palestinian problem was not only one of frontiers, but also, and principally, of people. In this context I put forward the view that only the Jordanian regime, under King Hussein's leadership, could provide the formula for real peace. His prestige among the Palestinians, and also internationally, made him the most suitable *interlocuteur valable* needed by Israel. If the King and the Prime Minister could meet together soon I felt that they might find a way out of the present impasse in Washington.

Rabinovitch replied that he would immediately convey my thoughts to the Prime Minister and asked me to call him on the following Monday, 28 March, with a view to a further meeting. On that day however he told me that because of the security situation in Israel he thought it better to wait for a few more days, but promised to get in touch with me as soon as he had received a reaction from the Prime Minister. I did not hear from him again.

Three days later I met with Martin Indyk, a National Security advisor and later on Ambassador to Israel. His main concern was whether King Hussein could succeed in by-passing Arafat, who was already being groomed by both the Americans and the Israelis as the Palestine *interlocuteur valable*. I insisted that Jordan was worried that agreements might be made which would marginalize Jordan's role: Jordan's interests were not confined to a few minor frontier disputes or the problem of water – without a solution to the problem of the Palestinian refugees and displaced persons there would be no security for anyone. Indyk admitted that the main problem between the Israelis and the Palestinians was the question of interim self-government: the Palestinians wanted to know what the end-game was, while the Israelis wanted that to be negotiated at the end of the process. He had correctly anticipated what would be the fatal flaw in the Oslo Agreements which were probably being drafted secretly at that time. My mission came to nothing, but later events proved that my estimate of a Hussein-Rabin collaboration was correct.

I presented a report on my mission to Washington to the palace, and returned to London. It was there that on 13 September I heard the news that Palestinian and Israeli delegations had met secretly in Oslo and made agreements which explained my failure, and opened a new, unhappy, and still unresolved obstacle to what I still believe must be the goal of any serious negotiations between Palestinian and Israelis – the establishment of the Palestinian State.

The announcement of the Oslo Agreements came as a tremendous shock to King Hussein, and I remember vividly his outrage expressed at a meeting in the house of the Crown Prince after my speedy return to Amman. Not only had he not been informed that negotiations had been carried on in Oslo behind his back, but the agreements removed Jordan from the scenario of the peace process, liquidated the role of the Palestinian team in Washington which represented a broad spectrum of Palestinian opinion in Gaza and the West Bank, and returned Arafat and his team to a role in which they had miserably failed in both Lebanon and the Iraq-Kuwaiti episode.

In book I of *An Unfinished Odyssey* I had compared the Palestinian problem to a ship floundering on the wide sea without a captain, and a crew at odds with itself. Now Oslo had appointed a captain who had already proved himself incompetent, who did not know the sea, its dangers, and its laws of navigation. It was inevitable that he should eventually run it onto the rocks, where it still lies waiting for a new crew to put it afloat again and bring it to safety; that team has yet to be found. By resurrecting Arafat from what seemed to be a decrepit decline, the Israelis believed that they had found in him both a partner and a willing accomplice; they were to be deceived and ended up with neither. The *interlocuteur* turned out to be not *valable*, and the partner a liability. Finding nothing to say which might have calmed the King's agitation I could only suggest that he should 'make the best of a bad job'. This he did: if Arafat thought he could make peace with Israel, the King would do it first, and the Jordanian-Israeli Peace Treaty was not long to follow in July 1994.

The Oslo agreements were subjected to intense scrutiny by Jordanians and Palestinians. The Palestinians were divided into two camps: the one rejected them out of hand as capitulation to an Israeli diktat, the other was ambiguous. Walid Khalidi, a prominent spokesman for the Palestinian cause, in a speech in Athens argued sophistically that although the agreements were bad, they should be accepted: he received a standing ovation! My own view was that the agreements contained the seeds of their own failure. Instead of starting with a clear definition of the final goal – the Palestinian state and its frontiers – and leaving the steps to reach that goal to the second phase, Oslo reversed the process: it began with the simpler problems, but as they went slowly on towards the still undefined 'final solution,' the Israelis found they were giving too much, and the Palestinians not enough. The negotiations floundered, then collapsed finally at Camp David in July 2000. The Israeli Prime Minister Ehud Barak and his side-kick Yossi Beilin had offered more than they could get their own public to accept, but laid the blame for the collapse of the negotiations on Arafat, who declined to play the role of stooge for which they had attempted to groom him.

King Hussein's decision to sign the peace treaty with Israel was taken to pre-empt any outcome of the Oslo Agreements which might prejudice Jordanian interests. I saw it, as I had seen Egypt's peace treaty, as an important step towards the resolution of the Arab-Israeli conflict, and published an article in *The Jordan Times* welcoming it. What I did not foresee was the negative outcome of the agreements on the situation of the Palestinians themselves, now left alone to face successive Israeli governments of fluctuating intentions. I was mistaken to believe that the Egyptian and Jordanian peace treaties could empower their governments to effectively pressure the Israelis towards the two-state solution, or indeed any solution at all. The assassinations of Sadat and Rabin, and the death of King Hussein, removed from the Middle East scene the three figures who had achieved enormous prestige and respect in Israel, and might have determined the balance of opinion between the Israeli proponents and opponents of peace with the Palestinians, and between the Palestinian advocates and rejectionists of peace with the Israelis. The death of King Hussein was a Shakespearian tragedy whose final act has still not been played out.

In the period between the signing of the Jordanian-Israeli Peace Treaty in the autumn of 1995 and 7 February 1999 when King Hussein died, I was frequently in Amman. It was an exciting time, and the prospects of peace between the Palestinians and the Israelis seemed to be greater than at any time in the past. The arrival of an Israeli Ambassador in Amman, and the appointment of a Jordanian Ambassador to Israel; the opening of the long-closed frontiers between the two sides of the river Jordan making it possible for Jordanians and Palestinians to visit each other after fifty years; the sight of Israeli visitors and tourists circulating quite easily between Petra and Amman; and tentative beginnings of joint commercial and industrial ventures between Jordanians and Israelis – all these new experiences created a hopeful though restrained atmosphere.

I thought it might be possible to start dialogues between Jordanian, Palestinian and Israeli academics and intellectuals to break down the fears, prejudices, and simple ignorance which over fifty years had inhibited contacts between the neighbours. A proposed meeting between three prominent Israeli academics and writers with some Jordanian and Palestinian equivalents failed when only one of the latter turned up. The director of Jordanian television liked the idea of a series of programmes to acquaint people on both sides of the river with each other's daily lives and problems: 'who are they?' was planned but never finalized. As the hopes of a negotiated Palestinian-Israeli settlement under the terms of the Oslo Agreements – hopes which I had never shared – faded, dark shadows fell over Jordanian-Israeli relations: the people on the East side of the river could not remain indifferent to the trials and tribulations of their brothers on the West. The assassination of Rabin in January 1996 removed one pillar of the hoped-for new structure of peace; the slow but relentless disease which killed King Hussein removed the other.

I had for some time been aware that there was an intrigue afoot to alter the succession to the throne. Public gossip seemed to emanate from a high source within the family, and the name of the hoped-for candidate cropped up from time to time in favourable mentions by the King himself. In the Shakespearean atmosphere which prevailed in the Royal Diwan it was not difficult to identify the source from which these whispers came.

King Hussein discharged himself from Mayo Clinic in Rochester where he had been staying for six months and returned to Amman on 25 January 1999. It was a bitterly cold and rainy day, and in the open car in which he insisted to visit his people the inadequate covering was visible. In an interview with CNN the following day the King hinted that he had taken an important decision. Early in the morning of the 26th Jordanian television broadcast the text of a letter from the King to his brother Amir Hassan announcing his decision to remove him as Crown Prince in favour of Prince Abdullah, the King's eldest son from his former English wife, Princess Muna al-Hussein.

The publication of the letter came as a tremendous shock in Jordan and around the world. The decision was clear but the reasons were not; the language was confused, the argument personal and at some points petty, and the contents hurtful to its recipient. The Amir replied in a discreet and dignified letter, only partially published at the time but later fully made public. Like many others I was disturbed: I not only disapproved of the decision, but I also saw that it was unjust and unmerited. What was surely to grieve Prince Hassan was not the loss of the kingship, which by now he must have seen as probable, but the loss of his brother, the companion of his career and the anchor of his life.

Although the motives and the circumstances in which King Hussein's letter was written may never be entirely clear, the consequences have not been happy. The elimination of Prince Hassan from participation in the political affairs of the kingdom which was soon to follow cut the thread of continuity with Jordan's Ottoman past – that 'last whisper' of the Dawlet which almost the last Turkish-speaking member of the family provided, and Jordan was deprived of the Amir's long-accumulated experience and wisdom. At the same time it placed on the new and 'unexpected' king problems and responsibilities which he had not been prepared to address. The erosion of Jordan's involvement in the events taking place on the other side of the river handed him an ambiguous legacy: was Jordan existentially and legitimately part of the Palestinian problem, or was it, like the other Arab states, an outsider, committed socially, culturally and emotionally to the cause of the Palestinian people, but not finally responsible for its success or failure?

History did not give the new King a clear answer. His great-great-grandfather Sherif Hussein had lost his throne because of his refusal to recognize the legitimacy of a 'national home' for the Jews in Palestine; his great-grandfather King Abdullah the First had been assassinated in Jerusalem by Palestinians who called him a traitor to their cause; his father almost lost his throne several times, and his father's best Prime Minister Wasfi Tel lost his life because of an attempt by armed Palestinians in 1970 to take over the country. His father's two proposals for a Jordanian-Palestinian federation had been rejected by the Palestinians, and although he had reluctantly agreed to accept the Palestinian Liberation Organization as the sole legitimate representative if the Palestinian people, it had gone behind his back and made agreements at Oslo which ignored Jordanian involvement in their problem.

When the new King acceded to the throne many Jordanians felt that they were being gradually demoted to the status of second-class citizens in their own country. A higher Palestinian birth-rate, and the greater commercial and industrial prosperity of many Palestinians stoked the natural resentment of a long-established community against a newly-arrived one. In an attempt to alleviate these domestic tensions the new regime adopted the slogan 'Jordan First'. This was widely interpreted to mean that its priority was the well-being of the Jordanian population. As a commitment to work for the improvement of the economic and social conditions of the population of which half at least were Palestinians, this was laudable, but it also seemed to imply the regime's intention not to get embroiled in the conflict next door – which indeed was the case.

To the outside world the existence of a Jordanian regime 'at peace' with Israel, concerned with the welfare and progress of its people, was seen as a rare and to-be-supported phenomenon in the region. It could tell the Israelis and Palestinians to stop killing each other; it could advise the Americans to exert non-existent pressure on the Israelis to stop building settlements, and it could join in the efforts of its fellow Arab governments to promote solutions which they had no means to implement. All this could not ignore the fact that the house next door was on fire. It is a dangerous gamble to watch the neighbour's fire and hope that it will die down whereas the wind might blow stronger and the fire spread.

Between a policy to resist involvement in the conflict between Palestinians and Israelis, and an inherited Hashemite vision of a common Arab destiny the choice may not be easy, but the failure to make any choice, and to drift along in the hope that by international or divine intervention things might get better is the worst scenario. If Jordan's role on the Middle East scene is restricted to its own small territory, that vision will have vanished, and with it any reason for the Hashemite Kingdom of Jordan to exist. There are many among both Arabs and Israelis, and even among some governments, who would view its disappearance with favour.[a]

---

[a] For Jordan's role, see The Missing Link, Appendix II.

Chapter 4
Albania: The Last Adventure

In 1996 during a visit to Amman I became engaged in an extraordinary crisis whose final denouement has yet to come. For many years I had dreamt of going to Albania: its mountains and its people were a secret land shut off from the world by the last and most extreme of communist regimes, and its identity muffled by its ambiguous past. I counted as a friend Julian Amery whose wartime record of events in *The Sons of the Eagle* unveiled a little of its mystery and its misery. What little I knew of its history, old and recent, seemed to me in many ways similar to that of Lebanon: Christian, Muslim, and small Jewish communities living for five centuries under Ottoman rule looked two ways - to Europe and the Mediterranean of which they were geographically a part, and to the Near and Middle East where were the roots of their faiths and cultures. And curiously, Albania and Lebanon shared the same Semitic consonants – L B N. What and where was Albania in the world? This was a question ill-formulated in my mind, waiting for an answer; chance gave me the opportunity to find one.

I knew that the King of the Albanians, Ahmed Zog had been evicted from Albania by the Italians who in the autumn of 1939 occupied it as their first contribution to World War II. In his book Julian Amery had recounted how the attempts he and other British officers and men to assist the Albanian partisans had been foiled by the war-cabinet in London, leading, as happened in Yugoslavia, to the eventual domination of the communist partisans. What I did not know was that there had survived the nucleus of a movement for the restoration of the monarchy, and that its members naturally regarded the son of Zog, who had died in 1961, as the legitimate successor to the role and title of 'King of the Albanians'. Nor did I know until I met him in Amman in September 1996 that the son, Leka the First, who was an infant of a few months when his parents fled to London, had accepted the role of successor and carried on a struggle from outside Albania to keep the monarchist cause alive.

My ignorance was corrected one day in Amman when Ihsan, a retired Jordanian air-force commander, told me that the Crown Prince would like me to meet King Leka. I visited him in his modest rooms at the Intercontinental Hotel, and found an immensely tall, fair-complexioned and booted figure whose gracious and modest demeanour reflected the manners of his aristocratic Hungarian mother. His father had become President of Albania and then chosen by the Albanian Parliament to be King in 1926. It was not an easy legacy to uphold, but my first impressions of Leka were that his kingship, now a title, might become a reality. He gave me a long and detailed briefing on the situation of the monarchist movement in Albania and his own relationship to it from abroad where he had remained ever since he left with his parents in 1939. He told me also of the difficulties of his own position, material as well as political, and revealed the reason for which he was in Amman.

At the age of eighteen Leka had entered the military academy of Sandhurst as a cadet; there he had met, and formed a friendship with another to-be King, Hussein bin Talal. Over the course of years Leka, who had lived in several European countries, but was now resident in South Africa, visited Amman where he was received as no ordinary guest. No stranger himself to pecuniary problems, King Hussein made a substantial investment in a future restoration of the monarchy in Albania. This had helped to keep the movement alive and the position of Leka as its head meaningful. His visits to Amman would, he hoped, continue to sustain the investment.

King Zog with the young Leka, in November 1940.

My first visit to Leka intrigued me. What were the realities of the situation in Albania, and was a return to the monarchy feasible; and what was Jordan's interest in sustaining a movement which even if successful held no obvious or immediate prospects of a return on the investment? These questions set me on a search for information, and a reflection on the historical position of Albania in the past, and what it might be after the crumbling of the communist era in the country and in the Balkans. There were not many reliable sources of information about contemporary Albania, and some of it, though academic in provenance, was in fact heavily weighted on the side of the now-fallen regimes of Enver Hoxa and Ramiz Alia. Nevertheless there was a considerable literature on the earlier history of the country, and I was able to form at least an arguable answer to the questions I was asking.

In the course of my research I learnt that Albania had a people, a language and a culture which were unique: they belonged to no European ethnic group, their language was not related to other European languages, and their culture was the product of centuries of contact with near and middle eastern cultures. Christianity and Islam co-existed within 'the Albanian family', and the emergence of perhaps the first European 'nation state' could be found in the extraordinary story of Albania's national hero, Skandarbeg, whose statue stands in the centre of Tirana, the modern capital created by King Zog.

George Castrioti was taken early in life by the Ottomans who had occupied Albania in the late 14th century, and, like many Christian youths, circumcised, educated and trained in the Ottoman army where he won distinction in many campaigns. In 1443 the Turkish army in Hungary was defeated at the battle of Nis, and Skandarbeg, as he was now called, and who had been present at the battle, returned to the family lands at Kruja, reverted to his Christian origins, and raised a revolt against the Turks which succeeded in wresting from them the major part of modern Albania. Successive attempts by both Sultans Murat the Second and Mehmet the Conqueror of Constantinople to crush the Albanian revolt failed, and it was not until after the death of Skandarbeg in 1468 that the Turks were able to recover control of all Albania for another 400 years. During the course of his struggle against the Ottomans Skandarbeg had made repeated attempts to convince various European regimes, including Venice, Naples and the Pope, to come to his aid, without success: but it was his defiance of their ambitions which were, in the long run, to save Europe from further Ottoman incursions into Italy.

Around the story of Skandarbeg successive generations of Albanians created the 'myth' – so necessary for all nationalist movements – of an Albanian nation to which all Albanians, wherever they lived belonged. When Zog accepted the role of King from the Parliament which offered it, he insisted on the title 'King of the Albanians', by implication refusing to accept the legitimacy of the amputation of Albania's historic fatherland by the European Powers in the late 19th and early 20th centuries. That title was to have a resonance whose notes can still be heard in Kosovo, as well as in other countries with large ethnic Albanian populations.

By 1996 the consequences in Albania of the end of the Soviet Union and the collapse of the communist regimes which had controlled the country since the end of World War II were disastrous both politically and economically. A weak government under Salah Berisha who had changed the red colour of his communist past into a democratic pink, was unable to control the unbridled 'free market' economy which followed the Chinese brand of communism by which the Albanian people had been brought to their knees: a series of 'pyramid' frauds emptied their pockets of anything which still remained there, and the country was on the verge of complete collapse. After the briefing I had received from Leka it seemed to me to be a propitious time for him to return to Albania and work for the restoration of the monarchy as the best, and possibly the only, way to stabilize the situation. A monarchist party in the country, the Albanian Legality Party, was working for that goal, but had no voice to the outside world and no capacity for public relations.

I therefore drew up on their behalf a 'Manifesto' on «the Albanian question» which presented a case for the restoration of the monarchy in terms of not only Albania's interests but also that of the Balkan region which was suffering from post-communist chaos, and of the European Community as a whole. The Manifesto referred back to the Constitution of 1928 adopted under the regime of Leka's father, Ahmed Zog, which established a secular state and a democratic political system. 'The Albanian State was thus, after Turkey, the second state with a Muslim majority to adopt a secular form of political and civil society. The preservation of this status within the new Balkan community where forces working for division, separation, and intolerance threaten to reverse centuries of co-habitation and cultural assimilation is thus of vital interest to the European family. A free, democratic, and pluralistic Albania can provide the forum for a renewed model of a liberal and mutually tolerant Muslim, Christian, and Jewish society.'

The result of local elections held in Albania in October 1996 which showed considerable support for the Legality Party, encouraged Leka to make the decision to return to the country which he had never known. Surprisingly too the major Albanian political parties agreed to the proposal of a referendum on the monarchy. I drafted a 'Proclamation' of his intention to return: it defined clearly the purpose and the conditions for that return, as, under the 1928 Constitution, the designated successor to his father, 'I shall not assert my claim or impose myself except through a clear and internationally-supervised national Referendum. Before it chooses its governors the people must choose the form of government under which they wish to live. It is logical and imperative that the national Referendum through which such a choice can be expressed should precede the holding of General Elections'. It ended with a reference to the pyramid scandal: 'I cannot give you back your money, but I can give you back your country.'

In Amman together with Ihsan, the Jordanian official who had introduced me to Leka, I drafted an operational plan for the 'rescue Albania' scenario. It envisaged a diplomatic initiative in the major European capitals, and a projection of a plan of action once Leka returned to Albania. This would include an immediate claim that the 1928 Fundamental Statute, or Constitution, was still operational. This would invalidate the presidency of Berisha in theory, but there would be no attempt to overturn it before the referendum.

On 29 March I received a letter appointing me as an Advisor to the Royal Court of Albania.

The decision by Leka to return to Albania was dependent on the availability of funds to conduct a campaign for the restoration of the monarchy. The financial support which he had received from the Royal Court in Amman had long been spent in the intervening years: resident in South Africa because of the low cost of living there at the time, he had to support his mother, wife and son, the considerable expenses of private security, and the minimal relations he was obliged to maintain with his followers in Albania and elsewhere. His several attempts to raise money through business deals had not been successful and it seemed to me that having supported his cause in the past it would be reasonable and desirable that the investment should not be lost just at the moment when it seemed possible that it could be justified. Ihsan and I presented this argument to the Royal Court without success, but eventually a meeting with the chief of intelligence produced the useful but inadequate sum of $150,000.

On 12 April Leka returned to Albania. He brought with him and broadcast a letter to 'My Brothers and Sisters' which I helped him to draft. 'In the perspective of history the events of these last months must not be condemned as a fall into anarchy but should be seen as the culminating point of the resistance that began with the invasion of 7 April 1939 and continued throughout the communist dictatorship... We reconfirm our stand that only a referendum under international supervision will grant the Albanian People, under their own free will, the means to choose the constitutional form of the regime which best suits the aspirations of the individual and the Nation, a Parliamentary Monarchy or a Republic. The People's choice will be binding upon us.'

On 29 March I received an invitation from Leka to join him in Tirana to observe events, and accordingly I flew there with Swissair on 5 May. The airport at Tirana was, after Beirut, my latest experience of the breakdown of law and order: there were no immigration or customs officials present, but I was met by a gendarme sent by Leka to meet and to guard me. As hotel accommodation in Tirana was either unavailable or unacceptable I accepted his invitation to stay with him at his modest rented house. I was thus able to witness at first hand both the strategic planning of his campaign, and some of its actual implementation, which consisted primarily in visits to different areas of the country. This was my initiation into the spectacular landscapes of Albania, and into the hearts of its desperate but courageous people. I loved them both.

There were several sides to the campaign to restore the monarchy. One was historical: the Italian invasion of Albania in 1939 was an act of force which did not abrogate the 1928 Constitution, nor did the end of that occupation and the succeeding years of communist rule. In the event of the referendum vote giving a majority to the monarchists, the Constitution would no longer be theoretical but operative, and Leka could legitimize and activate his role. Then there was the pragmatic and political side: without a hereditary Head of State the political parties on the ground, with years of both authoritarian and repressive experience, were incapable of bringing the stability which the fragmented and bewildered Albanian society needed. As in many other countries which had no long experience of constitutional and democratic regimes, elections were no guarantee of the peaceful transmission of power, and might lead to its abuse if there were no legitimately-hereditary Head. Constitutional monarchy thus was the most suitable form of government for Albania.

But there was another, and perhaps more convincing side to Leka's campaign. In spite of the fact that he was unknown in person to the Albanian people, and that his Albanian language, scarcely used in his involuntary exile, was intelligible but not oratorical, yet his tall and dominating height, the openness and simplicity of his bearing, and the graciousness of his human contacts,

Habib Bourguiba returning to Tunis, 1956.

combined with a nostalgia for a regime which in contrast to the years of wars, revolutions, and hardships seemed to have been a golden age, all these factors conspired to upset the calculations of the Albanian 'experts' in the outside world, and of many inside too: Leka seemed to be winning the battle!

Of this surprising and to me encouraging development I was a witness in the days in which I accompanied him on his visits to the towns and villages of the country. The enthusiasm and the increasing numbers of his supporters reminded me of the heady days when I had accompanied Habib Bourguiba on his visits to the Tunisian people after his successful return to the country in 1956, and I was no stranger to the frantic scenes in which I found myself sometimes engulfed, only to be rescued by a providential *garde du corps*.

Leka at a rally in Tirana before the referendum, June 1997.

In May the OECD meeting in Helsinki had decided that general elections should take place in Albania on 29 June, and as the Albanian Government and the twelve major political parties had accepted on 23 May that a referendum on the monarchy should also take place, the two events were scheduled to take place together under international supervision. The Legality Party had unsuccessfully resisted this combination on the grounds that it would give an advantage to the Socialist Party, funded by Greece and opposed to the monarchy, and suspected of having the backing of the OECD's head, the Austrian Dr Vranitski. In view of the urgency of finding further financial support for Leka, whose funds were running out, and of informing international opinion of the turn of events in Albania, I decided to leave Tirana on 19 May and return to Amman. There I presented a report to the Royal Court on what I had observed, and what I believed to be the real possibility of Leka succeeding in his campaign: 'It is my estimate that with a fund of $2-3 million the Legality Party could make a good showing at the referendum, but that with $4-5 million it would be certain to succeed'. On a more pessimistic note I predicted to the Crown Prince that without funds the campaign was certain to fail. Once again the Royal Court did not wish to listen, due I believe to the negative view of Leka held by Zeid Rifai, a former Prime Minister. At the same time letters were sent to a number of Arab Governments, asking for support: this was *'a historic opportunity for the restoration of a Muslim monarchy in Europe for the first time since the fall of Granada in 1492'*. Not having much use for history

The crowds at a campaign rally for Leka in northern Albania.

these Governments did not respond.

On 28 June I returned to Tirana to be present on the day of the referendum and general elections. By now the enthusiasm generated by the monarchist campaign had reached its climax, and I attended a vast meeting around the symbolic statue of Skanderbeg in the centre of the city. Early on the morning of 30 June the BBC announced that the monarchists had won the referendum, Reuters, Italian and Turkish televisions followed shortly after. By ten a.m. journalists from the international press began to arrive at the house, anxious for an interview with the prospective King. The mood among his entourage was jubilant but not triumphant: although the Albanian Prime Minister Bashkim Fino had officially announced that the monarchy had won, we were aware that the result would not be palatable to Dr Vranitski and some members of the OECD, and that the results of elections could always be manipulated by their organizers. This what indeed was to happen: on the ground that the final counting of votes in some of the areas of Tirana had not been made, the announcement of the final result was delayed for several weeks, and when it was announced it gave the monarchist vote only 33% of the total. As the number of delayed votes could not have swayed the results to such a large degree, the decision was not credible, and transparently falsified. More objective estimations of the result gave a majority of between 55-60% to the monarchist cause.

The delay in announcing a final result to the referendum created a difficult situation for Leka: his supporters, many of whom had come down from the area in northern Albania where his family had their roots, had to be sustained in Tirana, while funds were running low. A large and pacific demonstration on 1 July resulted in some bloodshed due to the intervention of government forces, and this was used as a pretext to accuse the monarchist movement of attempting a *coup d'état*. Leka was faced with a difficult choice: in his message to the people on his return to Albania on 12 April he had said 'the People's choice will be binding upon us', and that meant that the positive result of the referendum legitimized his position as King, and put him in the obligation to act accordingly; on the other hand he did not have the financial means to be able to assert his right. The hostile reaction of the government to the monarchist success in the referendum, and the evident unwillingness of the OECD's direction to accept it, made it clear to Leka that he had either to mobilize his supporters for a show-down of force, with the probability of bloodshed, or leave the country and continue the struggle from abroad.

I was acutely aware of Leka's dilemma. Fearing for my safety he was adamant that I should leave immediately. I was in no position to advise him to take a risk that I was not ready to assume myself, although I felt that the cause would be better served by his remaining to face the challenge – but he had no money, and he was unwilling to face the possibility, or probability, that his supporters and others too would shed their blood in his cause. His decision to leave the country was noble, but it was a serious, but not necessarily fatal, setback to the restoration of the monarchy.

I left Tirana on 2 July. Leka left a few days later. In a Note addressed to the European Chancelleries on 17 July he repeated his pledge that he would 'only assume the responsibilities of my heritage as the legitimate successor to my father King Ahmed Zog if there is a clear expression of the wishes of the Albanian people for my return. The true and not the announced results of the referendum were such a clear expression.'

Chapter 5
Lebanese Dilemmas

My first book of memoirs was in part the story of my search for identity. Like many children of the emigration the question 'who am I' first troubled me in adolescence. I knew of Lebanon through my parents' description of its landscapes, and of its food through our kitchen, but before I went there for the first time in 1939 I thought of myself as Syrian, which was how the members of the small Near Eastern community in Manchester who came from what are now Syria and Lebanon called themselves.

Those who had come before 1914 were mostly from Beirut, Damascus or Aleppo. Marjayoun and Ibil al-Saqi from where my parents came was not part of 'Mount Lebanon' which had enjoyed a semi-autonomous status after 1861, but belonged to the *Vilayet* of Beirut, not Damascus. Anxious to discover the area from where we derived our family name, I once visited the town of Ezraa in today's Syria. The Hauran is now divided between Syria and Jordan, and when my ancestors left some three hundred years ago there were as yet no Syrian, Jordanian or Lebanese States. When the Syrian and Lebanese states were created out of the former Ottoman territories and placed under a French Mandate, its citizens were given the choice of nationality of either one or the other.

My father chose to be Lebanese, but I did not understand what that meant until Nadim Dimishqiyye later a prominent diplomat and Lebanese personality, corrected me when I called myself Syrian. Himself a life-long Arab nationalist, he was however always strongly conscious of both his membership, through his father, of the Beirut Muslim Sunni community, and of the fact that his mother was a Christian lady from the Chouf mountains. It was my first introduction to the very special characteristics of Lebanese society in which a shared language, way of life and culture transcend religious affiliations and form a distinctive 'Lebanese personality'.

When my brother Albert appeared as a witness for the Arab Office set up to represent the Palestinians' cause before the Anglo-American Commission of Enquiry in 1946, he was asked by the chairman what he was, and he replied that he was Syrian. I myself, in Cairo at the Middle East HQ of the British Army, and in touch with both Lebanese and Syrian personalities coming there to press the cause of independence, saw no difference, and felt no preference between Camille Chamoun and Hamid Frangieh on the Lebanese side, and Jamil Mardam and Husni Barazi on the Syrian. My sense of a common cause and a shared identity continued in London when Lebanese and Syrian Embassies were established, when I was as much welcomed by Najib Armanazi in the Syrian as by Camille Chamoun in the Lebanese; and later in Washington, when I was as much at home in the house of Costi Zurayk at the Syrian Embassy as that of Charles Malik at the Lebanese.

These happy relationships were to continue in the corridors of the newly-established United Nations first of all in Lake Success and then in Manhattan, where although I was a member of the Lebanese delegation in 1949 I was on such good terms with the Syrian delegation that I wrote two of the speeches of one of its members on the subject of Israel's application to join the organization, and the problem of the future of the former Italian colonies.

A change in my perceptions came as the first regional consequence of the wars which accompanied the creation of the state of Israel in May 1948. The dismal failure of the Arab armies which attempted to thwart that event inspired the first of the many military *coups d'état* which swept away the fragile democratic systems set up by the French mandatory authorities in Syria and by the British in Iraq. Until Husni Zaim seized power in Damascus in 1949, the parliamentary systems in Lebanon and Syria functioned quite well, and their deputies were often as much as at home in Beirut as they were in Damascus: a financial and customs system of common interests, and joint banking arrangements facilitated common industrial and commercial ventures. Newspapers, journalists and writers, reported, discussed and wrote about the same events and the same problems. And it was still possible, to visit Syrian friends in Damascus or Aleppo – as I did often with my wife – to enjoy the spectacular springtimes at Jisr al-Shughur, and explore the many Roman and Byzantine ruins without any problem at the frontiers.

Little by little, as *coups* followed *coups*, all this conviviality eroded. The 6-Day War of 1967 made the change very clear to me: between Marjayoun and Jaulan and Hauran in Syria there were old trading and friendly relations between its people, and I was often able to make visits to Kuneitra and the Jaulan where some of my family had houses or shops, and go from there on to Damascus. The war ended all that when Israeli forces occupied what they now call the Golan Heights, and cut the main road from Marjayoun to Syria at Banias, whose beautiful gushing sources of water and Crusader castle of Nimrud I can no longer visit. The war also introduced a change in the character of the Syrian regime which survived the loss of that vital territory. They became more authoritarian, and under the influence of the Arab nationalist ideology of the ruling Baathist governments, less constrained from interfering in the affairs of neighouring states. The end of the ephemeral Egyptian-Syrian union in 1961 did not end Syrian involvement in Lebanon's political problems: rather it increased their involvement as Lebanese society was now fragmented between those who believed in either Baathist or Nasserite versions of Arab unity, those who believed in the Greater Syrian ideology of Antoun Saadeh, and those who clung to the idea of *Grand Liban*.

The Syrian regime headed by Hafez al-Assad was astute in exploiting these divisions which were not only ideological, but also sectarian, and the serious deterioration in Lebanon's stability which began in 1975 gave the opportunity to the Syrian army to enter into the country and participate actively in its affairs. The key to that opportunity was the presence in Lebanon of the Palestinian 'armed struggle' against Israel organized by those who had been expelled from Jordan in 1970, and headed by Yasser Arafat and his associates. Syria had its own Palestinian 'armed struggle' whose unit – the

Saiqa – was integrated into the Syrian army, as well as a variety of Palestinian parties of different degrees of intransigence.

The territory of Lebanon thus became a pawn in the hands of the Syrian regime in its confrontation with Israel, and South Lebanon was its trump card. While making sure that no incidents on its frontiers with Israel on the Golan threatened the Syrian regime's control of its people, it believed that a war by proxy from Lebanon's frontiers would strengthen its hand in negotiating a settlement of its problems with Israel.

From the entry of Syrian forces into Lebanon in 1976 until their departure in 2005 following the assassination of Rafiq Hariri, the Syrian regime was able to exert almost total control over the Lebanese political scene, with the willing collaboration of many Lebanese politicians and businessmen. This resulted in a dichotomy in my attitude towards Syria: on the one hand I could not obliterate my past empathy for its country and its people, nor my consciousness of the social and cultural connections of my family with its land, but on the other hand I deplored the way in which Lebanon was being manipulated and exploited.

However my greatest regret was to witness the Syrian regime's transition from a real though fragile parliamentary system of government similar to Lebanon's to a secretive and authoritarian one. I could see how Lebanon's political social and intellectual freedoms were also being eroded, and feared that they could not survive under Syrian control. At the same time I persisted in distinguishing the regime from the people, and could not share in the violent anti-Syrian opinions expressed by some Lebanese politicians and parties which transformed what is only a conflict of interests into mutual national enmity. I could not accept that in order to be a true Lebanese 'patriot' Syria had to be an enemy.

The dilemmas which I faced in my own perception of the events taking place in Marjayoun, which, after my return from Tunisia in the late 60s and early 70s became my frequent base, were the same which on a much larger scale faced its inhabitants and the Lebanese officers and men of the Lebanese Army stationed there. From 1976 until 1978 the town of Marjayoun and the surrounding area were the centre of a semi-autonomous administration controlled by the Lebanese army under the command of Major Saad Haddad.

After 1978 the area was enlarged by an Israeli invasion to the borders of the Litani River. In 1982 Israeli forces again invaded Lebanon and forced out the armed elements of the Palestinian Liberation Organization, which were then replaced in south Lebanon by Hizbullah and other anti-Israeli organizations. In 2000 the Israeli forces which had been inside their 'security belt' and assisting the 'Free Lebanese' administrations of Major Haddad, and his successor General Antoine Lahd, withdrew. Now nominally under the complete control of the Lebanese state, with the assistance of the United Nations forces (UNIFIL) since 1978, South Lebanon remains an area in which different parties play out their open aims and hidden agendas. Geographically contiguous to northern Galilee, and on the strategic road to Damascus which skirts the southern slopes of Mount Hermon, the control of its territory engenders rivalries and conflicts which impinge negatively on the security and well-being of its inhabitants. Trapped between the Palestinians' struggle for statehood, their Lebanese supporters' armed presence, Israeli concepts of security, and outside manipulation of its problems to serve other ends, the people of South Lebanon still face the same dangers and dilemmas. The actors on the stage may change, but the scenario is the same.

Among my documents there are two in which my views of both Palestinian and Syrian interference in Lebanon's internal affairs are clear. The first is a letter which I prepared at the request of Major Haddad, initially addressed to President Carter in anticipation of his re-election on the autumn of 1980, but re-drafted for President Reagan on his election. The letter summarized the dilemmas which events in Lebanon posed for Major Haddad and the soldiers under his command as well as for the civilian population. For them their loyalty to the Lebanese state and their responsibility to defend its sovereignty in the South conflicted with the Palestinian armed struggle against Israel. When the government in Beirut failed to provide them with any assistance in this role, and indeed appeared to be obstructing it, they faced a tragic dilemma: should they surrender their role and do nothing, or assume the responsibility with which they had been entrusted, and risk being denounced as disloyal, or even traitors?

Saad Haddad and the majority of his soldiers and the civilians under his authority adopted the second choice. The letter gives their reasons, and describes the consequences of their decision: Selim al-Hoss, the Prime Minister, expelled Haddad from the army and cut off the salaries of the soldiers. They then had no choice but to accept Israel's offer of support. How difficult it was for this loyal Lebanese army officer to become a dependent of Israel can be understood from a poignant statement he made to an Israeli journalist - 'It took me about two months until I got used to being in Israel and talking to Israelis. Every time I crossed the border from South Lebanon into Israel I felt uneasy, queasy in my stomach'.*

The dilemma which Saad Haddad, his successor Antoine Lahd and their men faced was between loyalty to Lebanon and the risk of being viewed as traitors. I believe they were indeed loyal and suffered the consequences, and I still regard them as victims of a situation which was forced on them, for which they should not be blamed, or punished, as they were later on to be. These events in the South forced me to reassess my views on the Palestinian problem. I had never been convinced that Yasser Arafat and his role in organizing the armed struggle against Israel could succeed in forcing Israel to accept a Palestinian state: the tactics of the Palestinian Liberation Organization in its unsuccessful attempt to overthrow the Jordanian regime in 1970 were followed by its efforts to exploit the weakness of the Lebanese regime, and to carry on its armed struggle from inside Lebanon and on its southern frontiers with Israel.

Not only could I see clearly that the PLO, instead of weakening Israel, was actually strengthening it, but I could also see, and at close quarters, the effects of its behaviour on the towns and villages of the South. It was only because of the existence of 'Free Lebanon' that the area had not been annexed by Israel, and that the town of Marjayoun had not

---

* Beate Hamizrachi, The Emergence of the South Lebanon Security Belt: Major Saad Haddad and the Ties with Israel, 1975-1978, New York 1988.

suffered the devastation caused by Israeli retaliation against attacks by the Palestinians which had devastated Khiam, Ibl al-Saqi, and many other locations. These events did not change my belief that the Palestinians have a just cause which deserves support, but I could then, and still see that a cause is one thing, and the people or organizations which claim to represent it may be quite another.

The election of President Reagan involved me in another dimension of the conflicts in Lebanon: a document marked 'Secret Guidance on Lebanon,' dated 9 March 1981, but with no address, was sent from Washington to the leadership of the Kataeb Party in Lebanon. In late 2008 I was surprised to be informed by friends that I had been mentioned in a popular Lebanese television programme devoted to the life of President Beshir Gemayel. Shaykh Beshir, who was then head of the Lebanese Forces, a militia linked to the Kataeb Party, had wished to reply to the letter, which stated that:

> The US supports the independence, sovereignty, territorial integrity and national unity of Lebanon. The US remains opposed to partition. The US supports the legitimate, constitutional central government and Lebanon's national institutions. It is important that legitimacy be preserved. The US recognizes that there are proponents of a reorganized governmental and constitutional structure. The US has no views about particular changes. That is for the Lebanese to decide, but any such changes, in our view, should be brought about through peaceful political processes.
> The US would therefore warmly welcome the development of a genuine political consensus on the shape of the new Lebanon, in which the views of all of Lebanon's many communities would be reflected. The US has a deep concern for the safety, security, and well-being of Lebanon's communities, including the Christian community. We recognize that the large Palestinian community in Lebanon constitutes a problem for the Lebanese. We believe in addressing the Palestinian problem, including its

Lebanese dimension, though a comprehensive Arab-Israeli peace. The US intends that any overall resolution of the Palestinian problem should not damage Lebanon's national interests.
The US deplores the violence in Lebanon, wherever it takes place. The US strongly opposes resort to terrorism. The US strongly opposes efforts to attack Israel from Lebanese soil. It creates an almost endless cycle of violence and adds to the suffering of innocent people, in both Israel and Lebanon.
The US supports a stage-by-stage withdrawal of Syrian forces leading to an ultimate end to any Syrian military presence in Lebanon. This should be accomplished through steadily expanded control by the Government's army and police in areas of tension which the Syrians now control. Syrian withdrawals, however, should take place in ways which do not incite a renewed civil conflict or major hostilities among the various militias and Palestinian fedayeen groups.
We hope that the Phalange (Kataeb Party) will exercise restraint and patience, even in the face of provocations and challenges which could come from Syrian and Palestinian groups. We would encourage any efforts at a dialogue between Lebanon's Christian leadership and the Muslim and Druze communities.
We believe that the Phalange and other Christian organizations are in a position to influence the future course of Lebanese history. We hope that the Phalange will pursue its objectives through peaceful political processes and will cooperate with, rather than challenge, the central government and the national army.

In the course of the television programme, Dr George Frayha, one of the participants, recounted how Beshir Gemayel had not been satisfied by drafts proposed by Charles Malik and others. George Frayha then suggested my name, unknown to Beshir, who asked Frayha to bring me to see him. I accepted George's invitation to accompany him to the headquarters of the Lebanese Forces in the Qarantina area of Beirut.

At that time Beirut was sharply divided between East where the Lebanese Forces were based and whose population was mainly Christian, and West which was the stronghold of a mixed Lebanese and Palestinian population and some foreign militias. To cross over from one side to the other was hazardous, and I had on one occasion heard the whistle of a sniper's bullet uncomfortably close, but I thought the occasion was worth the risk. I had for some time been intrigued by the phenomenon of Gemayel, a young man daring to challenge the military and political Syrian presence in Lebanon. How were his aims and his strategies related to those of Saad Haddad in the South, and what were, or could be, the relations between the two men, were questions I hoped to answer. I was not disappointed by the meeting: I found him frank, forceful, and certainly charismatic. I listened carefully to the exposition of his belief that the moment was propitious for an attempt to enlist American support for his campaign to liberate Lebanon from the Syrian grip on the country. He asked me to draft a letter in reply to the American message.

The Kataeb Party had for many years been unfairly represented by the international media as a fascist Christian organization, and the term 'right wing' was regularly used by some of the journalists and Middle East 'experts' to distinguish it from the mixture of socialists, radicals, Palestinian resistance groups and their foreign supporters, who liked to call themselves 'nationalists'. The 'right wing' label was also stuck onto the senior Christian politicians and intellectuals who formed the Lebanese Front, and who supported the efforts which began in 1975 to resist what they perceived as a Palestinian attempt to take over Lebanon as their base for operations against Israel after they had lost their base in Jordan in 1970. The 'national movement' frequently accused members of the Lebanese resistance of seeking to partition Lebanon on sectarian lines, and of looking to Israel to implement their goal.

Although the message was written in the fuzzy language typical of washington bureaucracy, I could read into it some of these misconceptions of the realities of the conflict in

Lebanon. I was already conscious that, between Lebanese resistance to Palestinian infiltration and Palestinian 'armed' struggle against Israel, a favourable prejudice towards the Palestinian cause seemed to prevail not only among most of the foreign journalists posted in Beirut, but also among some of the American diplomats and officials in Washington. In the letter which Beshir asked me to draft in response to the 'secret' message, I tried to dispel some of these misconceptions, and to present a true picture of what both Gemayel in the north and Haddad in the south were attempting to achieve, each in his own differing set of circumstances.

I had in fact been somewhat surprised and disappointed by what appeared to be Beshir's reservations about the actors and the situation in the South. I did not know at the time that he had sent some members of the Lebanese Forces there with the task of assisting Saad Haddad's army, but that they had not behaved well, and been sent back by Haddad. He also cast doubt on the truly 'Lebanese' character of the population, describing them as closer to Palestine than to Lebanon. This was geographically true if Lebanon was confined to Mount Lebanon and the Maronite hinterland, but it was an unfair judgment on Haddad and the soldiers and civilians who were supporting him. I did my best to correct his views, and gave him a copy of Haddad's letter to Reagan in which he associated his actions in the South with those of Beshir in the north.

After expressing gratitude with the 'secret message's reiteration of American support for Lebanon's independence, sovereignty, territorial integrity and national unity, my draft went on:

> The Kataeb party reiterates to the U.S Administration one of the central theses of its philosophy and program: that Lebanon belongs to all its communities which give their fundamental and unique loyalty to the Lebanese State and to the ideals of Lebanese society. It has always been prepared to enter into dialogue with the Sunni, Shia, Druze, and any other Lebanese community which shares the desire of the Christian leadership to establish a broad political

consensus within the framework of Lebanese sovereignty and independence.

Further, the Kataeb, which is a Lebanese party, naturally supports the legitimate authority of the country, and is always anxious to co-operate with, rather than challenge the central government and the national army in the pursuit of genuinely national policies and interests.

The Kataeb believes that the strengthening of the army and of the central government, the regulation of the status of the Palestinians, the prohibition of the use of any part of Lebanese territory for international or local terrorist activities, and the solution of the problem of South Lebanon can only be achieved within the context of an early and total Syrian withdrawal.

The withdrawal of the Syrian forces, in the opinion of the Kataeb Party, should not be made conditional on the prior achievement of any of these objectives, and the fears of the US Administration that this withdrawal might incite renewed conflicts in the country have no justification. It is the presence of the Syrian forces rather than their withdrawal which is the basic cause of the prevailing lawlessness and instability in Lebanon, and the fundamental obstacle to the attainment of a broad political consensus among the Lebanese.

The Kataeb Party believes that the early and total withdrawal of the Syrians would rapidly lead to reconciliation and agreement between the Lebanese; that the government which would reflect this new consensus would be able to deal effectively with the problem of the armed Palestinian presence and re-establish Lebanese sovereignty over all the areas now under Palestinian control; and that the presence of UNIFIL in South Lebanon would then become unnecessary.

In the meanwhile the Kataeb Party views with deep concern efforts being made by the

Secretariat of the United Nations, with the apparent support and encouragement of the US Administration, to engage UNIFIL and the still embryonic Lebanese army in operations in the South which, instead of forestalling violence, may only provoke it, and may have the effect of totally de-stabilizing the South, and with it the rest of the country.

The Kataeb Party believes that the restoration of Lebanese sovereignty over the whole country cannot begin on the frontiers with Israel, but must start in the capital, Beirut, and spread from there throughout the areas not presently under the control of the central government. The Kataeb Party is co-operating with the Lebanese army in the areas where the Party has been able to maintain a Lebanese presence, and is ready to assist the army in extending its deployment in other areas once the major obstacles to that deployment have been removed.

Finally the Kataeb Party believes that the restoration of a genuinely independent and sovereign Lebanon consequent on the withdrawal of the Syrian forces, and the regulation of the presence and status of the Palestinians is in the interest not only of the Lebanese, but also of the USA which would find again in Lebanon a people responsive to the same ideals of freedom as it cherishes for itself.

Beshir was happy with my letter, and asked me to come again and discuss his efforts to liberate Lebanon from the Syrian grip. In the years after my departure from Tunis in 1967 I had decided that I would henceforth try to be self-employed, a hazardous decision. In the following years I had spent much time in Washington and New York as a consultant to the Ford Foundation, ARAMCO and other oil companies, a semester as lecturer at Princeton and talks in other universities, occasional journalism, and the cultivation of many friends. It was to Washington and New York therefore that I went to advise Beshir about what might be expected from there, and to discover how the cause which he was pursuing might be helped.

I arrived in Washington at the height of a serious clash between the Lebanese Forces and the Syrian Army in the town of Zahle in the Bekaa Valley. The situation was of acute concern in Washington because of the introduction of Russian missiles into the area by the Syrians, and the possibility of a wider zone of conflict involving Israel. At this time also an Arab Peace Force, of which Saudi Arabia was a part, was also in Lebanon attempting to put an end to the almost total collapse of the government in Beirut. I believed that the Saudi's influence in Washington could be useful in weaning away American policy from what seemed to me to be a too-biased support of the Syrian role in Lebanon. In Washington I met David Tanter at the National Security Council, Bob Basil, Beshir's representative in the USA, and old friends from previous visits with Middle East connections. In the light of what I found out I drafted a memorandum as well as a number of newspaper articles in which I placed the Lebanese crisis within a wider regional dimension, which at that time was still dominated by the Cold War. The memorandum was sent to the State Department and to the Saudi Foreign Minister, Prince Saud al-Faisal who had been particularly concerned at the degradation of security in Lebanon. By substituting 'Iran' for references to the Soviet Union the following extracts demonstrate that the situation in Lebanon has not much changed since 1982:

> It is possible to discern two currents of thought about Lebanon and Syria within the policy-making bodies in Washington. The first sees the Lebanese crisis as the occasion to mend Washington's bridges with Damascus: to act, for example, as the honest broker trying to save everyone's face, and to be the intermediary through whom Syria's relations with the Arab Governments closest to Washington can be improved. The restoration of Arab financial contributions to the Syrian 'peace-making' forces in Lebanon, it is argued, would make Damascus see the benefits of improved relations with

Washington; would counter-balance Syria's exclusive one-way relationship with the Soviet Union; and would wean the Syrian Government away from its close ties with the rejectionist front into a closer relationship with the moderate Arab States.

To this way of thinking what happens to Lebanon or the Lebanese is of secondary importance. Even if the policy outlined above resulted in a bargain or a compromise between Syria and Israel at the expense of Lebanon, and under American sponsorship, this would not worry its advocates... on the contrary such a bargain would have the advantage of bringing under control not only the territory of Lebanon, but also the Palestinians and their resistance movement, which would not be unfavourably regarded in Washington or Tel-Aviv.

The second school of thought views the current crisis, and the American efforts to diffuse it, as a means of gaining time for another kind of policy. This views the Lebanese situation and the Syrian involvement in it within the framework of countering Soviet penetration into the Middle East. If the Syrian grip on Lebanon were to be strengthened to a point where the Lebanese State and Government would completely disappear - this would bring Lebanon fully within the orbit of direct Soviet influence, and permit the introduction of Soviet weaponry and military personnel into Lebanon's strategic coastal and mountain areas, and into a position of direct confrontation with Washington's closest military ally in the area, Israel.

From this point of view the restoration of a genuinely sovereign and independent Lebanon, with close links to the USA and the West, would be preferable to Lebanon's disappearance or total subjection to Syria. It would prevent the opening-up of a new front between Syria and Israel at a time when the front on the Golan

Heights is stabilized. Nothing frightens Washington more than the possibility of another Israeli military victory, for which it is feared America would have to pay the price. An independent and perhaps neutralized Lebanon would also set a limit to direct Soviet influence, and confine it to Syria. And it would also permit the re-establishment of Lebanon as a centre for western financial commercial and even political contact between the West and the Arab world, and provide a viable alternative to America's exclusive reliance on Israel.

In an effort to defuse the crisis the State Department appointed Philip Habib, a former diplomat of Lebanese origin, to mediate between the Lebanese Forces and the Syrians, and to pre-empt an Israeli threat to take out the Russian missiles if they were not speedily removed. Like many other American and European initiatives to prevent crises from becoming explosive it succeeded in its immediate aim: the missiles were removed, but the causes of the crisis remained, and eventually resulted in a still bigger crisis - the Israeli invasion of Lebanon in the summer of 1996. It is arguable that things might have turned out better had they been left to follow their dangerous course without Mr Habib's initiative.

This was only one of several other examples of the way in which outside intervention in Lebanon's internal problems did not solve but only aggravated them. In the spring of 1996 I was staying together with my daughter's family on holiday in Marjayoun when the Israeli Government headed by Shimon Peres undertook a massive onslaught on positions held by Hizbullah and other anti-Israeli groups within the 'security belt'. On the morning on which it began I was weeding in the garden of our house accompanied by my English son-in-law, for whom the experience of missiles was unusual. Following a warning widely broadcast over the area to the inhabitants to leave certain towns and villages before the operation, named 'Grapes of Wrath', was to begin, a large number of civilians were taking refuge at an UN military post when it was hit by Israeli shelling, and many were killed. The massacre at Qana caused an international storm of anger and criticism of Israel, and the Israeli government was obliged to end the campaign.

The sequel, instead of leading to a solution of the problem of South Lebanon which had begun in 1976, further complicated it. Under the terms of an agreement hosted by the American administration between the Lebanese and Israeli governments on 24 April, the Israelis would only retaliate when attacks on its territory came from Lebanese territory outside the 'security belt': this left the 'belt' as an area where the anti-Israeli groups were free to continue their operations against the forces of Free Lebanon over which General Antoine Lahd had taken command after the death of Saad Haddad in1984. The war 'to liberate Palestine', as in the days when Abu Iyad had commanded the *fedayeen*, was still being carried on inside Lebanon, and the main target of their attacks was still not Israel, but the Lebanese soldiers and civilians – Christians and Muslims – who were attempting to preserve the South as an integral part of a Lebanon which they hoped would one day be able to liberate itself.

The situation however was now much more dramatic and dangerous for them than when they were in conflict only with the Palestinians. Until the PLO and its armed forces were forced out of Lebanon in 1982, Amal, the Lebanese Shia party led by Nabih Berri was also engaged in fighting Palestinians in areas outside the security belt. Now, after the departure of the PLO, Hizbullah had taken their place and Amal's anti-Palestinian posture ended; a new inter-Lebanese conflict then began. When the Israeli government under Ehud Barak unilaterally evacuated Lebanon on 24 May the result was disastrous for the Lebanese soldiers and citizens who, in circumstances beyond their control, had been forced to choose between betraying what they saw as Lebanon's real interests, and collaborating with the Israelis, and who now had no protection against the accusation that they were collaborators, traitors.

The reasons for Israel's evacuation of its 'security belt' are clear: the Israeli public was weary of a situation where its soldiers could be killed with impunity inside Lebanon. General Barak, a better pianist than politician, while campaigning for election as Prime Minister had promised to withdraw the Israeli army by the end of July 2000. The circumstances in which the withdrawal took place, however, are not as clear. Though hailed as a military victory by Hizbullah, there had been behind-the-scene negotiations going on well before the July date between the Israelis, the Americans and the UN, from which the Lebanese government was notably absent. The Americans and the UN had been irritated since 1978 that UNIFIL had not been able to function in the South: Saad Haddad and Antoine Lahd were seen as inconvenient *protégés* of Israel, although on all other dimensions Israel was America's favourite *protégé*. A UN representative who had played a major role at Oslo between Israeli and Palestinian negotiators became the broker of a still-undisclosed deal whereby Israeli forces would be withdrawn, and combined Lebanese and UN forces would take over the evacuated territory.

It did not happen like that. Taking advantage of a temporary absence of General Lahd from his base in Marjayoun, the Israelis withdrew suddenly in the night of 24 May instead of the announced date in July. Neither the Lebanese army nor UNIFIL were on the scene, and Hizbullah, who were certainly aware of what was impending, immediately replaced the Israeli forces in all their strong points, and carried away the vast quantities of arms and equipment abandoned by the Israelis in their precipitous exit dash.

Once again the Americans and the UN, instead of trying to solve a problem which they had themselves caused had only addressed its consequences. A combination of errors of judgement, ignorance, and often stupidity, not only failed to achieve the immediate aim, but magnified the crisis so that it rebounded on themselves. The problem of South Lebanon was not solved for Lebanon where it still festers, but a much greater problem for Israel, the Americans, and the UN now emerged. By early 2000 negotiations between the Palestinian 'Authority' and the Israelis that followed the Oslo agreements had reached a deadlock, and popular Palestinian support for Hamas and other groups who opposed those agreements was growing. What appeared to be a victory for Hizbullah and its philosophy of resistance in Lebanon now stimulated a second Palestinian *intifada* in September and greatly increased the prestige and the influence of Hizbullah throughout the region. In the unwinnable war against terrorism the USA and its allies added Hizbullah to their list of enemies, so that what they thought they had won in Lebanon they found they had lost in the Middle East.

The people of Lebanon have been blessed by a land of great natural beauty, a climate in which the seasons are well-defined, a rainfall which if properly managed could irrigate vast areas of its territory, and a combination of coastline and mountain ranges which make it as attractive to foreigners as to its own people. When I first arrived in Lebanon in 1939 it was still possible to see the city and its landscapes of sea and mountain as it was described by the 19th-century American missionary, William Thomson, in *The Land and the Book*: 'neither pen nor pencil can do justice to Beirut... this is decidedly the most beautiful and healthy locality at the head of the Mediterranean.'

I have witnessed with growing concern and despair the rapid desecration of this beauty as unregulated and largely hideous construction spreads along its coastline and up into the mountain ridges. The demolition of the architectural heritage of Beirut at the hand of developers threatens to reduce it soon to the banal status of the worst resort cities of the world; its inhabitants increasingly alienated from their mainly rural origins, now constitute three-quarters of the entire population of the country. While their present is rootless, their past is becoming largely folklore.

As the physical landscape has deteriorated, so has Lebanon's political society. By its constitution a secular state, its functions are dominated by sectarianism: its high and low offices are distributed on a fictitious balance between its Christians and Muslim communities in which the first are assumed to be united, and the second divided. This no longer corresponds to realities, and gives rise to a permanent struggle to redistribute power and to gain more advantages. A permanent state of tension paralyzes government, and leaves the country at the mercy of outside forces and events. As no community can claim absolute majority, all acquire the complexes and ambitions of a minority, and live together in a permanent state of mutual grievance. In such conditions truly representative government cannot function, and no consensus of a common interest inspires the country's policies. As each constituent looks to outside powers to gain advantages over their rivals, the country becomes hostage to forces and events over which it has no control. At the present time one side of the sectarian divide brandishes the spectre of an American-Israeli 'project' for Lebanon and the regions, while the other conjures up the spectre of an Iranian-Syrian 'project'.

A precarious balance between the two conflicting narratives poses a problem for the Lebanese people: while the majority are anxious to preserve their free society, they can with difficulty restrain those forces which identify Lebanon's interests with one or other of the protagonists of the regional conflicts which surround them. For one of these forces the Palestinian-Israeli conflict provides the justification for a Lebanese involvement in efforts to solve it: 'resistance' finds some support in Lebanon and much encouragement from outside. Another view opposes any Lebanese involvement which endangers once more the lives and properties of its citizens, and threatens the very existence of the state.

Both these views reflect a genuine frustration with the failure of all international efforts to end the conflict. From a Lebanese perspective this failure may justify the argument that peace with Israel is not only impossible, but also undesirable, while from an Israeli perspective peace may seem neither necessary nor desirable. The impasse in all the proposed 'road maps' strengthens these irreconcilable Arab and Israeli positions, which unless circumscribed must lead inevitably to military confrontation. In such a scenario no state in the area can stand aside, and some may disintegrate. Among these Lebanon will be high on the list of endangered species.

To face this danger Lebanon needs a new definition. It must start with a recognition that the situation which led to the creation of the *Grand Liban* in 1920 has changed. The name referred to the territorial enlargement of the autonomous Mount Lebanon which the European Great Powers forced out of the Ottoman administration in 1861. The constitution of the new state established a parliamentary and Presidential system of government which in practice but not explicitly was advantageous to the Christian over the

Muslim population. These advantages eroded when Lebanon became independent in 1945.

Demographic changes, and the civil strife which began in 1975, initially provoked by a Palestinian attempt to take over the country, encouraged efforts by some Muslim parties and personalities to alter the Christian-Muslim balance in favour of the latter. This attempt succeeded at the conference in Tayef in 1990 in reducing the power of the Christian community, but created a new problem between the Sunni and Shia components of the Muslim community. The *Grand Liban* now faces a fragmentation of power which risks a territorial fragmentation on confessional lines.

While the Republic of 1920 was territorially 'Grand' relative to Mount Lebanon, a new definition would relate to the human expansion of the Lebanese people into the Middle East regions of which it is geographically and culturally a part. Some Lebanese intellectuals and politicians still debate whether they are Lebanese or Arabs, but it is evident that there is no dichotomy between the two, and that there is no advantage, and many disadvantages, in the separation of the two identities. In the past, when the Lebanese men and women left for the Americas, Europe, or Australia, they went as emigrants, most of whom would by choice or necessity never return, except as tourists. Today when they go to the Gulf or any part of the Arabian Peninsula, or even North Africa, they do not go as emigrants nor are they foreigners in their new locations. Whatever their political status, they become part of the societies in which they work by reason of their language, culture, and in the case of the Muslims, by religion.

Lebanon's space, its *Lebensraum*, has thus been enlarged beyond its territorial borders, into a wider entity which, if the terms were valid, might be called '*Plus Grand Liban*' or Greater Lebanon. In any future changes in the political structures of the Middle East and North Africa such as I envisage in the Epilogue of this book, Lebanon's role would not be marginal but central.

To play that role in keeping with its authentic tradition of freedom, changes will need to be made to its constitution and the legislation. The Lebanese Diaspora will have the right to return to the body-politic of the state; new laws will ensure that elections reflect the genuine wishes of the electors; a national code of personal status will equalize men and women in all their rights, and ensure their freedom of choice in all their personal relationships. The new Lebanon will not only be 'Greater' in its new-found regional space, but also in the horizons it opens for its citizens to live a wider, more secure, and happier life.

Chapter 6
Garlic Identity and Language

The journey, the 'odyssey', from one world into another – in my parents' case from a Near Eastern village society to an English urban one – must have provided a series of cultural shocks. The education which both my parents received from the American missionary schools which they attended in Beirut and Sidon provided them with an adequate knowledge of the English language to enable them to enter into the Scottish Presbyterian community in whose church, St. Aidans in Didsbury, they worshiped and made friends.

My mother in her wedding dress.

They participated in the social activities of the church – the charity bazaars, the harvest festival, Sunday school for their children – invited the pastor occasionally to Sunday lunch and ladies to tea, but with the wider cultural dimensions of English life, such as the worlds of football, cricket, pubs, music halls, and both low and high life, they had no contact. It must have been an uncomfortable cultural shock to my father to have to exchange the comfortable Lebanese *qumbaz* and tasselled tarbush for the starched high collar and necktie, but photos of my mother before marriage, and in her wedding dress, show that late-Victorian fashions in dress had already penetrated into Lebanon at the end of the 19th century.

It was the transition from the ingredients and tastes of a Lebanese mountain diet to the Lancashire menu which must have been the hardest to digest. My mother brought with her a popular Arabic cookbook by Khalil Sarkis which included some European dishes such as macaroni and beef-steak, but it was difficult, and usually impossible, to find the basic ingredients of Lebanese food in the English groceries and markets. They never abandoned their native tastes but there was one ingredient which provided them with a cultural dilemma: garlic, so essential to many of the dishes of their childhood, never entered our house. My father indeed claimed to have a positive distaste for it, but I believe the real reason was his wish not to be identified by smell with his fellow-Levantine Jewish merchants who took the same trains and buses to work downtown in central Manchester, and who, along with the Arabic language which they spoke to each other, clung to their garlic as a way to preserve and not to conceal their identity. What originated in my parents' wish not to be 'different' became for my sisters and brothers a genuine gustatory rejection of the precious onion.

My father with his mother in her nineties and his five sisters in 1921.

Unlike the Jewish members of our Near Eastern community, who made their children take Arabic lessons with Rabbi Mendoza at the Spanish-Portuguese synagogue in West Didsbury, my parents assumed that we would neither need the language nor tolerate a taste for garlic. Both my brothers and myself, to the delight of my father, eventually learnt Arabic, but I alone was to acquire an obsessive taste for the forbidden fruit, no doubt to prove to myself, if not to anyone else, that I belonged ethnically, if not culturally, to a non Anglo-Saxon species.

In my case it was a hope to re-connect with 'the old

country' which motivated my wish to learn its language. Brought up without knowing grandparents on either side, my closest substitutes were my father's five aged sisters, with whom I went to live when I first went to Lebanon at the age of twenty-one, and who spoke no other language. I learnt it then as an adult exactly as if I had been a child, acquiring a vocabulary before an alphabet, and learning to read before writing. Later in my life my grandchildren were sent by their mother to a Saturday Arabic school in London. There they were taught in exactly the opposite way – to write, and then to read, before speaking it. Unable to follow the teacher, and sometimes scolded for not performing, they naturally hated not only the school, but also the language, and sometimes their grandfather for taking them there.

When living in Beirut I became aware of another dimension to the problem of teaching Arabic. It was not only English-speaking children, but also Arabic-speaking children and adults who had difficulty in learning it: our cook Kerimeh, married very young, had had no education, and my wife attempted to teach her to read. Although she had learnt by herself to read some words – shop signs, for example in French or English, she was unable to learn the Arabic alphabet, because she was confused by the way in which some letters would change their shape according to their place in the word. It was children also who were learning to read French or English – or any language using Latin characters – faster and more easily than Arabic. Here then was an enormous problem: if a child whose mother tongue was Arabic was able to acquire a vocabulary in a foreign language, and to read it, and then speak it more easily than its own, the process of alienation from Arabic culture must start very early in life. This process is aided by the fact that the French or English book is superior in design, and especially in typography, to the Arabic.

These educational and cultural problems were to occupy a considerable part of my life over a number of years, and still interest me. My interest was focused on possible solutions by a Lebanese architect and type-designer in Beirut: Nasri Khattar when I met him in the 70s was convinced that he had found the solution to both problems, and could demonstrate it. His Unified Arabic alphabet had reduced the number of letters from the hundreds of varieties currently used in print to twenty-eight: they would, he claimed, be easier to learn and easier to read if they were to be accepted by the two key players – the printers and the teachers.

In order for this bold project to succeed, there was a basic premise to be accepted: that typography and calligraphy are two variants of the same sounds which, ever since the discovery of the alphabet, have been written down on stone, wax, paper or any other solid material. This distinction is still not made in the process of printing Arabic. When Arabic started to being printed in the 16th century the printers cast metal type to reproduce all the variants and combinations of shapes used in calligraphy.

This was enormously time-consuming and sometimes erroneous as some of the early, and even recent, font-designers did not know Arabic. Nasri Khattar had studied both architecture and typography in the USA, and was commissioned by IBM to design a new electric Arabic typewriter. This concentrated his mind: the typewriter clearly could not reproduce all the variants as the metal-type printing machines were doing, though it could do a few, so Nasri decided on a radical step; his typewriter would not only print one shape for the letter, but it would print them separately, rather than using the joined letters of the cursive script which change contextually – according to the preceding and following letters.

Samples of Nasri Khattar's Unified Arabic font.

When I first met Nasri he was a very frustrated man. He had made some considerable progress in promoting his project: he had made signs for display in Unified Arabic and sold them in Lebanon and Saudi Arabia; he had convinced the editor of the literary supplement of *al-Nahar*, Lebanon's most prestigious newspaper, to use it in its weekly edition; he had written and printed an illustrated first text-book for children; and he had designed and had manufactured four different Unified Arabic transo-typefaces in Germany. But he was meeting resistance from many quarters, some because of the novelty of any new typeface, some for cultural and aesthetic reasons, some from prejudice or simply misunderstanding.

One such was the claim that Unified Arabic resembled Hebrew, although this was a proof of its possible validity, because the transition from cursive Hebrew to unified typefaces, except in four cases where the letters do not change contextually, was successful. The most-widespread myth ascribes a religious sanctity to the Arabic script, as if the Quran had come to the Prophet Muhammad in writing! So strongly has this belief prevailed that until recently editions of the Holy Book were not type-set, but only hand-written and reproduced either by lithography or photographically-offset, on the view that the word of God should not pass through a machine. Now with the coming of the computer this argument has broken down, and versions of the work can be seen on-screen in a variety of Arabic styles, some clearly not traditional.

The greatest obstacle to the acceptance of Nasri Khattar's project, however, has been the development of the computer, and the argument that it is now unnecessary to simplify or unify the Arabic alphabet as the computer can reproduce the correct contextual shape for any letter by a touch on the keyboard. This has been widely hailed as a great advance for Arabic communication, although it is in fact a serious setback. It ties the Arabic text even more closely than before to calligraphy with all the defects of the cursive as body text which would be revealed if a daily newspaper, *The Times* for example, were to be printed in hand-written designed letters. By making it possible for anyone to 'invent' letters on the screen, the way has been opened to a proliferation of hideous typefaces designed by amateurs some of whom claim they can create a whole new alphabet in a day! The aesthetic values of Arabic calligraphy based on the skilled use of the pen or the chisel owe their beauty to the movement of the writing implement, the flow of the letters and their decoration; now the keyboard reproduces a jumble of dots on the screen which follow no set of rules or aesthetic canon.

Mustafa Atatürk had solved the problem of the Arabic alphabet by abolishing it; but this was done at the expense of hundreds of years of Ottoman literary culture, now no longer accessible to the following generations. While I was in Tunisia, Habib Bourguiba, more deeply versed than Atatürk in Muslim and Arabic culture, had been attempting to bring his people into the modern world without changing its roots, so I thought that we might find in Tunisia a greater openness and encouragement for Nasri's project than elsewhere. I found it in his son, Habib Bourguiba Jr. He kindly organized a meeting in Tunis for us with a group of printers and publishers. After giving a lecture expounding his ideas, Nasri projected on screen a text in two Unified Arabic typefaces; in the first the letters in Nasri's Beiruti Unified style were separate, and the group was puzzled; then he showed the same text in Kufic with the letters joined. The reaction was immediate: they shouted that this was nothing new! Because the vernacular handwriting in Tunisia, as elsewhere in North Africa, is a form of Kufic they had not realized that the letters were unified. Encouraged by this, we presented the project through the Tunisian Ministry of Culture to the cultural organization of the Arab League, then based in Tunis. There it was successfully buried by the Egyptians.

After the Tunisian experience I realized that if the project were to survive we would have to accept a compromise and proceed by stages. In the first stage the letters would be designed, as Nasri had done for Kufic, to be separate or joined as cursive; when joined, the reader would gradually get accustomed to them without realizing that they had been modified. In the second stage they would be completely separate, but designed as true type. Nasri, however, was not a man of compromise: for him the alternative to total acceptance was total rejection. He continued to add to his catalogue of beautifully-designed Unified characters, but we parted not altogether amicably, to my distress. I then turned to a friend who I believed could develop these ideas in a more pragmatic way. I asked Mourad Boutros, a Lebanese calligrapher and Arabic typeface designer living in London and already well-integrated into the real and hard world of publishing and advertising, to design a 'compromise' alphabet, not as a challenge or rejection of Unified Arabic, but as a stage on the way to its final development.

Basic Arabic was conceived and born as both a typographic innovation and a method of teaching, and is now available along with the many other 'Boutros' typefaces. It has already been used as headlines where its easily-read words conceal their innovation. My experiences as a consultant and frequent visitor to Jordan convinced me that this country might well be the first sponsor of 'the alphabet revolution': its open society and readiness to challenge embedded or fossilized perceptions encouraged me to propose the project there and I found a readiness to respond. As a trial an entire page of a Jordanian newspaper was printed in Basic Arabic with its unified letters joined together. With an effort it is legible. If it were to be promoted through its use on signs, advertisements, and headlines it would soon become familiar. Its effectiveness in facilitating the learning process needs to be tested in a school where it can be taught parallel to the conventional methods of teaching reading and writing. I am hopeful that one day soon this new dimension to the Arabic language, so essential to its cultural evolution, may come to be accepted.

Chapter 7
From Iran to Tunisia

A happy consequence of one of my unsuccessful efforts to promote Nasri Khattar's Unified Arabic project was an episode in a brief partnership with Fadhl Haeri. This unusual and enigmatic figure entered into my life as have so many by chance; I do not remember the occasion, but only the instant empathy. There was the name and the family's background: the Haeri family have over centuries produced teachers and scholars in Iran and Iraq, and in the 19th century some were involved in one way and another in the turbulent times in which Furugh's ancestors provoked a new controversy about evolutionary Shi'ism. Fadhl's grandfather was a *mujtahid akbar* in Karbala, but had himself sought a 'modern' education in England where when I met him he worked for a computer-based company. At the same time he was also deeply involved in one of those centres of retirement and meditation which in the 60s and 70s flourished on the Indian sub-continent. From the banal necessities of earning a living, and perhaps also from the exchange he had made of the warmth of Iraq for the dampness of London, he would retreat periodically to his ashram, motives with which I was entirely sympathetic. It was from these retreats, I believe, that he learnt to combine with no incompatibility the pursuit of spiritual and material strivings, and the pleasures of the mind and of the senses.

It was at this point in his life that we met. To the chemistry of instant empathy was added on my side an urgent need to improve my unstable and often precarious financial situation, on his side a perception that my chaotic but extensive experiences in the murky world of middle-eastern politics might be organized and channelled into profitable avenues. We set up a company which we called

'Communication and Support' that seemed to suggest a capability to operate in almost any field of human activity.

Our joint efforts produced some successes but also some frustrations. Among these latter was an attempt to help Nasri Khattar exploit his typographic talents more successfully than he and I had been able to do. Fadhl recognized that Khattar's typographic revolution had great potential for the newly emerging world of electronic communication; the problem was to find the capital to exploit Nasri's work. Fadhl found in Saudi Arabia a person willing to invest in the project, but the process of negotiating a contract which would satisfy both inventor and investor proved impossible: the investor quite normally expected to both manage and benefit from any profits which might be generated, but Nasri, for whom the concept of 'exploitation' provided the proof that he was being cheated, refused the deal with considerable indignation, some of it directed against myself for bringing him such unworthy characters.

Fadhl left his employment and became increasingly involved in the financial and commercial markets of the Middle East. This drew him back into the cultural worlds of his family and their historic roots in Islam. The pantheistic teachings of India and the pleasurable experiences of the ashram could not satisfy him intellectually, and the rejection of worldly goods could not satisfy his material needs. He found in the Arab-Iranian Gulf the possibility of benefiting from his acquired skills at a time when such benefits were becoming increasingly attractive, and still relatively easy to enjoy.

The move to the Gulf was not one I could follow; the possibilities of a fruitful partnership died a natural but not painful death. I followed with wonder and admiration Fadhl's progression from a successful man of business to a teacher and communicator of the beliefs and culture of Islam. Transporting himself and his family to the United States of America he founded a mosque and a *madrassa* in San Antonio whose landscape and climate replicated those of Iraq, and opened a school in the tradition of his scholarly and educational ancestors. 'Karbala' he told me, at the time when Saddam Hussein was wreaking vengeance on that Holy City, 'will be ours again'. In the meantime – how ironically in the light of later events – Karbala was being kept alive in Texas.

I do not know where Shaikh Fadhl will, if ever, find a final home, but the pamphlets and books which he and his family continue to publish ensure that his mission to enlighten both believers and the still-to-be enlightened will continue. The Islam which he radiates is not one which inspires fear or terror, but a message of charity, humanity, and hope, not in essence different from the teachings of the humble Man of Galilee on which I was brought up. I have benefited on more than one occasion from his generous friendship, and retain the warmest admiration and affection for this mirror of the Iranian-Iraqi world into which my marriage to Furugh had introduced me.

My first contact with the cultural world of Iran preceded my marriage to Furugh Afnan and my friendship with Fadhl Haeri. The town of Nabatiyyeh, situated on the road to Marjayoun, has for centuries been the religious and cultural centre for the Shia population of Jabal Amil in South Lebanon. There the events at Karbala in the year 680 AD are re-enacted annually at the *maidan*, a wide plain outside the town. The ceremonies of Ashoura commemorate the battle scene in which Hussein, the son of the Imam Ali (peace be on his soul) was killed. I was a spectator at these scenes a number of times during my first years in Lebanon; it was a moving but bloody tragedy as young and older men inflicted serious wounds on their heads and chests and invoked the names of the martyred Hussein and his father. Nabatiyyeh was not only a centre of Shia learning and culture, but the architecture of some of its houses indicated that there were Iranian families living here, and I well remember often seeing old and bearded gentlemen wearing green turbans, and clerics in the black transparent goat-hair robes still woven in Karbala.

It was much later, while I was living in Tunisia, that I became more aware of the old relationships between the towns and villages of south Lebanon and Iran. In 1961 Furugh and I accompanied President Habib Bourguiba on a state visit to Iran. At the reception ceremony Bourguiba introduced my wife as 'Furugh Afnan', the name by which he had known her in the early days of our friendship. The Iranian Prime minister, Amir Abbas Hoveida, later to be unjustly executed by the regime which overthrew the Shah, was startled; he clearly recognized the name. His family had lived in Beirut at the same time as Furugh's and according to rumour were followers of the message of her great-grandfather. We were taken to Isfahan and it

Cecil, Furugh and Habib Bourguiba in a Beirut café, 1952.

was there that the connection between Jabal Amil and Iran was most splendidly evident. Two mosques dominate its famous square: one large and 'royal' which perpetuates the memory of the city's grand patron, Shah Abbas; the other small but exquisitely elegant, known as the mosque of Shaikh Lutfullah, a scholar whose family came in the 16th century from Mays al-Jabal, a small town in South Lebanon. When the first Safavid ruler decided that Iran should follow the Shia practices and rules of Islam there were few to teach them, so it was from the towns and villages of Lebanon, where they had been preserved, that Shah Ismail and his successors recruited scholars, teachers and builders. I understood then that the Iranian presence in Lebanon is not new, and cannot be viewed only as a one-way road: Lebanon had, and still maintains a presence in Iran.

My fascination with Iran in fact preceded both my first visits to Lebanon and my fascination with Furugh. During my stay in Cairo during the Second World War I had met and become a close friend of Paul Kraus, whose sad story I related in my earlier memoirs. Paul Kraus came from the traditional school of 'orientalism' which flourished in Germany and Central Europe in the 19th and early 20th centuries, and which applied to Arabic, Persian, and Hebrew texts the rigid canons of scholarship which the humanists of Renaissance Europe had imposed on Greek and Latin. Between the texts which they collated, annotated, and sometimes translated there was often a divorce from the real world they depicted, and 'dead' languages seemed sometimes to mirror 'dead societies'. At some point in his life – perhaps due to his collaboration with Louis Massignon on the thoughts and martyrdom of Mansur al-Hallaj in Baghdad in 922 AD Kraus ventured into the then largely unexplored territory of 'unorthodox Islam' in its Shia forms. The proximity of Central Europe to the Ottoman Empire tended to concentrate the minds of western scholars on Sunni interpretations of Islamic doctrine and history; but in the early years of the 20th century their horizons widened, and they began to explore the intellectual histories of those eastern areas of the Empire and North Africa where Shi'ism had once flourished and is still alive. Kraus was fascinated by the obscure paths by which offshoots of Shia political and theological movements had spread to the Maghreb. The Fatimid movement which took power in Tunisia in the 10th century once dominated the greater part of the Near East, and even when overthrown politically by Turkic dynasties from the north, left a social and cultural legacy not yet fully extinct or explored.

In Tunisia I experienced some still-detectable emanations of that legacy of which my friendship with a number of scholars and men of culture gave me some insights. Hassan Husni Abdulwahhab, Shaikh Fadel Ben-Ashour, Lamine Chabbi, Mahmud Messadi, Mahjoub Ben-Milad, Jellal Ben Abdullah, had each in their own way explored and radiated aspects of it: Tunisian popular art, with its persistent theme of birds and flowers; the architecture and landscapes of public and private buildings and gardens transplanted by Arabs and Persians from Damascus and Baghdad; a freedom of thought, an openness to new ideas, a respect for 'the other' greater than what I experienced in the Mashreq; an ability to digest another culture without losing their own – all these seemed to me to be still audible voices from the past. As a Lebanese I also liked to think that farther away in time these whispers came from Tyre and Carthage.

Unlike the majority of 'orientalist' scholars in European centres who had rarely lived for long periods of time in the Near East, Kraus passed the last years of his life in Egypt, with frequent visits to Syria, Lebanon and Palestine. The Arabic language became the medium of his every-day life, and no longer an instrument to study the distant past. I believe it was this fact which led him into a new field of research: the relationship between the Hebrew texts of the Bible, and in particular of the Pentateuch, and the Arabic language, of which the earliest literary works date from what has come to be called the pre-Islamic period. In the absence of a written culture, memory transmits historical facts and creative thoughts, and poetry becomes the medium. Kraus believed that he had discovered, or deciphered, the poetical structures of the Hebrew texts which corresponded to the structures of that early Arabic poetry. This was a revolutionary approach to the understanding and interpretation of the Biblical texts: 'the epic recitals of the Hebrew Bible were actually composed in a meter resembling that of classical Arabic poetry'. In a letter to a friend in December 1942 he wrote: my work on Semitic metrics... the results pass every expectation... The consequences for Hebrew, for the Old Testament, are inestimable.'*

It was not surprising that Kraus's revolutionary theory should encounter strong resistance from orthodox Biblical scholars: his ideas had implications not only for Hebrew scholarship, but also for the wider field of Jewish-Arab relationships. In the early days of the Zionist movement the question of what language the new Jewish 'returnees' should adopt in Palestine was argued: one view was that it should be Arabic since that was the language of the country, but another was that Hebrew, hitherto the language of the liturgy, should be revived, or recreated, to become the language of daily speech and literature. The latter view prevailed. Instead of absorbing the newcomers into Palestinian Arab society, language became a mark of distinctiveness, a gesture of disagreement, a social barrier. The idea that the two languages might have had a common origin, and that the sacred texts of one religion could be interpreted through the structures and even the meanings of another, had controversial implications.

I do not know to what extent Kraus was conscious of the political implications of his theories: in his twenties he had been attracted to Palestine and spent time on a kibbutz, but later seemed to have distanced himself from the political

---

* Joel Kraemar, *The Jewish Discovery of Islam*, Tel Aviv, 1999.

problems of which he must have become aware in Egypt and other Arab societies, although he continued to have close relations with the Hebrew University in Jerusalem, and had he lived might have gone there after Cairo. It was the criticisms from scholars in his own field which frustrated him: among my papers is a document which sheds light on Kraus's view of orientalist scholarship in traditional centres of learning. The occasion was a dinner which Albert and I organized in Cairo in June 1994 to enable Kraus to meet Brigadier Iltyd Clayton from whose one-manned office influential views were disseminated to British policy-makers. We had been discussing with the Brigadier ways of conveying a better understanding of current political thinking among a wide selection of Arab intellectuals to official British opinion, and at the same time to promote among these intellectuals a greater understanding of what motivates British policies, and what might be done to influence, or even to change them. I still have a list of proposed Arab members of this imagined foundation. Kraus's letter read:

> Dear Sir,
>
> I take it for granted that you do not mind my writing to you when still under the spell of our charming evening. In the early hours of this morning I was suddenly struck by the name which alone would suit your foundation and evoke the whole complexity of its living reality.
>
> You certainly noted my apprehension with regard to the name of the Institute. Institute in my vocabulary means all those numerous departments for diploma-hunting postgraduates at the Cairo University which is so proud of its Institutes of Archaeology, Journalism, of 'Higher Studies' and even of Oriental Studies. Institute means those very respectable foundations throughout the Near East, where some European savants and would-be savants are attending to their research work, behind water-tight walls and closed windows. Institute finally means, (cf. *membre de l'Institut!*) a company of self-conceitedly beaming 'beards', buried alive and embalmed by their mutual assistance... And all

this should not be your Institute.
I would call it a centre: 'Centre of Oriental Studies', *'Centre d'études arabes', 'Markaz Al-Dirasat Al-Sharqiyya'*. Centre evokes something living, like a cell destined to the incubation of thought, it means the co-ordination of all the 'diametrically' opposed efforts and energies which exist inside the circle and its periphery. And as the 'cercle' of its activities is infinite and its actual 'centre' is not bound to any particular place, I am curiously reminded of those remarkable definitions of medieval Platonists (*liber* XXIV *magistrom*): *'Deus est infinita cuius centrum est ubique circumferentia nusquam'*, and still more paradoxically *'Deus est sphaera cuius tot sunt circumferentias quot sunt puncta'*.
I really think your foundation already exists.
Yours very sincerely
Paul Kraus
6 June 1944
7 Ahmad Hismat Pasha
Zamalek

The kernel of Paul Kraus's visionary philological interpretation of Semitic texts did not die with him. It is significant that it was in Beirut, where he gave a series of lectures in February 1943, and through the medium of the Arabic press to which he contributed a series of articles, that he found the most receptive and appreciative audience. Although not directly inspired by Kraus's work, in Beirut my cousin Tony Naufal is now following a parallel approach to the relationships between Hebrew and Arabic.

Kraus's definition of a centre as 'something living, destined to the incubation of thought' was fifteen years later to provide me with the inspiration to create the International Cultural Centre in Hammamet, Tunisia. Hammamet seemed an ideal setting for Kraus's 'incubation of thought'. In the lovely undecorated spaces of George Sebastian's house, scholars, writers and artists could meet, and in the vast and flowerless gardens overlooking the sea a theatre could be built to inspire and illustrate a new dimension to the still-embryonic Arabic performing arts. The Centre was not just a beautiful house and garden, but an instrument to promote what I believed might become a new Arabic culture through exposure to and participation in the international culture of our times. In many discussions with Jean Duvignaud, and exchanges of ideas with Denis de Rougemont, I came to hope that Hammamet would inspire fellow centres in Egypt, Iraq, Lebanon and Syria.

Paul McCartney, Jane Asher and Cecil in Hammamet in 1965.

Chapter 8
Cheese

It was in the garden of our family house in Didsbury, Manchester, that I enjoyed my first taste of the pleasures of the soil. While I had some success in planting seeds for flowers and radishes my greatest joy was the hen which I was allowed to keep in a small shed which I contrived out of a packing-case and wire. My hen co-existed peacefully with the cat which was our indoor pet, but though she never produced an egg I felt that she was a more useful member of the animal family, and deserved at least as much care and affection as we bestowed on Tinkerbell.

Our house at 22 Pine Road, Didsbury, Manchester.

It was to the soil and to the animals which lived on it that I turned for comfort after the frustrations of my life in the world of politics. To prove to myself that I was not only a manipulator of words and ideas, but could produce something tangible, useful, and, why not, also pleasurable, seemed to me a worthwhile goal. To make cheese, for example, satisfied all these goals. I liked cheese, and I had often experimented with the goat or sheep milk which I could sometimes buy from Cypriot families who lived in north London.

The occasion to satisfy this craving to produce, to create,

came through my French friend Patrice Bougrin Dubourg, who told me of a then-unused cheese factory in the neighbourhood of Poitiers. The Cypriot cheese *haloumi* was not known in France in the 1980s. In Cyprus the production of *haloumi* was limited to the season in which goat or sheep milk was available, namely spring and early summer, whereas in France the proximity of Spain with its vast supply of both kinds of milk made it possible to produce it all the year round. I decided that this was a venture worth trying. Chance brought me in touch with a Cypriot in London who, though a butcher by profession, knew how haloumi was made. I entered into partnership with him, acquired the use of the factory in Mirebeau near Poitiers, repaired its outworn facilities, and started to produce the cheese.

Maria the goat.

The sight of those vats full of milk being churned and heated, the curds being cut by hand, the scooping into moulds, the reheating of the whey to produce floating isles of ricotta, was exciting. I felt I had outgrown the character of an intellectual and become a farmer, close to the land and to the animals which transformed its fruits into milk. The cow, the sheep and the goat replaced in my mind the students of my academic years, and the politicians of my later days: they were more malleable than the former, and more faithful than the latter.

From one point of view the venture was an enormous success: at the inauguration of the newly-reopened factory at Noiron, Madame Edith Cresson, the Minister of Agriculture, declared that France now had its 367th cheese. Since then *haloumi* has become widely produced in France and elsewhere in Western Europe. But my venture was premature, and commercially unsound. There was no publicity to announce its arrival on the market, and no distribution chain to make it available. Inevitably the sales could not provide sufficient revenues to assure the constant supply of milk which had to be contracted, and the partnership was soon forced into liquidation.

As long as I was able, and at considerable financial loss, I staved off the end, until a tragic event opened my eyes to what I had been reluctant to believe. One day, when the factory was still functioning, I had seen on market-day in Mirebeau a truck standing in the square with a solitary and mournful-looking goat. I enquired of its owner what he intended doing with it: 'she's old and useless so I'm taking her to the *abattoir*'. I felt an irresistible urge to save the sad creature, he agreed to sell her, and delivered her to the farm at Noiron. There I released her to the fields, christened her Maria, and gave orders that she was to be treated as my guest. Over the months she put on a new coat of hair, fattened up, and lived a life of goat-like luxury. Then one day, after returning from London, I was astonished to find that she had produced two beautiful white children. Without any visible signs of a partner this was indeed a miracle: I took it as a sign that my venture was to be blessed, and that the two kids were a divine assurance that all would be well.

My faith in providence, and in the human race, was soon to be shattered. Returning again from London I did not find the happy family, nor was my Cypriot partner to be found. In my absence he had invited relatives to the farm, and had prepared a Cypriot feast for them, of which my two beloved kids had been the main dish. This came as an enormous shock: I had for some time been suspicious of the financial probity of my partner; now my suspicions had been confirmed: if he could eat my goats, why not my money also? This was far worse than any miserable monetary fraud - this was a blow to my affections. From that day onwards I could see no redeeming features in my partner, and parted from him with less regrets for the inconveniences to my life which the end of my venture into the world of cheese had brought about than for the fate of my lovely kids.

Though the cheese venture failed, my interest in the production and producers of food did not end. One day in a bookshop on Madison Avenue in New York my eyes fell on a book with a strange title, and the name of an author clearly Lebanese: *Songbirds, Truffles, and Wolves* by Gary Paul Nabhan recounts the author's journey in Italy described as 'a spiritual quest as well as an ethnobotanical field trip... to discover what is useful in the old ways, what remains wild in the civilized world, and what in ancient science has survived to make its way into contemporary culture'. I was at the time making frequent visits to Jordan, and Nabhan's book sparked a new impulse to reconnect with the natural world. I had become intrigued by the absence of any Jordanian cookbook, or any Jordanian restaurant by that name, although Amman and other towns and villages had cafes and bistros where *ful beans* and *hummus* were eaten; but what was Jordanian cuisine? What did the farmers plant and what did the people do with their produce? The answer I almost always received was: 'We don't have a Jordanian cuisine – we only have one dish, the *mansaf* (a sheep or goat cooked on a bed of rice or *burghul*).

So what do the ordinary people of Jordan eat in their homes? There was no-one to tell me, so I decided to find out for myself. Cooking was not considered a serious subject for academic study, Jordanian men relied on their womenfolk to provide them with their food, and educated young Jordanian women were being increasingly wooed by the culture of the supermarket and fast food, so it was to old ladies, taxi-drivers and soldiers that I went for answers. The results were surprising. I discovered that there really is a distinctive and traditional Jordanian cuisine based on a combination of what the people produce: the villagers their wheat, cereals vegetables and fruits, and the Bedouins their meat and milk. Water being seasonal and frequently scarce, the conservation of food plays an important role in the activities of the kitchen.

And there was another dimension to Jordanian food: immigrants into Jordan from the Caucasus and Anatolia in the late 19th and early 20th centuries brought their own cuisines with them, and while they are now fully integrated into Jordanian society they have preserved their cultural specificity, including their own cuisine. My first introduction into their food was an extraordinary lunch at the house of Sitt Makarem Hagandouqa, a hospitable Circassian lady. So what began as a simple curiosity, stimulated by frequent visits to the farms of friends and to the food markets in downtown Amman, became not only a collection of recipes, but also a reflection on the role of culinary culture in a people's identity. The Jordanians' uncertainty about their culinary affiliation reflected an uncertainty about their social and national identity. I decided to write a small book to try to answer the question: *Jordan: The Land & The Table* is an attempt to show that the cuisine of Jordan reflects the multi-ethnic and multi-cultural character of its society.

Might there not be also some connection between the identity of the individual and what he or she eats more complicated than the over-quoted dictum 'you are what you eat'? Here again it was in a book which Nabhan kindly sent me that I found an answer: *Some Like it Hot** describes Nabhan's and other ethnobiologists' research into 'the dynamic connections between our culinary predilections, our genes, the diets of our ancestors, and the places that our ancestral cultures called home for extended periods of time'. The scope of their work is vast, and their hypotheses still tentative, but there seem to be serious reasons to believe that *'we are what our ancestors ate'*.

Who are our ancestors, and what did they eat? 'Evolutionary gastronomy' was a phrase which seemed to reflect at least in its first word some relationship to the work of Charles Darwin: my grandchildren have inherited some of the genes of that venerable man, in addition to a variety of genes from their paternal and maternal grandparents, so if they should ask the great question 'who am I?' the answers must be complicated. I decided to help them, to tell them in *Ancestral Appetites*, an essay in gestation, some stories of their families, their ancestries, their lives, and the foods they ate.

---

* Island Press, Washington DC, 2004

Epilogue

Recent events in the Middle East and North Africa have lightened the gloom which permeates some of my memoirs and reflections. I had almost come to believe that my earlier enthusiasm for the Hashemite vision of an Arab polity continuing the Ottoman heritage of multi-ethnic and cultural pluralism was futile. I had written already in 1967 that 'the Arab League, faced with the difficulties of achieving its final goal – Arab unity – never did anything seriously at all.' As military and autocratic regimes destroyed the fragile democratic and parliamentary constitutions left behind by the former European powers, the main concern of the new rulers was to preserve themselves in power. To this end there grew up a complicity between them and the international purveyors of arms: the stability which endeared the dictators and autocrats to the great and small powers in Europe and America was paid for by the peoples, the revenues from oil and gas which could have developed their lands and educated their youths went back to the economies of the industrial countries and into the large pockets of the rulers, and the arms they had bought to fight their fictitious enemies were only used to suppress their own peoples.

For the young generations who grew up under these regimes the slogans of their rulers grew stale. Democracy and Socialism became dirty words to conceal dirty facts; religion became the instrument of power and not its inspiration; Arab Unity turned into Arab Disunity; the Palestinian Cause became an excuse for emergency laws, and anti-Israeli words a cover for inaction. As desperate attempts by some regimes to prevent the spread of information among their own populations and abroad failed, the now-growing computer generations saw through these frauds and rejected all their slogans. The common theme of all the uprisings – whether

successful as in Tunisia and Egypt or on-going in other areas
– is not an ideology or a doctrine, but simply freedom. How
could I not be thrilled to witness this, and see what vast
horizons of hope and happiness have opened up for the Arab
peoples? Is it conceivable that after overthrowing one kind of
dictatorship, the Arab or any other people, will accept the
chains of another?

It is no accident that Lebanon is the one country in which
there has been no demand for the change of the regime: its
constitution is secular, its system of government a
parliamentary democracy, its society free in all its intellectual
and material dimensions; its churches, mosques, and the
recent restoration of a synagogue in central Beirut,
demonstrate the will of the people to preserve the image of a
free Arabic multi-confessional and cultural society. Although
that image is today tarnished by the behaviour of some of its
leaders who represent not the nation, but their communities,
the aim of the growing movement among the Lebanese young
of all ages is to abolish political confessionalism, to restore
the authentic interpretation of the constitution, and to
change, not the regime, but its leaders: this is Lebanon's
spring revolution. Its success or failure will have a far-
reaching impact throughout the Middle East, and particularly
in Lebanon's southern neighbour, now deeply divided
between the irreconcilable protagonists of Israel as a shared
state with its Palestinian people, and Israel as a Jewish state
in which there will be no room for the Arabs.

So I now ask myself, is it not possible that the 'Hashemite
vision' may now be re-discovered and freshly formulated? In
the Middle East the frontiers which were imposed on the
territories of the Arabian Peninsula after the First World
War no longer correspond to the needs and the aspirations of
their populations: the combination of rapid demographic
growth in some of these territories and the discovery and
exploitation of oil and gas in others has created an imbalance
of wealth and power. It is no longer reasonable or acceptable
that the vast revenues from the underground be spent on
absurd projects in the sea instead of developing the semi-arid
and desert lands which surround them; nor that the funds
needed to build the schools and universities and hospitals for
which the people crave be spent on arms and planes to defend

against imaginary enemies. More urgently, the problem of the Palestinian people, now faced with total eviction from its homeland, threatens the whole area; the individual sovereignties of the Arab states have obscured the need for a common policy; the failure to contain Israel threatens them all.

Without changing the existing boundaries, larger political units now need to be formed which will strengthen their interior solidarity and increase their external influence. Within the Peninsula one such unity would be between the countries of the Fertile Crescent, another a unity of the heartland and coastlines of the Peninsula. In North Africa the unity of the countries under former French and Italian control is foreseeable, and the unity of Egypt and Sudan would provide the territorial and human link between Africa and Asia. Together the four units would constitute the new 'Arab Polity'. Its fundamental Charter would include equal legal, political and individual rights for all citizens of whatever racial, ethnic, religious and cultural affiliation, and of both genders; adhesion to international codes of Human Rights and respect for the codes of international conduct; constitutional government in all forms which provide for the separation of powers, equal representation, transparency, and the peaceful transfer of authority. A Council made up of an equal number of elected members from each of the four units would constitute the supreme authority of the Polity.

The formation of these regional unities would eliminate the dangers now threatening the area of further fragmentation into separate ethnic or religious mini-states, and restore the geographic, historic, and economic links between their populations. And the supra-national Arab Polity would offer the best, and indeed the only viable solution to the problem of Israel. By choosing to build its national home in Arab Palestine, the Zionist movement committed itself historically and morally to co-existence with the already existing population, as even Theodor Herzl recognized in his prophetic novel Alt-Neu Land. The establishment of the state of Israel, and the transformation of its citizens from Palestinian Jews into Israelis removed the political raison d'être of Zionism, and faced the new state with a historic choice: either to accept the legitimacy of the

Palestinian Arabs right to statehood, and strive to revive an Arabic-Jewish culture and way of life such as had existed in the past and is still alive among Jewish communities in the Middle East, North Africa and their Diaspora, or to repudiate that right and heritage, and attempt to remove the Arab population, first politically, and ultimately physically from the land of Palestine.

There will be a place for Israel within the supra-national Arab Polity if its citizens accept the conditions of its Charter: in so doing they will have nothing to lose, and everything to gain; but if, under the influence of out-dated American Zionists or newly-arrived immigrants from Russia, they make the second choice, Israel will face a bleak and ghetto-like existence, and permanent insecurity.

Within this perspective of a 'rassemblement' of the populations of the Arab Peninsula and North Africa in a new supra-national Polity, is it too visionary to imagine a similar process of change taking place in the hinterlands of Iran and Turkey, both of which states have multi-ethnic and multi-cultural populations, and which also face the dangers of fragmentation? Or to envision some kind of union of common interests between the three new entities? In the not-so-distant past, the mark of an educated and cultured gentleman from the East was a knowledge of the Arabic, Farsi and Turkish languages and cultures; his world stretched from the Atlantic to the borders of India and China and the lands of Central Asia. The restoration of that lost world of culture commerce and conviviality need not be just a fantasy, nor the road impassable between Dream and Deed.

Marjayoun, April 2011

Appendix I

Moment of Truth 2003

Another Road Map: Going Forward not Backward

The 'Road Map' for a solution to the Palestinian-Israeli conflict now being promoted by the American administration is just one more attempt to go backward in time and space and to draw a map of the situation on the ground as it was on the day before 5 June 1967. This new one is likely to fail for the same reasons as they did previously: in the thirty-six years that have gone by the situation on the ground, and in the minds of the protagonists, has changed. The road that leads back to the past cannot lead to a sustainable future.

To understand why the 'peace process' which began in Madrid in 1992 has led to the present impasse, one must return to the circumstances in which the confrontation between Arabs and Jews in Palestine under the British Mandate was transformed from a local to an international conflict. The decision taken in November 1947 by the General Assembly of the United Nations to recommend the partition of the country into an Arab and a Jewish State was not intended as the ideal or even the final solution to the violence to which the terms of the British Mandate had inevitably led. The partition proposed was not total, because it was qualified by the inclusion in its project of 'economic union' between the two states. This was a recognition that the two could not be completely separated from each other, and that while frontiers would define the political dimension of sovereignty, there was an economic – and by implication a social – dimension in which the interests of both populations would be their joint responsibility.

The acceptance by the Jewish population of the United Nations' proposals, and their rejection by the Palestinians resulted on the one side in the establishment of the State of Israel, and on the Arab side in a failed military attempt backed by neighbouring Arab governments to prevent partition. The Palestinian parties refused the idea of a Palestinian state in a divided country, and requested the Jordanian monarch King Abdullah bin Hussein to accept provisional sovereignty over what territory remained in Arab hands after the armed confrontation between the two communities ended in armistice agreements in 1949. Thus the project of economic union never saw its implementation, and only the Jewish State – Israel – came into existence.

After the war in 1967 in which Israel occupied all the Palestinian territories on the West bank and Gaza, Israel assumed responsibility for the economic – and indeed for the entire social – interests of the Palestinian population. This situation prevailed until the Oslo Agreements in 1994 accorded that responsibility to the so-called Palestinian Authority set up in the West Bank and Gaza. The Jordanian state, which had exercised sovereign authority in those areas since 1949, seemed to relinquish its claims to sovereignty by default, and thus the present situation was created in which a sovereign Jewish state exists alongside a non-sovereign authority and separated only by no finally-defined or internationally recognized boundaries. This is a situation in which disagreement, vocal and violent, is built-in. Within the parameters of this situation there is no way in which the theoretically irreconcilable claims of Palestinians and Israelis to the land on which they co-exist, or the practical problems of daily life, can find solutions; all that can be expected – and this is both difficult and precarious – are temporary cease-fires or lessening of the scale of violence.

The agenda of the Madrid Conference as set by letters from Secretary of State James Baker to the participants imposed Security Council resolutions 242 and 338 adopted after the 6-Day War. These resolutions did not address or even mention the problem of the Palestinians or of a Palestinian State, but only the situation between the parties which had been at war, namely Egypt, Jordan, Syria and Lebanon. They were interpreted by the Americans, the Russians, and the Arab participants as a formula for achieving a final solution of the Arab-Israeli conflict: the Israelis would return the land they had occupied in the war, and the Arab governments would recognize and make peace with Israel. 'Land for Peace' became a magical formula which is still being chanted, although it has long been revealed as a mirage which disappears as soon as its seems to be near.

Nothing in the wording of Security Council Resolution 242 contained any reference to 'Land for Peace' either explicitly or by implication; in fact, at the tortuous negotiations at the United Nations at which I was an observer, it was deliberately phrased by its main protagonist, the late Lord Caradon, to make it ambiguous. It was not made clear whether all or some of the land occupied during the war should be evacuated; and as there was no mention of the Palestinians it was also not made clear how the resolution could be reconciled with the terms of the original partition plan which set up both an Arab and a Jewish state, unless Jordan was substituted for the Palestinian Arab state. Did resolution 242 negate that plan? And what would happen if Jordan did not accept to substitute itself for the Palestinians – as indeed did happen?

It can be only either naivety or obstinacy which motivates those who still cling to the illusion that 'Land for Peace' could provide the key to success, or that the two-state solution based on a return to a past that has changed could possibly succeed in ending the conflict. The demographic, territorial, and psychological changes which have taken place, and the fact that Jordan seemed to relinquish the sovereignty it exercised over the West Bank after 1949, has left the Palestinians in an unequal and disadvantageous situation relative to Israel. While soon after 1967 and even later Jordan might have recuperated nearly all the territory it lost to Israel in war, the Palestinians' chances of doing the same even with the backing of all the Arab and Islamic states – if it were to be forthcoming – are nil so long as the imbalances between the two parties to the conflict are not redressed.

The Oslo Agreements did not introduce any real change into the process which Madrid laid down: they only sought to liquidate whatever traces remained of Jordanian sovereignty, and led to the Jordanian-Israeli Peace Treaty which left the Palestinians even more on their own. The Oslo Agreements also re-imposed on the Palestinians a leadership originally created by the Arab League from among Palestinians living outside their country, and removed from the scene an emerging new Palestinian leadership distinct from the exiled groups in Tunis and Cairo, and more representative of the population on the land. The newly-created Palestinian Authority, without a clear mandate from the Palestinian people, and under either the illusion or the genuine but naïve belief that the agreements they had secretly negotiated would lead to a Palestinian state, proceeded from a position of weakness to negotiate with players who had almost all the cards in their hands.

When they came to the problem which has never been resolved since the original refusal to accept partition, namely the question of the boundaries between the Jewish and the Arab State, the Palestinian leadership made claims based on the results of a war which had been lost, not by them, but by the Arab states. As a people without a nationality in their own homeland they succeeded in enlisting the sympathy of the outside world for their plight, but no effective support to alleviate it. Frustrated in their efforts to achieve what was not within their reach from the beginning, and anxious to prove to an increasingly sceptical population that they were their sole legitimate leaders, they decided to play the card of violent confrontation, which had only led to disaster in the past, and which could only lead to the same result in the future. As a gesture of frustration the new *intifada* did win a renewed international concern for their plight, but as a policy it could not succeed either in sustaining that concern, or in moving successive Israeli governments to accept their terms; on the contrary, the more they gained in intensity, the more they lost sympathy in the outside world, and the harder public opinion in Israel grew against a recognition of even their legitimate demands.

What then needs to be done to end the present cycle of violence and break out of the deadlock which was programmed into the now-defunct peace process? The first step is to recognize that in the climate of mutual distrust, fear, and revenge which now prevails between Palestinians and Israelis there are no immediate solutions, but only possible settlements of issues which are the cause of immediate violent confrontation. To be more than temporary postponements any sustainable settlement must contain within its conditions the seeds of future solutions. Separation, for example, may be necessary for reasons of security or as means of restraining opponents unwilling or incapable of controlling violence, but it should not be an end in itself, and its terms of reference should ensure that it does not exclude its eventual replacement by closer ties, and perhaps by an eventual re-union.

The second step is to define the parties to the conflict and its scope. Is it an Arab-Israeli or a Palestinian-Israeli conflict? And what is the territory on which the conflict takes place? Historically, geographically, and demographically the Holy Land includes both sides of the Jordan, a river which does not divide but rather unites them. Their political and administrative separation was decided by the British Government for its own reasons, but this could not alter facts: the fact that the Arab population on both sides constitutes one ethnic and cultural family, and secondly that the populations on both sides share a common sky and climate, and resources of both land and water which make their material interests and needs complementary, and their way of life similar.

Since 1948 the Jordanian state and people have been involved in all the conflicts, political changes, and human disasters generated by the United Nations decision to partition Mandatory Palestine, and are affected for good or bad by whatever happens on the other side of the river. Jordan then is a part of the equation of the conflict, and must in one way or another be brought back into attempts to resolve it. A truncated Holy Land leaves Palestinians and Israelis in a cage in which they fight out their frustrated passions; restored, it provides the stage on which their conflicting goals and claims can be reconciled if there is a will to do so.

Instead then of trying to go back to the de facto situation created by the military confrontations in 1948 and 1949 and which was ended by the 6-Day War in 1967, the problem must be rethought in terms of today's realities, taking into account the experiences of the last fifty-four years: the tragedies, the failures, but also the successes and the promises.

APPENDIX I

One Land

In 1947, when the partition of Palestine was decided by the United Nations, the population, two thirds Arab one third Jewish, was small. The Mandatory regime had provided a political, administrative and judicial framework within which both communities had lived for twenty-four years, and had developed economic and social relationships which, though fragile, seemed to the advocates of partition strong enough to enable the two states, in each of which there was to be a mixed population, to exist peacefully alongside each other.

This hope, excessively optimistic, was shattered by the wars which followed. The demographic relationship was altered by massive Jewish immigration, and the development of Israel as a Jewish state took place independently from the Arabs and in conditions of conflict. On their side the Palestinians clung to the hope that somehow the partition could be reversed and a unified country restored, until they finally accepted the idea of a separate Palestinian state. In the meantime the Arab states' failed war against Israel in 1967 evicted the Jordanian and Egyptian presence, and left the Israelis free to expand the frontiers of their state which had been frozen in 1949, to create new facts on the ground in the form of settlements in Palestinian areas, and to declare Jerusalem as the eternal and exclusive capital of their state.

These changes in the demographic balance and the division of territory diminished the prospects of reaching a settlement acceptable to both sides. The Jewish population became too large to fit into the original partition plan, and the areas left to the Palestinians became too small to accommodate a population with a high birth rate, and to allow the creation of a seriously viable state. The options open to both sides were narrowed down to two: the first – ideally the best, but not in the present circumstances realisable – is a return to the idea of a bi-national state in which Jews and Arabs would be partners sharing equal rights; the second is a division of territory satisfactory to neither, and pregnant with the probability of future conflict. The first option would dilute the Jewish character of Israel; the second, would lead to an eventual take-over of Jordan by the Palestinians. Frustrated by the truncated and tiny area of their own state which would make them totally dependent on Israel, and incapable of sustaining any return of their displaced people or supporting future generations, they would turn to the neighbouring territory where they are already strongly implanted, and create in fact what they have always rejected in words – the *Watan Badil*, the Alternative Country.

While this might be an appealing prospect for some extremists on both sides, in the long, but not very long, term – it would be disastrous not only for the Palestinians and the Israelis, but for the region as a whole. Once in control of the Jordanian state, the temptation and the opportunity to convert it into a confrontational challenge to Israel's existence would be great. Encircled by neighbouring states which might seem to threaten its existence, or which might give it the excuse to present it as such, an embattled Israel would use its weapon of last resort, and so say 'good-bye Damascus, Baghdad, Beirut, and perhaps Tel Aviv as well'!

The Three State Solution

Since then in the present climate of hatred and insecurity neither the Israelis nor the Palestinians can envisage living peacefully with each other in a shared state; and no territorial division of the former territory of Mandate Palestine can satisfy their mutual needs for viability, security, and development; the only way to break out of this dilemma is to enlarge the framework within which the two can exist and develop, and this means enlarging the equation by including the state of Jordan. This would be a natural sequence of the events which started with the Peace Treaty between Jordan and Israel, and which set a pattern for a tri-partite *modus vivendi* between the inhabitants of the Holy Land.

The three-state formula would restore the natural unity of the two sides of the River Jordan; create a greater demographic balance between Arabs and Jews, and give them benefits of which they are all in need. The collective benefit, which the three-state solution gives, would be security. The Palestinians will feel secure within their frontiers finally established and internationally recognized; the Israelis will feel more at ease with the inclusion of Jordan within the framework of this new entity, and the Jordanians will feel a greater sense of regional security if they have both Palestinians and Israelis as partners. And above all the problem of the refugees and displaced persons and of Jerusalem, insoluble in the two-states formula, will find a logical and sustainable resolution within the larger entity. Each state will break out from the narrow perspectives which now limit their horizons, and give their citizens a greater space within which to live, to work, and to develop creatively.

The New Entity

To be successful any project for peace must take into account the people who live on the land, and the land itself – its location, natural resources, and its historical and cultural associations. Independently of how the inhabitants may identify themselves – as Palestinians, Israelis, or Jordanians – they are obliged, and indeed condemned to live together by the environment in which they exist. Physical separation between them cannot be a solution, but only a formula for endless violence. What then are the conditions in which they can hope to end violence and construct a viable and sustainable peace?

There are three conditions which any project for peace must satisfy: the Palestinians' legitimate longing for a national identity embodied in statehood; the Israelis' longing for security based not only on their own strength and international support, but also on a sincere acceptance by their partners of their mutual rights and interests; and the Jordanians' assurance that they will preserve their national and cultural identity within whatever framework of institutions the three entities agree to establish between themselves.

The project for peace, to be serious must therefore come from the people of the three entities themselves, be based on their own experiences, fears, and hopes, not on ideas or proposals emanating from outside governments, international bodies, 'Middle East experts', propagandists, or well-meaning but ill-informed friends. The international community cannot successfully initiate, but should encourage and support any project which originates from the peoples and from the land on which they live, and which represents their collective will to live together.

What will be the nature of the new entity created by the association of the three states? Somewhere between confederation and federation would seem to be the answer. Confederation is too rigid, would involve the unnecessary duplication of expenses and services which can best be shared, and might erect more barriers instead of helping to break them down. Federation on the other hand is premature: neither institutions nor peoples are ready to live too closely together. Constitutional experts, international lawyers, political parties and public discussions must co-operate to find acceptable compromises between theory and practice, between sovereignty and common interest, between exclusivity and commonality. And a wider perspective should encompass the possibility of enlarging the scope of this new initiative to open the door to what would be a further step towards the vision of the Fertile Crescent.

The experience of the founding fathers of the American Constitution may provide a useful example of a compromise between exclusivity and commonality. That Constitution was framed to define their common interests and to leave to the individual states the control of what they saw as particular. A similar though not identical compromise could inspire a constitution for the Union of the Holy Land States: their representatives – elected or chosen – could find common interests in the joint control of their natural resources, their financial systems, and their economic and social development. What would provide the cement of their populations' relationships to each other would be their common interest in attaining comparable standards of living, equal opportunities for development, and conditions of internal and external security.

The experience of Europe also demonstrates that it is possible to create areas of common interests and to establish institutions to administer them without abolishing national sovereignty. In the Holy Land it should be easier than in Europe to discover and define these areas. The British Mandatory period in Palestine and Transjordan left a legacy to their successor states of similar administrative and judicial systems. There is also no long history - only a recent one - of conflict between the populations, although it may take time for the distrust and hatreds of today to subside. Unlike

Europe there is no multitude of languages and cultures to make communication difficult: as more Palestinians speak and understand Hebrew and more Israelis speak and understand Arabic the beginnings of a common culture can already be perceived which may in time transcend but not erode national identity. Palestinians, Jordanians and Israelis will all retain their distinct identity but all will enjoy the privilege and the responsibility of sharing the Holy Land.

The inhabitants of the Union will further share a common interest in striving to bring back the international community to its true role, and to a recognition of its responsibility in creating chaos where it had hoped to establish peace. By initiating partition but failing to implement it the United Nations has been unable or unwilling to remedy the consequences of its failure; instead it has spent vast amounts of money to alleviate the conditions of the Palestinian refugees without either returning them to their homes or compensating them for the loss of their properties; and it has created a variety of agencies which benefit its employees as much if not more than its intended beneficiaries. To repair and to compensate for the enormous human and material prejudice done to all the populations of the Holy Land will require a massive injection of funds. It is in the interests of the United Nations, and in particular of its major players – American, European and Arab – to provide those funds, and to remove from the Middle East and the world scene the running sore of the Arab-Israeli conflict.

It is not too rash to predict that the arrival of the Union of Holy Land States on the human and political stage of the Middle East would play a vital and beneficial role in the development of the region. The three associated states would constitute a powerful political, industrial, financial, and cultural force, which could exert a strong influence on the development of systems of government and social relationships in the other countries of the area. They could set an example of constitutional and democratic government and civil society which would erode the present hold of military and authoritarian regimes on their unhappy populations throughout the Middle East. They would demonstrate the importance and the possibility of overcoming historical ethnic and sectarian enmities, and of sharing natural resources. They might well become the nucleus of a new regional order based on both political and social pluralism, in which all its peoples could learn to live together in peace and prosperity.

Nowhere more than in the Middle East is the necessity of transcending the boundaries drawn in the imperial age evident. The two great inventions of the 20th century – the aeroplane and the computer – have made territorial frontiers irrelevant to the needs and to the potentialities of their populations. Space cannot be divided, and ideas cannot be compartmentalized. While national sovereignty will still prevail its limitations and drawbacks must be recognized, and ways found to overcome them. And the frontiers of the mind which have made religions and ideologies exclusive and mutually intolerant must be superseded by a new openness, a new acceptance of the Other, and a new dedication to a universal order of justice and peace.

Appendix II

The Missing Link
The decisions by the General Assembly of the United Nations in November 1947 to partition the territory of Palestine between an Arab and a Jewish State led to a de facto situation in which the borders between the Arab and Jewish populations, as well as between the Israeli State established in May 1948 and Egypt, Jordan, and Lebanon were crystallized by Armistice agreements.

Later on both Egypt and Jordan made Peace Treaties with Israel, while between Lebanon and Israel there still exists a nebulous situation in which the Armistice agreement is in 'suspended animation'. This leaves the Palestinians in limbo: they have no internationally-recognized status but only agreements on the ground between the Palestinian Liberation Organization and the Israelis to negotiate solutions to their problems and to arrive at a 'final settlement'.

The agreements made in Oslo in 1993 have not resulted in this 'final settlement', and this failure produced two Palestinian *intifadas*, or movements of desperation. The Palestinian Authority set up by Oslo was unable to control the violence or prevent Israeli governments from unilaterally creating facts on the ground which prejudice the final delimitation of the frontiers between the two states in favour of Israel. This led to the rise in popular Palestinian support for Hamas which challenged the strategies of the Authority, accusing it of recognizing Israel's rights to statehood in Palestine without securing a reciprocal right for the Palestinians. In elections for a representative Palestinian body held in 1996 Hamas won 46% of the Palestinian votes.

The strategy adopted by Hamas of refusing to recognize Israel's right to statehood without a reciprocal right for the Palestinians was interpreted by successive Israeli governments as a terrorist position and they succeeded in bringing the American administration under President Bush into line. The American administration in turn succeeded in convincing the other members of the Big Four – the UN, the EU and the Russian Federation – to outlaw Hamas, and to recognize only the Palestinian Authority as the legitimate representative of the Palestinian people. The Palestinians have thus been effectively divided between themselves, not by their own opinion, but by decisions taken by the Big Four which under Israeli influence have substituted themselves for the international community.

This was the situation which resulted in the crisis of Gaza in which neither the Israeli government nor the Palestinians could act responsibly: Israel claimed that it is only answerable to itself, and the Palestinians were divided by the outside world. It is the unfortunate fact that the international community also has not acted responsibly to its own commitments in the past, nor to its duties in the present. All that can now be expected in these conditions is a cease-fire, a temporary truce, and the expectation of a further conflict sooner or later.

It is therefore necessary to address two basic problems: who represents the Palestinian people, and what are the conditions in which negotiations between them and Israel can lead to a positive result. The answer to the first is that once there is a cessation of hostilities in Gaza an international body or commission composed of neutral powers should organize a referendum in the West Bank and Gaza to determine the question of Palestinian representation. It will then be possible to address the second and larger problem.

Ever since the Madrid conference all attempts to organize successful negotiations between Israel and the Palestinians have failed because the framework within which they have been conducted has been based on Security Council Resolutions 242 and 336. These resolutions related to the consequences of the 6-Day War in 1967 in which Israel took the West Bank from Jordan, Gaza from Egypt, and the Golan Heights from Syria. These resolutions have been interpreted as a formula under which Israel would restore these territories in return for peace. For the West Bank the 'Land for Peace' solution did not answer the questions of 'return to whom', or how Jordan's acquired sovereign rights were to be transferred to the Palestinians. On two occasions the Jordanian sovereign (King Hussein) unilaterally designated the PLO as the sole representative of the Palestinian people, but this was never sanctified by any resolution taken by the United Nations as the original source of international legitimacy. As Israel has never recognized Jordanian sovereignty over Palestinian territories, this has created the limbo in which the Palestinians now stagnate, and which has allowed Israel to disclaim its role as occupier, and to justify its rights to act solely in its own interests.

The role of Jordan in clarifying and legitimizing the Palestinian participation in the peace process is therefore crucial. The Jordanian-Israeli Peace Treaty in 1990 did not cancel that role, or abandon the Palestinians to face Israel alone. In fact the Treaty explicitly and implicitly linked Jordan to both the final and the permanent settlements of the Palestinian-Israeli and the Arab-Israeli conflicts. It could be said that the Treaty contains the embryonic solutions to both these conflicts.

The 'two-state' solution originally proposed by the UN in 1947 now needs a midwife: Palestinians and Israelis cannot by themselves, for reasons explained above, give birth to peace. They both need a partner to strengthen their will to conceive it, and to produce a healthy child. Because it is already intimately involved with both, by contiguity, demography, and a shared history, Jordan is better placed than any other government to play that role.

The framework within which negotiations between Palestinians and Israelis can be successful should therefore now be enlarged. None of the three major problems which face the Palestinians and Israelis – frontiers, the refugees, and Jerusalem – can be resolved without Jordanian participation. The definition of the frontiers between Israel and the Palestinian State must take into account the contiguity between both and Jordan. Jordan hosts the largest number of Palestinian refugees who constitute at least half of the population of the country; and in Jerusalem and other religious areas, Jordan has rights and responsibilities recognized by Palestinians and Israel. Once these negotiations achieve their principal aim – namely to establish the Palestinian State – it will be up to the three States to decide whether they wish to remain as three distinct sovereign entities, or whether they choose to enter into bi-lateral or tri-lateral relationships, federations, confederations, or Benelux-like arrangements.